Fantasies of Flight

Fantasies of Flight

DANIEL M. OGILVIE

OXFORD
UNIVERSITY PRESS

2004

OXFORD
UNIVERSITY PRESS

Oxford   New York
Auckland   Bangkok   Buenos Aires   Cape Town   Chennai
Dar es Salaam   Delhi   Hong Kong   Istanbul   Karachi   Kolkata
Kuala Lumpur   Madrid   Melbourne   Mexico City   Mumbai   Nairobi
Sao Paulo   Shanghai   Taipei   Tokyo   Toronto

Copyright © 2004 by Oxford University Press, Inc.

Published by Oxford University Press, Inc.
198 Madison Avenue, New York, New York 10016

www.oup.com

Oxford is a registered trademark of Oxford University Press

Library of Congress Cataloging-in-Publication Data
Ogilvie, Daniel M.
Fantasies of flight / Daniel M. Ogilvie.
p. cm.
Includes bibliographical references and index.
ISBN 0-19-515746-X
1. Levitation. 2. Levitation—Case studies. I. Title.
BF1385 .035   2003
154.3—dc21   2003001367

9 8 7 6 5 4 3 2 1

Printed in the United States of America
on acid-free paper

PREFACE

This book is about fantasies of flying. The topic is my port of entry into discussing human personality in ways intended to interest and spark the imaginations of readers. It borrows from and builds on a tradition of studying lives that was initiated by Sigmund Freud but fell on hard times when academic psychologists grew suspicious of storytelling and became reliant on numbers and relationships among numbers as preferred ways to create and affirm knowledge.

I am something of a numbers person myself, but numbers are of no assistance in understanding when and why *Peter Pan* was brought to life by his creator, J. M. Barrie. I wouldn't know what to count in the process of seeking to understand what the discovery of the collective unconscious meant to Carl Jung. What was Larry Walters looking for when he was lifted sixteen thousand feet into the air by weather balloons that he had attached to a lawn chair? Did Marshall Herff Applewhite really believe that he and his Heaven's Gate cult members would be rescued by a spaceship after they swallowed lethal doses of poison? Why did Perry Smith, the "hero" of Truman Capote's book *In Cold Blood*, repeatedly dream of being swept away to a better place by a parrot-faced bird? And what elements of his own experiences and desires did Marc Chagall express for all to behold in his paintings of levitated objects?

On the surface, none of these questions appear to be urgent questions requiring immediate answers. But they are *interesting* questions that can only be addressed by "getting in there," by getting beneath the surface and resurrecting the idea that the human brain does a great deal of its work behind the scenes. This brain, after all, is the same brain that creates symphonies, arranges gardens, writes stories, and loves to solve problems. It is also the brain that prefers one god against another god, an organ that propels us to abuse our neighbors, to slaughter our enemies, and to ignore long-term consequences of short-term gains. Exploring the topic of fantasies of flying provides us with a side door entrance into some fundamental questions of our design and, given that, perhaps some of our questions *are* in urgent need of answers.

My strategy for deciphering the meaning of flying fantasies involves recovering some old territory in the field of personality psychology and charting some new territory that I believe is on the horizon.

The old territory involves a debate about the value of conducting case studies. The view of the majority is it is virtually useless as a scientific activity. I am in the minority, taking the position that it is a mistake to dispense with case studies. Case studies earned a bad reputation in personality psychology because they were often used for the purpose of locating examples that support preexisting agendas and arguments. But done well—and there are a number of difficulties to overcome to do them well—case studies can be rich sources for discoveries and for generating new ideas.

Although case studies are viewed with great suspicion in personality psychology, brain scientists and neurological specialists who write about the effects of lesions in specific locations of the brain make liberal use of them. For example, Oliver Sacks's book *The Man Who Mistook His Wife for a Hat* would not have been nearly as engaging and informative had it not been for his ability to give case-by-case examples of brain-challenged individuals struggling to make sense of their lives and the world around them. It is unfortunate that what has become the bread and butter of some neuroscientists is viewed as chicken feed in a field that is devoted to a thoroughgoing understanding of human development and behavior.

The chapters in part I of this book review the role of case studies in psychological research. Questions that have been raised and charges that have been made against their worth are considered. I then describe the approach taken by one of the leading advocates of case studies, Henry Murray. Unmoved by the booming voices of his critics, Murray began to champion in-depth studies of individuals in the 1930s and continued to do so throughout the remainder of his life. He invented the term "personology" to separate the methods he used for understanding lives from the crosspersons comparative methods that characterized work in "personality" psychology. Murray also addressed and made recommendations about ways to resolve a major problem in case study research. The problem involves the blurring of psychological boundaries between an investigator and his or her subject and the resulting tendency to unwittingly study oneself under the pretense of analyzing the life of another person. I discuss that trap more thoroughly in chapter 6 in connection with Freud's psychobiography of Leonardo Da Vinci.

Most of the chapters contained in part II feature a partial psychobiography of J. M. Barrie. Here I ask readers to roll up their sleeves and join me in a quest to identify and make sense of the conditions that gave birth to Peter Pan. The project of investigating the psychological significance of this character, half bird/half boy, to the Scotsman who brought him to life presented a difficult challenge. On some occasions, I nearly joined the forces opposed to case studies, not because case studies are a waste of time but because they require so much mental effort. In the end, however, the work paid off: Some ground was broken that enabled me to tell a gripping, stand-alone story that also nurtured ideas about the origins of flying fantasies that might apply to some other individuals who entertain them.

The last two chapters in part II, chapters 13 and 14, deal with Carl Jung's concept of the collective unconscious. In contrast with Freud's argument that flying dreams and fantasies are sponsored by the sex drive, Jung conceived of them as being among the products of a towering, transcendent force that generates symbols that remind us of our true nature, our true selves. That force and its involvement in sightings of disk-shaped objects from outer space (UFOs) are described in chapter 13. Chapter 14 presents the case that Jung's early sense of abandonment by his mother at a critical age in his development propelled him into a lifelong mission to mold an omnipresent substitute for the earthbound mother whose betrayal had left him with a fractured sense of self.

The recognition of a degree of similarity between the childhood experiences of James Barrie and Carl Jung and the prospects of these experiences leading to both the creation of Peter Pan (for Barrie) and the invention of a source of timeless psychic energy that skirts conscious recognition (for Jung) opens a gate into a new province of psychology, where I ask readers to accompany me. This new territory involves what I perceive to be promising links between discoveries in brain research and certain matters that reside at the heart of personality psychology, particularly in the area of stages of self-development and the onset of consciousness. We are on the brink of discovering ways to combine old ideas with new knowledge about the operation of the human "psyche" and the operation of the human brain. Once again, an attempt to understand what inspires some individuals to want to fly is my window into this arena. In part III, chapters 15 to 18 specify portions of a more general vision of how progress can be made in understanding what for many people is humankind's most illusive and haunting puzzle. I put that puzzle as a question: What is meant by the "self" and what is its bearing on consciousness? I explore that forest just long enough to emerge with a theory of what Barrie and Jung were compelled to seek. I argue that they were driven to restore conditions of early maternal protection—to restore sensations that had been associated with childhood experiences of intersubjective union with their mothers.

In part IV I explore further the hypothesis that flying fantasies can be expressions of nonconscious yearnings to go back to a time prior to the onset of painful disruptions of a world of intersubjective union with a primary love object, a time when the child's sense of self was "at one" with the mother. I begin with a playful chapter about the story of Dumbo, an elephant whose ability to fly brought his mother out of captivity. I then apply the framework for understanding hidden meanings of flying fantasies to "real" people I have studied directly (e.g., a young man who devoted two years to creating a flying backpack) or know about through secondary sources (e.g., Marc Chagall). None of these applications "proves" my point, but together they add a degree of credibility to my thesis.

The last chapter summarizes the gains that can be made by thinking carefully and deeply about individuals' lives. What began as a narrowly focused and reasonably simple question about how Peter Pan arrived as a character in the imaginary landscape of his creator has expanded in directions that make it possible to ask and make progress in answering more difficult questions: questions that pertain to the development of the self, the onset of consciousness, the evolution of the human brain, and the ongoing role of subjective experiences in the ways people conduct their lives and construct their fantasies. These are the sorts of issues have the potential of bringing new life to the field of personality psychology, a discipline that is currently mired in borrowed methods that have precious little bearing on understanding a person—any person.

A brief appendix deals with women's fantasies of flying. I caution against the temptation to squeeze women with ascensionistic desires into a model designed to understand the latent meanings of imaginary flight for men. I suggest that an awareness of the potential of gender differences might reduce the prospects of operating within a framework that sets boundaries around what otherwise could be discovered.

WRITING STYLE

Some sections of this book are written in a lighthearted manner. The tone reflects the joy I experience when I study lives and observe some of the pieces falling together. My language is an alternative to the jargon-filled literature of personality psychology that has the effect of distancing the reader and obscuring the pleasure and privilege of deepening our understanding of human beings. Although I occasionally make fun of myself and take a few jabs at the discipline of psychology, I treat my "subjects" with respect. My style is intended to entice readers to reconsider any notion that issues in psychology are beyond their grasp, and to question and assist in the collapsing the walls that form boundaries around and limitations on a full and rich understanding of our place in the animal kingdom.

INTENDED AUDIENCES

This is not a book that must be read word by word, chapter by chapter, from cover to cover. It is written for several audiences and straddles the line between an academic book and a trade book. One impetus for launching the project that became enlarged into this book was to address the concerns of college students that the field of personality psychology takes statistics more seriously than people. There are many ways to study people, and statistics are indispensable tools for separating facts from fictions. A pendulum labeled "methods of choice" is currently tilted strongly in the direction of tracking variables, but it isn't locked in that position. It will loosen up with a little nudging and eventually move in the direction that honors the fact that we are human objects with subjective lives.

There is another audience that I hope will take an interest in my attempts at integrating various "outside in" and "inside out" theories about early self-development and the onset of consciousness: graduate students and colleagues in psychology and other disciplines who may find the model created in part III robust enough for further consideration and refinements or so outrageously speculative that it provides an example of why scholars should stick with their own fields of specialty. In either case, love it or hate it, the model is my best shot at answering the simple question of why Sir James Barrie, the author of *Peter Pan*, was so desperate to get his mother to smile.

Sometimes the word "theory" evokes grimaces and yawns. I have seen it happen in my teaching with such frequency that I hesitate to even use the term. I don't want that word or its companion term, "model," to discourage the readers I most hope to reach. If you are one of these, you are interested in lives and in ideas about lives. You like mysteries and are aware (or at least suspect) that a lot of unconscious mental activity directly or indirectly influences behavior. You sometimes think about the "self" and wonder about what "it" is. Perhaps you have taken a course in psychology at one or another point in your life and have maintained a modest interest in developments in the field. Irrespective of any formal exposure to psychology, you enjoy reading and thinking about lives and coming to your own conclusions. If this composite or any portions of it fits, I recommend that you begin by reading about James Barrie and Peter Pan (chapters 7 through 12) and decide where to go next.

ACKNOWLEDGMENTS

The creation of this book has been aided by many students at Rutgers University who over several years have listened to me prattle on about the topic of imaginary flight and have read portions of earlier drafts of the book. Their endurance is much appreciated. I have put their criticisms, and especially their expressions of confusion, to good use in making "reader friendly" revisions and stylistic adjustments.

Catharine Carlin at Oxford University Press became an important person in my life in 2001 when she took an interest in this project. I had become accustomed to feedback from editors and publishers who wished me luck but noted that my manuscript fell through the cracks of their marketing categories. Printing an unusual book on an unusual topic is not a risk most publishing houses are willing to take. Despite the odds, and encouraged by enthusiastic comments of anonymous outside reviewers whose opinions Catharine solicited, she and her associate, John Rauschenberg, did whatever needed to be done for Oxford to agree to publish the book.

Some of the original and a few additional anonymous reviewers were given another crack at critiquing the manscript that I had the audacity to think had nearly reached its final form. The book has benefited from their criticisms and suggestions, and I am as unreserved about my gratitude to this very talented group of scholars as they were forthright in their critiques.

The tradition this book is intended to forward is one that has been maintained by others who have kept the case study candle lit through times of stiff opposition. Several of these scholars have played such important roles in the history of biographic research that I have devoted a portion of chapter 2 to noting their contributions. That is a more fitting tribute to them than bunching their names together here in a few lines of text would be. This book is dedicated to these and other individuals who make up the Society for Personology, an organization whose once-a-year meetings were inspirations for me to begin and, most important, to complete this book.

It is largely due to the work of these individuals, who have remained faithful to the idea that people need to be studied as people instead of carriers of variables, that Oxford University Press has decided to reissue Henry Murray's 1938 book *Explorations in Personality* at or near the same time this book is being published. As one of Murray's last students, perhaps his very last student, I am thrilled about this arrangement and hope that *this book* assists in bringing the Murray tradition back into the spotlight.

Finally, I acknowledge the support of my wife, Renee, and my children, Troy and Sam. They have tolerated my early morning departures from home and weekend jaunts into the seclusion of my office. I thank them for their patience.

CONTENTS

PART I *Flight Preparations*

ONE *Come Fly with Me*

Chances are you have dreamed of flying. I have had a few of such dreams. They tend to be restricted to times when I am dreaming about being at a social gathering, usually a reception of some sort. Suddenly and without effort I float up toward the ceiling. I engage in a few conversations as one normally does at such affairs, and later, still in my midair suspended condition, I announce to others that they, too, can fly. "Come on up, join me," I tell some people. "All it takes is intention combined with an element of Zen-like doing without doing." The problem is nobody is interested in my instructions. In fact, only one person even notices that I am doing something exceptional, and I hear him mumble "What a jerk!" I hate to admit that I am so easily grounded, but those words are sufficient to bring my feet to the floor.

Now if only "jerks" are able to fly in their dreams, I am in very good company. I have asked students, hundreds of them at a time in large lecture halls, to raise a hand if they have ever had flying dreams, and usually about a third of the class indicates "yes." In fact, dreams of levitation are so common that some people have taken them to be evidence that human beings descended from birds. No less a person than Lord Montague Norman (1871–1950), an admired former governor of the Bank of England and not thought to be a crackpot by those who knew him, believed that "dream-flights were memory impressions going back to conditions of life more ancient than man . . . when the normal method of locomotion might have been a kind of gliding, skimming, and floating."[1] However, over millions of years, humankind became pampered and civilized and developed unnatural habits like wearing clothes and breathing incorrectly.

3

We thereby lost the wonderful powers we once had at our command. Although Lord Norman had some notable supporters, like Hugh Dowding, who was appointed air chief marshal by King George VI after World War II, his theory that flying dreams are atavistic echoes of primitive times when our wings or spirits could catch the breeze did not achieve the kind of prominence he must have wished.

This book takes a different approach to understanding flying dreams and fantasies. For most people, images of flying that appear in their dreams quickly fade as they go about their daily activities or are reduced to memory fragments of passing curiosity. But there are others for whom flying is such a recurring feature of their dreams that they extend them into their waking hours and imagine themselves soaring above trees, or drifting slowly among the clouds, or taking spectacular airborne voyages to outer space. Some even take serious interest in the prospects of transforming their nighttime reveries into reality. Clive Hart,[2] a historian on this topic, documents centuries of mostly failed efforts to design and execute artificial wings that their creators hoped would take them aloft. Broken bodies were the usual results. Less courageous (and probably wiser) people prefer simply to imagine being able to fly, and some do so to the extent that it becomes a major theme in their lives.

A few specialists in imaginary flight are the primary focus of this book in its quest to penetrate beneath the surface of such fantasies. There is evidence that the desire to fly can, in fact, be traced to lingering remnants from distant times, but not as distant as Lord Norman would have us believe. We need only to go back to periods in these individuals' own lives when earthbound reality presented them with obstacles that they subjectively experienced as so threatening to their survival that they desperately sought to resurrect sensations that accompanied feelings of earlier safety.

I will show that there are many different forms for expressing the urge to fly. One form I will give special attention is stories whose main character(s) are endowed with the ability to fly. Peter Pan is one example I will consider. One would be hard pressed to find more than a few people who are not familiar with the story of Peter, Wendy, Tinker Bell, Captain Hook, and the rest of the gang. When most people think of Peter Pan, the Disney movie or a play based on the script usually comes to mind. Fewer people know that Peter Pan originated from the productive pen of J. M. Barrie, who was a literary giant during the early part of the twentieth century, particularly in Great Britain. As a consequence of his success, a great deal has been written about him. The most valuable source of information is Barrie himself, whose personal paper trail is extensive. Other authors, some who knew him personally and some who did not, have written biographies and commentaries about him to the point where an abundance of facts and speculations about his life and its circumstances are available to ponder.

The large amount of information about Barrie, particularly about his early years, provides us with an opening to explore the psychology of fly-ing. On the basis of strategies for interpreting stories in the context of major underlying concerns of their creators, I will operate with the propo-sition that Peter Pan was partly crafted as a means for granting outward ex-pression to some of the internal needs of the author who brought him into existence. I will use convincing evidence to support this assumption and thereby gain a foothold on decoding the meaning of flying fantasies. The ideas that emerge from considering the life of Barrie will then be extended to the study of the lives of others for whom various forms of flight were of special appeal. This exploration will lead to a deeper understanding of Carl Jung's vision of himself in space, Marc Chagall's striking canvases of levitated figures, and Marshall Herff Applewhite's tragically enacted fan-tasy of himself and his Heaven's Gate followers being lifted from Earth by a comet. I will also consider the lives of less well-known figures, for exam-ple, a boy who devoted several years to the project of creating a flying ma-chine, a man who flew in a lawn chair with weather balloons fastened to it, and a murderer awaiting execution who regularly dreamt of being rescued by a bird and taken to heaven.

As I proceed, I will pause at times to take advantage of some unfore-seen intersections that will appear among ideas from scholars whose works may supply us with important building blocks for shaping our understand-ing of the yearning to fly.

But before delving into these and other matters, it is necessary to make a few comments about the origins of this project. This arena of ex-ploration requires the use of methods and ways of thinking about lives that are less common today than they were during the formative years of the discipline called personality psychology. In fact, this project began with my desire to provide students taking a survey course in personality psy-chology that I have taught for nearly three decades with something to read that represents a tradition that has been nearly forgotten in the current state-of-the-art computations of traits, or that is lurking in the distant back-ground of rigorous statistical analyses for tracking the operation of a few selected variables. On balance, personality psychology is currently being driven more by the study of variables than by the study of individuals. For the most part, a particular version of "hard" science has replaced a "softer" brand that is more willing to bring a combination of methods, including intuition and a degree of art, to the task of studying lives, and I saw no harm in exposing students to "old" ways of thinking about personality and its development. So, as I made progress in setting forth my ideas, drafts of what I composed reached the status of assigned readings to supplement the course's primary textbook.

Then, gradually, the project took on a life of its own. What had started out to be the creation of a reasonably confined instructional device soon engaged more of my attention and *much* more of my time than I had anticipated. Some fascinating leads to understanding the phenomenon of fantasies of flying started to emerge, and I was hooked. In addition, the college bookstore kept running out of copies of my supplemental reading packet because students who were not taking my course were purchasing it. That was a gratifying problem to hear about. And it encouraged me to think about writing with a broader and more diversified audience in mind.

My dual aim became one of holding the attention of readers with a background in psychology and then introducing both them and readers with more casual interests in psychology to ways of thinking about and studying individuals that are different from the world views and procedures that currently prevail in the field of personality psychology.

The process of my promotion of person-centered research in the context of studying the inner lives of people who entertain fantasies of flight has resulted in a guiding theory that a core component of flying fantasies is the manifestation of underlying yearnings to return to less troubled times. Intensive studies of individuals for whom such fantasies are prominent reveal that each of them generated interests in things on high for the common purpose of recapturing feelings associated with a lost protected innocence that they sensed had once been theirs. This is a counterintuitive conclusion—sure to raise the sorts of objections that have already been brought to my attention by scores of individuals. Some have been raised by good friends who are more concerned about my scholarly reputation than I am. They fear that I might embarrass myself, and them as well, by taking a stand on flight that flies in the face of the obvious. The most frequent criticism of my views on the matter is the assertion that flying symbolizes freedom. Birds are free to fly wherever they wish, I'm told, and symbolize the desire to depart from the drudgeries of earthbound realities. (In reality, of course, birds spend most of their time constructing nests, looking for food, and, when the season is right, seeking sexual partners, but I withhold that information because I don't want to be a fantasy destroyer.) Flight can also be considered a metaphor for ambition. Some people tolerate the tedium of their everyday existence by hoping that some day their careers will take off and they will soar to new heights. We speak highly of individuals who are at the peak of their professions. Kings and queens are seated on elevated thrones that symbolize their authority and power. Superman flies for the purpose of defeating evil and preserving what is good. (He was also an orphan, but that would get us much too far ahead in the story.) Freedom, goal attainment, power, altruism; that's what flying is about, my informants explain to me. And I agree! But I also have come to suspect that these and other motives, at least in a few dramatic instances, siphon energy from a still active earlier source that speaks to us not through words but through feelings that operate under the camouflage of more conscious desires.

In order to gain some credibility for the position I am taking, I must make my case carefully. I hope to have done so in several ways. One avenue I have taken is to present a good deal of the information, the "raw data" as it's called, on which my conclusion rests. Along the way, other perspectives for understanding flight fantasies will be compared with my own in a manner that shows I am aware that I have no exclusive rights to the topic. In addition, I take a few detours and discuss issues related to human development in general, and, in one chapter, the human brain in particular, and consider how current knowledge in these areas may be related to flying fantasies.

I ask readers to suspend their beliefs about what flying represents long enough to hear me out. I acknowledge that case studies are viewed as questionable by advocates of a specific set of scientific standards and summarily dismissed as fatally flawed by others. I have profited from and am a victim of an era that opposes the freedom I have granted myself. And, looking back, my "no-holds-barred" approach has not been reached without a struggle. The scholarly words and positivistic advice of intellectual leaders that are lodged in my head, with a united voice, have cautioned me against suspending conventional standards. At times I have used the title of Richard Feynman's 1989 book *What Do You Care What Other People Think* to bolster my confidence, silence my internal critics, and throw another card on the table. "Surely You're Joking" was contained in the title of an earlier Feynman book[3] and the spirit of that phrase has encouraged me to both lighten up my prose and take a plunge into mysterious territories of the human mind.

However, there is one area where I do care about what other people think—particular others, colleagues mostly, who may be prone to toss this book aside as soon as they sense its drift toward reductionism. "Enough!" their words ring out in my ears. "That pap was buried years ago." For the uninitiated, reductionism involves the conviction that past experiences shape personalities; in its strongest and most pessimistic form reductionism holds that personalities are *determined* by childhood events—they *cause* us to be the way we are. Furthermore, reductionism argues that if the determining experiences can be located, a life stands *explained*.

I operate with a less stringent perspective on causation. Certainly I am on the lookout for early experiences, especially turning-point events, to which the enduring concerns of an individual might somehow be linked. There is a recycling-of-old-issues quality to some lives (some would argue every life) and it is fascinating to both identify these patterns and trace them to their origins. But that is where the story begins, not where it ends. Although early dilemmas and recurring configurations of childhood events may be determining factors in terms of *what* is brought into adulthood, they do not determine *how* these issues find expression. There are, of course, some individuals who conduct their lives within the tight boundaries of monotonously repeated themes. But others, the vast majority I would say, are improvisers. All of the case studies in this book are studies of improvisers. Marc Chagall and James Barrie improvised on their basic themes in ways that thrilled the world. Carl Jung's improvisational work made him a celebrity among groups of people who seek their spiritual roots. To argue that these individuals were limited or restricted by early traumatic experiences would prevent us from marveling over what they *did* with their problems.

In summary, if I accomplish my mission, we will come to understand that the case studies that follow converge on the theme of levitation as a way to express latent longings that, perhaps, in various and fluctuating degrees, lie hidden in many other souls. What makes these individuals special is the intensity of their desires to manage disappointments, cruelties, and traumatic experiences by finding a way to return to a better time, a time of weightlessness, a safe and gratifying time of being at the source of love and comfort. What makes them unique is how each of them improvised on that theme.

I mentioned that my method for exploring the grounds from which flying fantasies emerge is at odds with methods that currently prevail in personality psychology. The next chapter addresses this matter so that readers will be able to situate this work in the broader context of the field. Readers who have no desire to be informed about the history behind this contemporary stalemate can move directly to chapter 3 without feeling left out of the loop.

TWO *The Shape of a Discipline*

This investigation into flying fantasies takes an approach to understanding lives that was tried in the field of personality psychology on a few occasions during the twentieth century but never quite survived countervailing forces. Most of this book is constructed from case studies. One of the premises of a case study approach is that if one is to understand the inner workings of personality and the various ways they manifest themselves, in-depth studies of individuals, one at a time, from multiple perspectives, is the most prudent path to follow. The antithesis to that position is that case studies, by their very nature, delve into the *subjective* qualities of a person's life and questions are posed to which no *objective* answers can be given. Furthermore, even if one were to come as close as possible to arriving at a comprehensive understanding of one life, a very time-consuming process in and of itself, what about the hundreds of millions of other lives? Ervin Staub summarizes one aspect of this problem by saying: "If we focus on the uniqueness of every human being, we cannot generalize from one person to another . . . [and] the aim of science is to discover laws . . . [that are] applicable to at least some, if not to all people."[1]

The problem of generalizing the results of studying one person to account for lives not studied is only one of many obstacles that have been thrown into the case study path. In their review of the "puzzling history" of case studies, Nicole Barenbaum and David Winter[2] note the following arguments. While a case study may be a place to begin, it is the least favored of all alternative methods. Case studies are primarily geared toward providing an account of the uniqueness of a single individual. While that ap-

9

proach may have had some value in shedding light on bizarre behaviors (of say a psychopath) in the early days of psychiatry, or may have provided useful examples of the effects of social class membership for sociologists during the first decades of the twentieth century, limitations of the method far exceed its virtues.

When the field of personality psychology began to take shape around the 1920s, it landed in the middle of heated charges that the case study enterprise represented a rebellion against science. Case studies were viewed as tricks in the subjective trade of making a point. In that "anything goes" world of impressionistic descriptions and speculations about the dynamics that drive the character, the authors of such meanderings knowingly or unknowingly simply located, intuited, or invented facts that support their "preformulated convictions."[3] The alternative to this travesty was to embrace science and its methods, particularly its statistical methods, and study "aggregates" of people instead of a single, isolated, soul.

Gordon Allport, acknowledged as the "father" of personality psychology by virtue of publishing the first textbook in the field,[4] struggled with this dilemma near the beginning and straight through to the very end of his illustrious career. He proposed that case studies be referred to as *idiographic* studies and referred to the array of normative approaches to aggregated data as *nomothetic* studies. Allport advocated both methods. While he considered case studies to be "the most revealing method of all," he struggled to design rules for how such investigations should be conducted and, in the end, all but acknowledged that he had not succeeded.

Traits were Allport's preferred units for studying personality. He argued that we *are* our traits, we know ourselves and are known by others by virtue of the traits we possess. We not only have traits, we are motivated by them. An extrovert is motivated to be extroverted. An introvert is motivated to be shy. (Circular reasoning, I know, but that was the position he took.) The advantage of this perspective is that traits can be observed and presumably measured, and when something can be measured, people can be aligned and compared according to their scores on particular instruments. Soon I will show that Allport's promotion of traits as the most promising focus for personality research spawned a tradition that is currently carrying the day. Allport knew what he created and was proud of his contributions to the scientific community. But he remained ambivalent about burying the unique person in the heap of statistical comparisons and urged others to develop methods that might bridge the gap between nomothetic science and the intuitive artistry that is required to do justice to individuality.

Henry Murray was also a looming figure in the 1930s. Both he and Allport were at Harvard University, and both were case study advocates. They agreed on that but on very little else. Murray's commitment to the centrality of case studies and the manner in which he conducted them is described in chapters 4 and 5 of this book. A summary of one of his cases is provided in chapter 3. As will be seen, Murray was interested in "unconscious" motives and was attracted to other psychoanalytic premises. By contrast, Allport was committed to disparaging depth psychology and latched onto traits as the only sensible foundation for creating a respectable theory of personality.

Despite the efforts of these two influential champions of person-centered research, critics of that aspect of their work relentlessly hammered them for promoting "pseudoscience." Both individuals were trained as scientists (Allport in experimental psychology and Murray in medicine and biology) and the criticisms leveled against them took their toll. Murray took more of a "devil-may-care" attitude than Allport was willing to muster, but both were sensitive to the charges against them and frequently defended their scientific credentials by pointing to the amount of research being conducted on the variables they had identified. Most of this research was nomothetic in nature. Scores of psychology laboratories across the nation were busy devising instruments for measuring traits. Allport had identified over five thousand trait terms listed in a dictionary, and a great deal of attention was given to narrowing that number down to a more manageable size. Some still fashionable statistical methods like factor analysis owe their existence to early solutions to the problem of determining which traits or trait clusters are to be granted most favored status for making crossperson comparisons.

What traits were to Allport needs were to Murray. Murray[5] observed that chemistry has its periodic table and botany has a system for categorizing plants and ethnologists classify species. He argued that psychology's equivalent to the elementary classes of other sciences would be a comprehensive list of needs. If such a list could be created and its units agreed on, the field would be provided with a set of primary elements for building a science for the study of "persons." He proposed a list of twenty needs to serve this purpose. A few examples of the basic needs he promoted are the need for achievement (abbreviated as n Ach); the need for nurturance (n Nur); and the need to understand (n Und). The summary label for a need to be humiliated was n Aba or need for abasement. (Murray sought an alternative summary label for this need as he grew weary of students and colleagues saying that they did not need a basement because they already had one.)

Murray's list of twenty needs became grist for the nomothetic mill. Needs, like traits, could potentially be measured, and "on average" scores could be computed for the purpose of studying individual or group differences at the level of motives. Operating with hard numbers derived from scores on various assessment devices offered the distinct advantage of earning psychology the respect it sought from scientists in neighboring disciplines. Enough tender-minded wallowing in subjectivity. Let us join the tough-minded men and women who specialize in the reality of numbers, who view anything that smacks of "soft" psychology with utter disdain and would relegate case studies to the province of serious novelists or hacks who eke out their existence by submitting confessional articles to popular magazines.

Barenbaum and Winter note a progressive decline in the number of person-centered articles in professional journals in their account of the history of case studies in American psychology. The only exceptions to that trend are a few journals in clinical psychology—particularly in the sub-field of "self" psychology. Case studies dominated the pages of journals in the 1920s (an average of 65 percent of the articles were of that sort, according to Barenbaum and Winter's count.)[6] But, as the historian Kurt Danziger points out, the drop became precipitous as "their place was taken by statistical studies based on group studies."[7] Eventually, the editors of most professional journals tightened up their criteria in ways that meant only articles that fit nomothetic formats were considered for publication.

One of the consequences of this trend for personality psychologists was their published research began to look a lot like the variable-tracking studies of social psychologists, so much so that any distinctions that once may have existed between the two fields were blurred.

Nowadays, most research being conducted under the name of personality psychology represents a person, any person, as one or a few data points in a scatter plot, or completely buries the individual in a dense forest of group-based statistical analyses—just as Allport feared might happen. Complaints about this trend are periodically published by a few who lament the disappearance of the "person" in personality psychology, but most of today's leaders in the field view these observations as the last vestiges of a tradition that refuses to enter the modern era of scientific psychology.

At the present time, complaining voices can barely be heard over the din of trait psychologists who in recent years have basked in the glow of the Five Factor Model of personality. The Five Factor Model, also called the Big Five, proposes that all people in all cultures can be profiled according to their relative places on five broad dimensions: Extroversion, Neuroticism, Openness to Experience, Agreeableness, and Conscientiousness. These dimensions have spawned a great deal of research and have provided trait psychology with a useful organizational structure. The success of this model and the recent contributions of cognitive social psychologists, who emphasize the role of rational consciousness in self-knowledge, have provided a platform for the declaration that psychodynamic psychology should be relegated to works devoted to the history of personality psychology. Using judiciously selected words so as not to completely offend remaining members of the old guard, Robert McCrae and Paul Costa, advocates and major figures in the Big Five movement, write:

We don't mean to disparage the thinkers who gave us classic theories of personality. Many of them were extraordinarily acute observers, careful scholars, and profound thinkers—truly grand theorists. But their theories, articulated in the infancy of the science of personality psychology, have been out-grown, and it is time to move on.[8]

And move on it will, because momentum in personality psychology is clearly on the side of trait psychology, as well as various other approaches that relegate "classic" theories and the methods associated with them to the backwaters of the current tide.

The problem is that personality psychology may have "moved on" too fast in certain respects. If migration into the American West in the 1800s had paralleled the recent history of personality psychology, it would have gone something like this. The land was up for grabs. A small group settled in the Farm Belt. Others paused only briefly in the region, found it not of their liking, and went further west to explore virgin territory. They attempted to grow some crops, but the soil was not deep enough to sustain them. They turned to ranching and became good at the trade, particularly in the area of developing a technology for categorizing their cattle. They debated among themselves about the number of categories that should be used to accomplish the task they set forth for themselves. One notable rancher proposed thirty-two categories and later settled for sixteen. Another believed that two categories were sufficient, but changed his mind and added a third. But the number that turned up with the greatest frequency was five. Eventually the majority of the frontiersmen agreed on that figure and proceeded to rigorously demonstrate their case. As word was spread throughout the land, many others arrived on the scene armed with new surveying equipment and other state-of-the-art instruments. They assisted with the task of molding the five categories into a model that dominated the news. Emboldened by their achievements and empowered by the plaudits of likeminded empiricists, they attributed their notoriety to having adhered to the dictates of the science of categorizing. Some of the leaders of the movement looked back with utter disbelief on those who had stayed behind. With a mixture of scorn, pity, and arrogance, they urged the stragglers to catch up.

Actually, some of the stragglers had ventured beyond the plains and initially had liked what they saw. They did some ranching themselves, but something was missing, so they returned to the Farm Belt where the topsoil reached depths of up to forty feet. They missed the soil and the underground streams that nourished it. They believed that there was more to the land than met the eye. They also believed that careful cultivation of their fields, although it would take a great deal of time and patience, could result in discoveries of a different sort than were the sources of well-earned pride of those who had ventured beyond the farmers' preferred territory.

I view myself as one who, in the latter stages of my career, has returned to the fertile fields that I all but abandoned when I picked up my gear and took leave of my intellectual roots. I have rejoined the stragglers, the guardians of an older tradition, and in the face of the shadow that is being cast on it by persons committed to branding-iron technology, I have surrendered to an internal call to resurrect elements of it for the purpose of generating greater understanding and appreciation of the excitement that characterized the field forty to fifty years ago, when psychoanalytic and other "classic" approaches were granted a more privileged status in the fledgling field of personality psychology. I argue that the soil is still deep and to a surprising degree remains unexplored. It is ripe for some "personological" crops.

However, I want to avoid the trap of declaring that the farmers are "right" and the ranchers are "wrong." They operate with different perspectives and use different methods for conducting research in personality and neither "side" need be viewed as superior to the other. A more productive way to view the matter is to understand that different methods are designed to investigate different problems. Person-centered research entails gathering large amounts of information about the lives of specific individuals for the purpose of making headway with the exceedingly difficult challenge of identifying recurrent themes around which a life is organized and describing the convergent internal pressures and external circumstances that contribute to enduring patterns of thoughts and behaviors. In this "long way" of studying people,[9] a good deal of thought is usually given to identifying childhood precursors to current interests, conflicts, and styles of coping.

Such matters are of little to no concern to scholars in other arenas of personality psychology, who use objective and standardized methods for the purpose of demonstrating the power of being able to test predicted covariations of one set of variables with other sets of variables in data gathered from a reasonably large number of respondents whose personal histories are of no interest. Less-than-tidy results in such "one-shot" studies are viewed as fallouts of uncontrolled variance, which represent unpleasant but acceptable losses that are offset by the "general" knowledge that is gained.

The field of personality psychology is currently in a cycle that emphasizes nomothetic methods to such a degree that today's students receive little exposure to a tradition that is largely written off as flawed and prescientific. So as the field moves forward, I am moving backward by providing an account of the kinds of issues and problems that, in some quarters, once occupied a share of the center stage. My resurrection efforts are intended to place a few ounces on the high end of the weighing scale that is presently severely tipped in the direction of nomothetic research. I do so, in part, to try to preserve a legacy that was the original source of my passion for psychology, a legacy that has been continued and has been built on by a few prominent—but widely scattered—scholars who withstood the storm of protests against person-centered research. If the tide is beginning to turn, as some say it is, they will be known as visionaries rather than as tender-minded obstructionists who refused to surrender to the dictates of the modern age.

PRESERVERS OF THE CASE STUDY TORCH

I want to acknowledge some of these more prominent "stragglers" who have remained steadfast to their commitment to whole person research and courageously withstood pressures to conform to the standards of an era that viewed their work as speculative, unscientific, and a waste of potentially salvageable talent.

Rae Carlson stands out as one of the nomothetic branch of personality psychology's most persistent pests. On several occasions, she managed to break the barrier that silenced the publication of laments against a tradition that treated the person as a score on one or another variable and further erased all traces of the person by merging his or her scores into a number that represented a group average.[10] That is a legitimate strategy to follow if one is interested in tracking and comparing variables, Carlson said, but call it social psychology or sociology perhaps, not personality psychology, because the person is missing. Carlson's fiery arguments were couched in statistics of her own, and journal editors surrendered to her insistence on being heard.

Carlson was also instrumental in founding the Society for Personology in 1985. She was joined by her friend and colleague Silvan Tomkins, a luminous scholar whose work on emotions and their central role in framing behavior established the base for a flourishing and increasingly popular line of research on reading faces for affects they both express and mask.[11] It will be evident in chapter 11 that Tomkins's theory of the onset and execution of "scripts" has profoundly influenced my thinking about lives.[12]

The Society for Personology now provides a two-day home once a year for stalwarts of the "old" tradition of studying lives. I have mentioned that most personologists work in relative isolation. A springtime mating call brings these individuals out of the shadows of their academic departments, homes, and offices, and about two dozen make their annual migration to the designated host's college or university grounds.

Willy-nilly, it once was determined that I serve as the outfit's treasurer that carries with it the daunting task of collecting a membership fee of twenty-five dollars a year. This chore, considering the owners of the purses and wallets I seek to raid, is less onerous than one might think. Not to downplay the sparkling work and lasting contributions of each member, I want to pay special homage here to just a few whose persistence in the midst of the field's frowning faces have been a source of inspiration to me.

Those who were most responsible for promoting person-centered, biographic studies prior to and throughout my extended leave from those studies include Irving Alexander, who is affiliated with Duke University, and Brewster Smith, who is affiliated with the University of California at Santa Cruz. Both are retired, and both were colleagues of Tomkins when they worked under the direction of Henry Murray in the late 1930s. Alexander and Smith are presently the elder statesmen of the Society.

The current elder stateswomen are Jane Loevinger, professor emeritus at the University of Missouri, and Ravenna Helson, whose home base is on the Berkeley campus of the University of California. Loevinger is well known for developing a framework and a method for studying stages of ego development, and Helson, through thick and thin times, has managed to conduct a precedent-setting forty-year longitudinal study of women.

Four middle-agers (an age range with a floating upward boundary) who have championed case study research throughout their careers and have been leading sources of support for my own work are Mac Runyan at Berkeley, Alan Elms at the University of California at Davis, Dan McAdams at Northwestern University, and Jim Anderson, a clinical psychologist who is also affiliated with Northwestern. These individuals have operated successfully at the touchy intersection between academic psychology and biographic studies without compromising their standards. Runyan provided a particularly valuable service during the lean years of the 1980s by publishing two books that probe the problems, pitfalls, and virtues of psychobiographic studies.[13]

Finally, I must mention my personal pest, George Atwood. For nearly thirty years, Atwood has been nipping at my heels in an effort to rejuvenate my interest in conducting case studies. Since we are both at Rutgers, he has been difficult to dodge. I stopped coteaching a graduate course on case study research in the early 1970s because I grew suspicious of the wheel-spinning, no-solid-standards aspect of the enterprise. Too often for my taste the course dissolved into a forum for students to engage in poorly controlled speculative analyses of "cases" interspersed with some "insights" that gave every appearance of having been derived extemporaneously from their personal free associations instead of being based on information that could be deemed objective. A stint of serving as my department's chair for much too long a period was followed by two dozen years of what amounts to nomothetic, group comparison, variable-centered research on various topics that were and continue to be interesting to me. However, I might mention that each line of research I developed over the span of twenty or so years began with case studies. That is how I began my work on the role of the "undesired self" in assessments of well-being.[14] In-depth studies of individuals led to ideas that found expression in my research on life satisfaction and aging.[15] My colleague and midlife mentor, Seymour Rosenberg, trained me how to use methods that he developed to empirically represent the structure of individuals' perceptions of the self and others.[16] Richard Ashmore and I applied these methods to studies of individuals' perceptions of themselves "when-with" others.[17] In order to prevent becoming lost in matrices of numbers and algorithms, I first applied them to single cases. I was unwilling to have a hand in conducting research on a multitude of participants until I felt comfortable that the procedures and methods resulted in reasonably valid representations of how individuals, studied one at a time, organized their subjective worlds.[18] So, looking back, I never really abandoned case studies. Instead, I have hidden the idiographic sources of nearly every "standard" study I have conducted, even in the face of knowing that Atwood would continue to view me as a coward for having abandoned ship.

In the meantime, I continued to teach my course in personality psychology. It kept me abreast of various trends in the field and its preference for variable-centered (versus person-centered) research. Year after year I witnessed the production of textbooks loaded up with the results of studies, hundreds of them, with occasional lessons on how to gather and manipulate numbers. Although I value the scientific tradition that many of these studies represent and occasionally am awed by the cleverness of some research designs, much that gets published under the heading of personality psychology favors methods over content. I could (but won't) give numerous examples of how a fascinating idea or a new concept reported in the literature can become butchered and buried by subsequent spinoff studies that tweak it this way and that until one is ready to scream, as several of my students have, "Who cares!" This phenomenon brings to mind the words of David McClelland, who several decades ago led the charge on motivational research, when he said that students were being well trained in methods and poorly trained in topic selection.

So I concluded that the time was right to stop complaining, heed Atwood's advice, and do something. At first glance, and even at a second, third, or final glance, it may appear that I violated David McClelland's "find a good topic" recommendation. Had he recommended that one find an unusual topic, flying fantasies would be very nearly perfect. In fact, my topic selection was a matter of expedience. I had previously written about the topic,[19] and it should be simple enough, I thought, to rifle through various notes and papers and produce a document that would serve my educational purpose. But during the process of looking over dated materials, another motive energized my plan. I recovered elements of my previous interest in what I had called the "psychodynamics of fantasized flight," and I got excited about the prospects of making more progress in understanding such fantasies than when I had previously toyed with various ideas. The impetus to write about flying fantasies as a way to introduce students to a fading tradition was now strengthened by a desire to come to grips with a topic of longstanding interest to me. The next chapter describes how the topic initially came to my attention.

THREE *An American Icarus Named Grope*

Flying fantasies first captured my interest when I read "The American Icarus" by Henry Murray, published in 1955 as a chapter in a book that contained several case studies by various authors.[1] Grope was the name Murray gave to the subject of his investigation. Grope was a reclusive undergraduate student at the time he was studied, a person whose presence on campus was barely noticed. He was a quiet young man; shy, apathetic, uninvolved, and uninspired. He never dated and belonged to no clubs or organizations. His social life was restricted to late night card games, bridge mostly, with a few regulars from his dorm. Studying was seldom on his agenda; books would be opened only when the pressure was on to obtain minimally passing marks in his courses. There was nothing at all about his inconspicuous outward appearance to indicate that his private life was filled with spectacular imaginary shows of personal heroism. Murray described Grope as "unsurpassed" in that regard.

A recurring theme in his imaginary exploits was flying. Such images were periodically accompanied by images of fire, water, and falling through space. The occasional interweaving of these images reminded Murray of the legend of Icarus. In that ancient Greek story, Daedalus and his son, Icarus, were trapped on an island with no means of escape. Daedalus's solution to the problem was to fashion wings from bird feathers for himself and Icarus by attaching them to their arms with wax. Tragically, Icarus did not follow his father's flying instructions. In direct disobedience of his elder's advice, Icarus soared toward the sun. The sun's heat melted the wax that held the feathers in place, and Icarus plunged into the sea and was drowned.

Murray discerned a sufficient degree of overlap among the themes in the legend of Icarus and the images contained in Grope's fantasies that he invented the concept of an "Icarus complex" that he used to structure a summary of his observations regarding Grope. Part of Murray's analytic strategy was to provide comprehensive definitions of each of the major components of the Icarus complex that comprised Grope's "covert personality." The theme of flying was included as just one element of a much broader concept that Murray called *ascensionism*. Murray's full definition is worth our consideration:

> [Ascensionism] is the name I have given to the wish to overcome gravity, to stand erect, to grow tall, to dance on tiptoe, to walk on water, to leap or swing in the air, to climb, to rise, to fly, to float down gradually from on high and land without injury, not to speak of rising from the dead and ascending to heaven. There are also emotional and ideational forms of ascensionism—passionate enthusiasm, rapid elevations of confidence, flights of imagination, exultation, inflation of spirits, ecstatic mystical up-reachings, poetical and religious— which are likely to be expressed in the imagery of physical ascensionism. The upward thrust of desire may also manifest itself in the cathection of tall pillars and towers, of high peaks and mountains, of birds—high-flying hawks and eagles—and of heavenly bodies, especially the sun. In its most mundane and secular form, ascensionism consists of a craving for upward social mobility, for a rapid and spectacular rise in prestige.

It is difficult to imagine a broader, more comprehensive definition of ascensionism. In fact, Murray's definition, while it served his purpose well, is so sweeping that it is rendered nearly useless for my present purpose. Everyone who has experienced a sudden burst of enthusiasm, or whose eyes have been attracted to high-flying birds, or as a child wanted to grow tall is, or for that moment was, an ascensionist. In that way, the cap fits us all. Nonetheless, I was struck by the concept of ascension when I read about Grope's aerial adventures, and in subsequent years I was reminded of them when I read about or encountered individuals in whose lives flying fantasies occupied a special place.

There have been times when I have returned to Murray's description of Grope and have concluded that Grope's ascensionistic desires had been merged with a need to achieve social recognition to the point where the two urges were indistinguishable from each other. For example, Grope concluded his written autobiography with the sentence: "I am just biding my time and waiting for the day when my soul will ignite and this inner fire will send me hurtling (two rungs at a time) up the ladder of success." Although what Murray wrote about Grope has remained a source of inspiration for me and periodically throughout this book I will mention some points of comparison between Grope and the lives I am considering, I am limiting my focus to only one element of Murray's far-reaching definition of ascensionism—themes of flight.[2]

It is fitting that a study written by Henry Murray got me interested in the topic of levitation, because it is a Murray-inspired tradition that I am endeavoring to resurrect. The next two chapters describe some of the pioneering work of Murray and his collaborators in the 1930s, what they believed were necessary components of comprehensive studies of lives, and some of the tools they developed for the trade. My description of Murray's interests in and treatment of imaginative stories will set the tone and orient the compass for several chapters that lie ahead.

FOUR *Henry Murray's Personology*

Hermeneutics is defined as the art and science of interpreting texts. It is used, for example, to describe the activities of priests, rabbis, and others in ministerial professions, whose jobs require them to decipher the meaning of religious texts. Normally, when one thinks about texts, the thought of words written on a page comes to mind. But there is a branch of hermeneutics that, taken to its extreme, considers the person to be a text. We all tell stories and in doing so provide bits and pieces, paragraphs and even chapters of our life sagas in progress. In some respects, one can say that we *are* our stories. Dan McAdams suggests[1] we are carriers of a grand text that, as Bertram Cohler has convincingly shown, is periodically revised and updated.[2] The application of hermeneutics to that text (read person) involves a subjective dialogue between the author and the interpreter who seeks to gain insight into the multilayered meanings of the text. That process may begin with a single story that the interpreter studies with an eye to speculating about what is packaged and expressed in it that, unbeknownst by the author, may be a prevalent issue in his or her life. A guiding assumption behind this process is that individuals, sometimes unwittingly, reveal meaningful information about themselves through the stories they tell. Some speculations and initial hunches may be incorrect and no additional support for them is forthcoming. Later on I will show that some interpretations provide more information about the dispositions and latent needs of the interpreter than of the person whose life is under scrutiny. In the meantime, other ideas may gain momentum and achieve the status of hypotheses used as guides for interpreting additional stories and shedding light on major themes that emerge in the text of the person.

In ensuing chapters I will apply these suppositions to J. M. Barrie as I endeavor to determine if and how he shaped the character, actions, and dilemmas of Peter Pan in ways that expressed major issues in his own life. This will require an effort to reconstruct Barrie's life in psychological terms, and in order to do that it is necessary to become familiar with as much information about him as is available. Only then are we in a position to explore the intersections between his life and his stories.

This strategy for studying lives was featured in the work of Henry Murray, who promoted the idea that there are no more fertile grounds than in-depth case studies for making progress in meeting the challenge of understanding the operation of the human psyche. The following description of how Murray became an early spokesman for person-centered, idiographic research will also present some of the premises and guidelines for case study work.

Murray's book *Explorations in Personality*, coauthored by many and published in 1938,[3] contains a compendium of methods for studying individuals. As the director of the Harvard University Psychological Clinic, and then as a senior faculty member and cofounder of Harvard's Department of Social Relations, Murray championed the position that one of the primary tasks of psychology is to understand the person—not just this or that piece of a person that may be represented by a score on particular test or measurement device but the whole person and how a particular life is organized. This ambitious undertaking required intensive case studies of "normal" people in "normal" settings using multiple perspectives and methods. As previously noted, Murray coined the term "personology" to separate his approach and formulations from other conceptions and guidelines for studying personality and defined it as the scientific study of the whole person.

One of the distinctive propositions of personology is that people reveal a great deal about themselves through their creative acts, including the stories they make up. Murray proposed that stories could be analyzed in ways analogous to Sigmund Freud's treatment of dreams. Here are a few of the basic elements of Freud's thinking about dreams. What a person recalls and reports about a dream is its manifest content, the dream as dreamed. Beneath the manifest content is the dream's latent content, and that is where the true meaning of the dream can be found. Dream work is the process of transforming raw desires into a nighttime reverie in a way that grants partial release of pent-up emotions and forbidden desires while disguising the true nature of the dream so the dreamer can remain asleep. Dream analysis involves reversing the direction of dream work so that one can weave one's way back through the dark passageways leading to the unconscious and, with a combination of luck and courage, confront the hidden material that is responsible for the dream's production. In patient treatment sessions, this was done through a process of having the dreamer, now awake, free associate to various figures, actions, and events recalled from a dream for the purpose of bringing to consciousness its unconscious determinants. This was an important aspect of Freud's clinical plan for many of his patients. He believed that dreams provided the "royal road to the unconscious," where the source of neurotic symptoms, often prefigured in childhood, could be located, dealt with, and resolved.

Following Freud's lead, Murray took a similar perspective on imaginative stories. He viewed them as avenues for giving partial expression to various tensions that rest beneath the conscious grasp of their authors. The phenomenon of nonconscious material bypassing consciousness and finding symbolic expression in dreams and stories was not restricted to individuals needing psychiatric assistance. It is true of everyone. It is how "civilized" men and women are designed. Sometimes we are forced to hide our innermost feelings and desires from others, and even from ourselves, for a host of reasons. Early on we learn that some impulses are shameful, that incest is forbidden, that even thinking about, let alone taking action on, unsanctioned behaviors might ostracize us from our families and from society at large. Even so, in the recesses of our minds, such desires remain active. They fester and seek avenues for release. The magic of dreams and stories is they grant partial release to threatening impulses and at the same time disguise them in ways that prevent us from being infused by anxiety or mortified by conscious recognition of reprehensible thoughts.

One of the side effects of this infiltration process is it spices up our imaginations. Without input from the unconscious, our dreams, as well as our stories, would be drab, lifeless, boring. I suspect that good storytellers, like many fine artists, engage in a sort of controlled seepage of unconscious materials into their creative works. Recognition is given to creative works that tap into and offer channels for discharging latent needs and concerns of the reading or viewing audience, particularly when such works succeed in symbolizing "shared" sources of internal restlessness.

In order to exemplify the interpretive power of this perspective on unconscious influences on story productions, Murray, intermittently over many years, studied the life and works of Herman Melville. He intended to write a definitive book on Melville but was unable to complete the project. Nonetheless, he wrote several essays on this topic, and one of them became an important item on the library shelves of Melville scholars. In that essay[4], Murray unleashed his enviable command of the English language in presenting his interpretation of Melville's novel *Moby Dick*. His central theme was that the monstrous white whale symbolized the puritan ethic of nineteenth-century America. It was the Calvinistic ethic of Melville's time that had built an "inscrutable wall" against the expression of anything other than righteous urges. Murray wrote: "As a symbol of a sounding, breaching, white-dark, unconquerable, New England conscience, what could be better than a sounding, breaching, white-dark, unconquerable sperm whale?" The stifling atmosphere of sermonizing that surrounded Melville's youth both in his church and in his home had been internalized and operated as an omnipresent guard against any temptation to waver from the Word. The whale, Murray argued, symbolized the rules that had been etched into Melville's mind by his God-fearing parents and by fire-and-brimstone pastors who reminded parishioners of long-term punishment the Lord had in mind for unredeemed sinners.

The actions of Captain Ahab symbolized Melville's desire to break the shackles constraining the expression of passions that, in the church's view, were inspired by Satan. The only alternative to becoming a purified puppet of Calvinistic dogma and thereby leading a life not worth living was to find the law-enforcing monster and destroy it. Billed as a battle between the "id" (Ahab) and the "superego" (Moby Dick), the mission to locate the mammal was complicated by its residence in the depths of the ocean, a metaphor for a superego that does much of its work in the unconscious reaches of the mind, making it an elusive enemy to locate, corner, and destroy. Finally, after the long, frustrating, and dangerous voyage of the Pequod, the White Whale rises to the surface, and a harpoon is hurled into its flesh. But Ahab's body becomes entangled in the rope, and he is dragged to his watery grave by the guardian symbol of society's unrelenting and unforgiving pressure to conform.

For Murray, *Moby Dick* was more than a captivating story about a tragic whaling adventure. In his opinion, Melville used his intimate knowledge of whaling cultures in small New England villages in the nineteenth century and the kinds of men who went to sea to create a saga through which he was able to vent his anger and frustration about the Presbyterian chains that had crippled his spirit. It was that latent story within the manifest plot that fascinated Murray, and he sought ways to incorporate this beneath-the-surface perspective into his grand design for personology.

The next chapter describes how Murray applied this perspective in his laboratory studies of individual lives.

FIVE *All the King's Horses and All the King's Men*

The participants in the first wave of individuals studied by Murray and his collaborators at the Psychological Clinic were male undergraduates attending Harvard College in the 1930s. There were fifty-one of them, all paid volunteers who had responded to a notice posted in a student employment office or had heard about the study by word of mouth. Given the makeup of the sample and the elitism of Harvard during those days, one might question the degree to which the volunteers met the requirements of "normal people" in "normal settings." And yet the participants, called "subjects" when that depersonalized term prevailed, were not patients confined to institutions or in treatment for various debilitating symptoms. So in that sense they fell within the broad boundaries of normalcy.

None of these students, as far as is known, were budding Melvilles. They were not armed with manuscripts they had written when they arrived at the modest wood frame building in Cambridge that housed the clinic. Since a portion of the long-term investigation of their lives was to involve interpretations of stories composed by each volunteer, a strategy had to be developed to obtain stories from them. That was accomplished in an innovative fashion that led to the most enduring product developed in the clinic. Murray and one of his devoted colleagues, Christiana Morgan, designed a set of storytelling stimuli that they called the Thematic Apperception Test (TAT for short.) The TAT, an instrument that some clinical practitioners and researchers still use, is not really a "test" in any formal sense. It is better thought of as an exercise that invites an individual to make up twenty separate imaginative stories in response to viewing twenty different drawings placed on eight-and-a-half by eleven–inch cards. The pictures are intentionally ambiguous, granting plenty of leeway for a person to "read" whatever he or she prefers to see in a picture and to fashion a story from those perceptions. For example, one card depicts the silhouette of a man or a woman against a bright window. The rest of the card is black. Another card shows a middle-aged woman standing on the threshold of a half-open door looking into a bedroom. Neither picture contains indications of what either figure might be looking at or thinking about. Storytellers must make up these sorts of details and, in doing so, are asked to follow the guidelines for most good stories. Specifically, it is recommended that each of their stories include a description of what led up to the situation depicted in the card, what is happening at the moment, what are the main characters thinking and feeling, and to conclude the story by describing its outcome.

One advantage of using the TAT method for eliciting stories from each of the volunteers is that all respondents compose stories to the same set of twenty cards, allowing investigators to identify stories that deviate from standard run-of-the-mill ones told by the majority to a specific card. But even a commonly told story can take on special meaning in light of other stories composed by a participant. An example of that will come up in chapter 22 in the context of the case of a person I named Tonka. He told a story about a man trying to decide if he should leave or stay with his mother in response to viewing a picture containing a young man and an older woman. In that drawing the man is looking at the floor while standing with a hat in his hands. The woman is looking out a window with her back turned away from the man. The gist of Tonka's story makes it similar to the stories generated by many others for the same card. But its meaning is enhanced by the fact that it is a variation of a theme that Tonka introduced in many of his stories—the theme of a young man's ambivalence about leaving a mother figure. In fact, the theme of maternal separation was the central plot of some stories he told against backdrops that contained no women figures.

Murray viewed such regularly appearing themes as expressions of the storyteller's dominant drives, emotions, sentiments, and conflicts. Repeated themes (called "themas" in Murray's system) were treated as clues to the contours of the "inner self," a place where past experiences, covert desires, and present wants are merged, amalgamated, and made meaningful. Just as liquid poured into a one-of-a-kind jug takes the shape of the jug, Murray surmised that experiences are processed or filtered in ways that conform to the needs, fears, and perceptual biases of the inner self. Call it an inner self, a subjective self, a phenomonological self—whatever "it" was, Murray sought to gain access to it.

Murray surrounded himself with an exceptionally talented group of Ph.D. candidates and postdoctorates who were tantalized by the prospects of bringing "depth psychology" into the lab. The 1930s were exciting times at Harvard's Psychological Clinic. New ideas, fresh insights, and inviting possibilities were almost daily occurrences. Some veterans of those heady days have told me that sleep was rarely on the agenda. The group had a floating membership of close to thirty people with backgrounds in clinical psychology, philosophy, anthropology, literature, and other disciplines, and lively subgroup discussions often continued in cafeterias and pubs well after midnight.

A task assigned to several senior staff members was to trace prominent themes that appeared in a person's stories to their origins. That involved arranging a large number of pieces of information gathered on each participant (autobiographies, interviews, TAT stories, responses to surveys, questionnaires, test batteries, etc.) into a coherent story, a psychological story, that specified the major themes around which a person organized his life, the primary experiences that determined these patterns and enabled them to be maintained, and how these and other forces were expressed in daily life. In short, the goal was to condense the story of a person's life into another story, a psychological narrative that dealt with a person's inner reality. Call it psychobiography.

Now psychobiographies make most academic psychologists uncomfortable, just as Murray himself made his academic colleagues at Harvard University and elsewhere uncomfortable. He was considered to be an outsider who lacked the training and credentials for making serious contributions to the science of human behavior. Prior to receiving a back-door faculty appointment at Harvard, Murray had been trained as a surgeon. He had become interested in psychology as a result of spending a few weeks with Carl Jung, a Swiss psychoanalyst, whom Murray claimed had introduced him to the unconscious. The last thing that a relatively new academic discipline struggling for respect from scientists in more established areas wanted to contend with was a maverick, albeit it a maverick with both an M.D. and a Ph.D. (in biochemistry) who eventually occupied a tenured position in a prestigious institution. Psychologists were invested in creating sound, reliable measurement devices that, when possible, could be used in rigorously controlled and preferably experimental studies of behavior. It was unsettling to hear Murray speak about nonconscious motivation. What's that? Latent needs. Sorry, that's armchair stuff. Fantasies, motives, inner selves? These are "black box" items that have no legitimate place in the behavioral sciences. And psychobiography? Perhaps there is a faculty position available for a person with such interests in a Department of Poetry.

Murray's spirit was not damaged by the majority's view. He was a towering figure whose confidence (always) and belligerence (sometimes) exceeded his tall frame. He was not one to mince words when it came to offering his opinions about the topics and methods that dominated the field. In one of his broadsides, he wrote that academic psychology

has contributed practically nothing to the knowledge of human nature. . . . It has not only failed to bring light to the great hauntingly
recurrent problems but it has no intention, one is shocked to realize,
of attempting to investigate them.[1]

Such mischievous words did nothing to endear him to his critics. He was
fond of heaving his own harpoons into the flesh of the academic establish-
ment and was careful not to get his legs tangled by the ropes that would
carry him into the realms of sanctioned research.

Secure in his knowledge of science and its limitations, Murray was
forthright about there being a component of artistry involved in writing
psychological narratives. He insisted, however, that narratives be written as
part of a joint venture with input from a team of researchers that consti-
tuted what became known as a "diagnostic council." The diagnostic council was one of the ways Murray endeavored to control for a very serious
problem in writing psychobiographies. This is the problem. People who
study the lives and stories of other people have stories and lives of their
own. Just as the target of an investigation may not be fully conscious of the
effects of his or her subjective experiences on the stories he or she tells, the
investigator may not be able to place a rein on the influence of his or her
own nonconscious issues and conflicts in the process of reading and interpreting another person's life. In other words, it is sometimes impossible to
disentangle the psyche of the psychobiographer from the major issues he
or she identifies in another person. People, all people, are inclined to see
in others things that have more bearing on themselves than the person
being scrutinized. A case study is a psychological story about another person's story and one must wonder about whose story is being told and
analyzed.

Murray's safeguard against the unknowing infiltration (he called it
"projection") of an investigator's own psychological dynamics into the life
of the subject under the pretext of objectivity was the diagnostic council
whose members served the function of all the king's horses and all the
king's men, making suggestions and taking positions and struggling to
agree about which piece went where in the psychological design of the
person. Group discussions served to counterbalance the effects of individual projective tendencies, enabling the group to evolve a working consensus about the major themes in a person's life. Speculations about the
influence of both early, recent, and anticipated future experiences on subjects' interests, their life patterns, the meanings they make of themselves
and others, and how such things sometimes find expression in their stories
were products of vigorous discussions and sometimes heated debates by
council members in their efforts to arrive at a consensus about how a particular life was best construed in psychological terms.

Traces of Murray's personological approach can still be found in psychology as they were carried forth by men and women who were trained in his lab. As shown in part by the names of a few current members of the Society for Personology I mentioned in chapter 2, a more complete compilation of the names of individuals who worked directly with Murray or were influenced by his ideas and the tools he created would constitute an impressive group of people who have contributed much to psychology. Nonetheless, psychobiographic work remains highly suspect in the overall academic discipline of psychology. Graduate students and young professionals who may be attracted to intensive case studies are quickly and correctly alerted to the subjective nature of the work by their mentors, who, again correctly in most instances, advise them to work on problems that can be contained within the boundaries of mainstream science if they desire to be competitive for prized faculty appointments.

Aware of the pitfalls of psychobiography and having no diagnostic council at my immediate disposal to issue objections and recommend alternatives to the direction my investigation might take, my first step at delving into the latent meanings of flight fantasies will be to follow Murray's lead and view the character Peter Pan as a fabricated image that gave expression to prominent issues in the life of its creator, J. M. Barrie. Before that challenge is tackled, however, a theory of the meaning of flying fantasies proposed by an influential protagonist—Sigmund Freud, who will occasionally accompany us on this venture—must be considered and, in the end, challenged. I do so in the context of full awareness that Freud identified and developed ways of understanding human behavior that are indispensable to the work that lies ahead.

SIX *Freud on Da Vinci:*

The Rocky Road of Psychobiographic Investigations

Flying fantasies are not exactly psychology's standard fare. Search the literature for key word references to *ascensionism* or *imaginary flight* on a computerized database, and the screen will declare that no matches were found. An advantage of this situation is that I have been able to stake out a territory and work on a puzzle without wondering if I should be spending more time thumbing through professional journals to keep abreast on the results of recent studies on levitation. That does not mean that there is no competition. Competition is "out there," as the current phrase would have it, and it is stiff. Enter the master himself, Sigmund Freud.

Freud wrote about dreams and fantasies of flight on at least two occasions, and in both instances he arrived at the same conclusion: images of flight in dreams and in daytime fantasies are to be understood as deflected expressions of sexual impulses. The latent meaning carried by manifest images of flying, for males anyway, is the desire for sex. Freud's position was that fantasies of levitation and interests in flight are formed and sustained as sublimated expressions of sexual instincts whose normal channels have been blocked. Sexual instincts, of course, would prefer more direct outlets. But when anxiety gets in the way, or when a person is confused about the raw nature of his or her desires, fantasies of floating above the ground or soaring through space provide at least partial release of primitive forces. Freud's interpretation of flying cannot be ignored. Nor are we obliged to let it go unchallenged.

This chapter presents Freud's application of his diverted sex-drive theory of imaginary flight to the life and works of Leonardo Da Vinci. In

the process of considering Freud's case study of one of the world's most famous artists who aspired to fly, examples will arise of the problem with psychobiographic investigations I mentioned earlier: the risk of biographers
observing in others what may be more true of themselves.

Dan McAdams defines psychobiography as "the systematic use of psychological theory to transform a life into a coherent and illuminating
story."[1] Among the best psychobiographers was Erik Erikson whose illuminating stories of Martin Luther[2] and Mahatma Gandhi[3] delved into the
conscious and nonconscious forces that shaped their lives and enabled
them to emerge as critical leaders of monumental historical importance.
Erikson masterfully interwove central themes in his subject's lives with the
cultural conditions that provided audiences that were receptive to the messages these great figures were psychologically driven to offer.

Erikson frequently spoke of his indebtedness to Freud for the conceptual tools for discerning the operation of latent subplots that give meaning
to actions that otherwise might appear to be unrelated. It is doubtful that
the term *psychobiography* would even exist were it not for Freud's lifelong
work on the topic of powerful unconscious forces that operate behind the
scenes of personal and historical dramas. Erikson took full advantage of
the conceptual tools provided by Freud. However, Freud's first foray into
psychobiography titled *Leonardo Da Vinci and a Memory from His Childhood* was more narrowly focused than Erikson's studies and was consider-
ably more shallow.[4] In fact, Freud's book on Leonardo backfired, in the
sense that it provided some of his critics with ammunition for discrediting
Freud and attempting to take the entire edifice of psychoanalytic "depth"
psychology down with him.

Freud set two kinds of standards for psychobiographical work in
Leonardo, high standards and low standards. Alan Elms[5] observes that
Freud created several rules, excellent rules for psychobiographers to observe (high standards), and proceeded to violate each one of them himself
(low standards).

VIOLATION 1

One guideline offered by Freud was to avoid arguments built on a single
clue. He managed to ignore this recommendation in a most astonishing
fashion in his analysis of Leonardo. He endeavored to understand
Leonardo's life and creations by arguing that they were derived from a single fragment of a memory that Leonardo jotted down in one of his scientific notebooks. There Leonardo wrote:

> It seems to me that I was always destined to be so deeply concerned
> with vultures; for I recall as one of my very earliest memories that

while I was in my cradle a vulture came down to me, and opened my mouth with its tail, and struck me many times with its tail against my lips.

This is how Freud interpreted the memory. First, the action of being struck many times on his lips was derived from Leonardo's fond memories of being nursed by his mother. It repeated

in a different form a situation in which we all once felt comfortable—when we were still in our suckling day and took our mother's nipple into our mouths and sucked at it. The organism's impression of this experience—the first source of pleasure in our life—doubtless remains indelibly printed on us.[6]

The mystery that Freud then attempted to explain was how it came to be that a bird's tail became a stand-in for Leonardo's mother's breast. In line with his theory that several desires and latent thoughts can be combined or "condensed" into one symbol, Freud argued that Leonardo's confusion about the source of babies was expressed in the fantasy through the image of a bird. Freud's reasoning was this. The fact that Leonardo was raised by his mother in a single parent household for the first three or four years of his life made the lad's "research" into the problem of the origins of infants more difficult than it would have been had a father been around. Freud notes that an important element of Leonardo's fantasy solution to the mystery of his birth bore resemblance to ancient Egyptian use of birds, *vultures* in particular, to convey the idea of mother. Freud elaborates on that idea by remarking that it was once believed that vultures impregnate themselves; a view that is said to have been endorsed by some Fathers of the Catholic Church in support of the phenomenon of virgin births. He suggests that Leonardo created his own version of an association between mother-goddess and vultures to explain how he had come into existence. In sum, the fantasy both represents and conceals his working solution to the problem of birth by conjuring up the image of a tail that represents both his mother's breast and her self-impregnating organ.

Freud used these ideas as a springboard for his thesis that Leonardo's artistic works (e.g., the fabled smile formed by the lips of Mona Lisa), scientific projects (e.g., early designs of heavier- than-air flying devices), presumed latent homosexuality, difficulty in completing paintings, and other facets of his interests and life patterns could all be reduced to a few elements of an early memory.

The links that Freud discerned between the memory and the consequences for Leonardo's psychological development demonstrates Freud's unsurpassed cleverness in applying his theory of infantile sexuality to a single case. One can learn a great deal about the hydraulic quality of Freud's theory of instincts and their deflections by reading the book. Unfortunately, he set a bad precedent for others who would follow his lead in attempting to explain a life on a single clue. The quality of Freud's analysis of Leonardo does not fit his legacy of introducing the power of unconscious processes to modern science. To make matters worse, Freud based portions of his argument on a text that had mistranslated the Italian word "nibbio," a word that refers to a bird commonly known as a kite, not a vulture.

VIOLATION 2

Another guideline for writing psychobiographies that Freud recommended was not to idealize one's subject.[7] Alan Elms constructs a well-documented and convincing argument that, in fact, Freud not only idealized Leonardo but in many ways identified with him. One parallel between the two that Elms stresses is the extent to which they devoted their full attention to their scientific pursuits. Freud believed that Leonardo represented a "rare and perfect" instance of sublimation of the sexual instinct that allowed it to operate freely in the service of intellectual pursuits. This, Freud believed, explained Leonardo's cultural and scientific achievements *and* the absence of sexual relationships in his life, the latter being an indispensable part of the former.

Prior to writing his analysis of Leonardo, Freud mentioned the absence of sex in his own marriage in correspondences with close colleagues. In fact, it is well documented that Sigmund and his wife, Martha, terminated all sexual contact around 1895. Freud was thirty-nine and Martha was thirty-four. One might speculate that abstinence was their version of birth control, but clearly other factors were involved. One explanation is that it was a manifestation of Freud's personal struggles with sex. Ernest Jones, one of Freud's most sympathetic biographers, claims that the problem had been initiated early in Sigmund's life when his "mother's tenderness was fateful to him. . . . The violence of the caresses . . . established his sexual inactivity for the whole of his later life."[8] Jones notes that his thoughts on the matter were based on a letter Freud wrote to him shortly after his (Freud's) mother's death. (I will say more about Freud's relationship with his mother near the end of this chapter).

The onset of sexual abstinence marked the beginning of Freud's greatest theoretical writings. His most impressive and lasting contributions to psychoanalytic psychology, a field that he was largely responsible for creating, were published during the dozen or so years after bedtime play had been abandoned. Increasingly, the psychoanalytic movement consumed all of his energies, and the numerous responsibilities he had taken on left him little time to write when, in 1909, he began his psychobiography of Leonardo. Bad timing, one might think, because he was overseeing new editions of two of his major works and was involved in training analyses, treating patients, presenting seminars, editing books and journals, maintaining the practice of writing voluminous letters to colleagues, and finding ways to expand the now international psychoanalytic movement.[9] A quotation from a letter Freud wrote to Carl Jung makes reference to his state of exhaustion. "My week's work leaves me numb. I would invent the seventh day if the Lord hadn't done it so long ago. . . . Quite against my will I must live like an American; no time for libido." Nonetheless, Freud completed his psychobiography of Leonardo in six months.

Elms raises the question of why the rush, why did Freud refer to the project as his "obsession" in another letter to Jung in 1909? Among the various answers Elms provides to this question is that Freud had begun to fear the waning of his intellectual prowess; prowess that, in accordance with Freud's theoretical principles, is sustained by the process of sublimation, the transformation of sexual energy in culturally creative acts. It is unlikely that he failed to notice the coincidence between the termination of his sexual life and the onset of his most productive years. The suspected failure of sublimation to sustain the flow of new ideas and major insights is perhaps one factor that contributed to the urgency behind Freud's writing about Leonardo as an example of a well-known figure whose "rare and most perfect" diversion of sexual impulses enabled him to sustain a lifetime of lasting accomplishments. Perhaps Freud believed that by understanding how Leonardo sustained his output, he (Freud) could rejuvenate his own intellectual powers.

Another of Freud's concerns, which arose just prior to and during the period of his frantic work on Leonardo, was the unwelcome awakening of homosexual feelings directed toward some of his younger disciples, including Carl Jung, Sándor Ferenczi, and Wilhelm Fliess.[10] Fliess had been the object of disturbing emotional feelings several years earlier, and in 1910 Freud acknowledged to a friend that he was once again working through the reactivation of former erotic feelings toward Fleiss.

Thus, two of the key observations Freud included in his analysis of Leonardo, his sublimation of sexual desires and his "idealized" homosexuality, were clearly pertinent to Freud's own life. Add to that Freud's emphasis on Leonardo's emotional and intellectual isolation, his rejection of religion and traditional authority in favor of dispassionate observations, and the refusal of Leonardo's contemporaries to understand and appreciate his genius, and one has reason to wonder about the degree to which Freud's analysis of Leonardo was actually an analysis of himself, as he too felt isolated, had rejected religious doctrines, and felt unappreciated by his relentless critics.

Going full circle with this possibility, which, in this instance, involves returning to Leonardo's fantasy, Elms brings our attention to the fact that Freud's earliest dream contained birdlike images. Freud described this dream as being one in which "I saw my beloved mother, with a particularly peaceful expression on her features, being carried into the room by two (or three) people with birds' beaks and laid upon the bed." His associations to this dream, thirty years after its occurrence, brought forth to his mind excessively tall figures with beaks that reminded him of deities with heads of sparrow hawks from an Egyptian tomb relief. Freud's first interpretation of the dream was that it represented a fear of his mother dying. Later, however, he traced it back to a "dark, plainly sexual craving, which had found appropriate expression in the visual content of the dream."[11]

It was for good reason that Freud warned against idealizing or identifying with the subject of one's psychobiography. The master succumbed to the trap he alerted us to and cautioned against. The title Elms gave to his chapter on Freud (a chapter from which I have borrowed extensively) is "Freud as Leonardo." It fits the essay and underscores the treacherous territory that anyone enters who ventures to describe another person's life in psychological terms.

PSYCHOBIOGRAPHERS BEWARE

"Projective identification" is sometimes applied to the phenomenon of the personal issues and concerns of the psychobiographer becoming entangled with the issues and concerns perceived in his or her subject. It clouds objectivity and renders the final product suspicious. The problem places a heavy burden on psychobiographers to be conscious about why they select their subjects and to take into account the fact that we sometimes unwittingly seek to become experts on our own dilemmas. Surely Erikson took that into account when he interpreted Martin Luther's "fit in the choir" as an expression of his crisis in identity. Erikson was a specialist on issues of identity and how one endeavors to resolve the questions "Who am I?" and "How am I to fit into the adult world?" It was a problem that Erikson himself faced as a young man in the situation of being a blondheaded Dane with the adoptive surname Homberger. But instead of being unaware of writing about himself in the guise of Martin Luther, Erikson saw and seized on the problem of identity by placing it front and center in a coherent reconstruction of the life and times of his subject.

By contrast, Freud's reconstruction of Leonardo was far less successful by nearly any standard. I suspect that one of Freud's intentions in hastening to write the book was to admonish colleagues who threatened to abandon the sexual instinct as the key to understanding psychological development. By demonstrating how his theory of childhood sexuality operated and accounted for the magnificent achievements of Leonardo, Freud was trying to put the lid on defections from the psychoanalytic camp. In this instance, he harmed the cause more than he helped it. His solution to the mysteries of Leonardo's life, particularly his interest in the flight of birds, while consistent with Freud's theory of the vicissitudes of sex, did not result in an illuminating, convincing story.

Freud's solution to Leonardo's attraction to birds and the prospects of contriving wings for human ascension are contained in the following passage.

> The findings which we have reached concerning the development of the mental life of children suggests the view that in Leonardo's case too the first researches of childhood were concerned with the problems of sexuality. Indeed he gives himself away in a transparent disguise by connecting the urge for research with the vulture phantasy, and by singling out the problem of flight of birds as one to which, as the result of a special chain of circumstances, he was destined to turn his attention. He probably hoped that he himself would be able to fly one day, and we know from wish-fulfilling dreams what bliss is expected from the fulfillment of that hope.[12]

Freud worded his concluding thoughts on the matter more succinctly when he wrote: "The wish to be able to fly is to be understood as nothing else than a longing to be capable of sexual performance." In fact, this conclusion reiterates a pronouncement on the meaning of flight in dream images that Freud had offered a dozen or so years earlier in his groundbreaking book *The Interpretation of Dreams*. There he wrote:

> The intimate connection between flying and the idea of birds makes it comprehensible that dreams of flying, in the case of male dreamers, should usually have a coarsely sensual significance; and we should not be surprised to hear that this or that dreamer is always very proud of his ability to fly.[13]

I am inclined to accept Elm's argument that there was a good deal of slippage between Freud's personality and his psychobiography of Leonardo. But so what? In the end, does it really matter how he arrived at his conclusions? The answer to that question is yes, it may matter a lot, particularly in light of the possibility that the intrusion of Freud's personal dynamics into his analysis of Leonardo resulted in his missing another interpretation worth considering. Freud, like many of us, may have operated with a "blind spot" that biased his objectivity. It is worth taking time here to sketch out what that blind spot may have been and in doing so to loosen up the common notion that flight is a disguised expression of sexual impulses.

Freud staked his illustrious career on his ability to track the course of sexual instincts. It was first featured in his theory of hysteria. He then extended his ideas to other forms of neuroses and proceeded to create a general model of the psyche to account for normal as well as abnormal development. It was an all-purpose model that featured the pleasure-seeking id as its primary energy source. The id generates a constant flow of libido, beginning at infancy and extending throughout adulthood, and its expressions cannot be denied. But civilization requires that the beast be tamed, and as a result the energy finds alternative tension-reducing outlets for expression. In the case of Leonardo, Freud argued that the beast had been tamed so thoroughly that most of its energy was sublimated into Leonardo's scientific and artistic activities. For Freud, Leonardo's attempt to design wings that he hoped would enable him to fly was sponsored by that portion of his libido that could not be completely converted into intellectual energy and latched onto levitation as a symbol for sexual fulfillment.

Freud seldom deviated from his views of the primacy of sexual instincts and berated any colleagues who thought otherwise. At the same time, he established the groundwork for alternative formulations that are less presumptive about the machination of id forces in human development. His observations about the infant's ties to its mother, bonds that are "altogether the most perfect, the most free from ambivalence of all human relationships"[14] and similar accounts of early experiences scattered throughout his prolific writings, were left in the hands of his revisionists to further elucidate. Initially Melanie Klein[15] and then other leading figures of the British "object-relations" school of psychoanalytic theory eschewed the idea that infants seek objects as outlets for sexual tension. Instead, human beings are instinctively driven to seek enduring ties with objects, particularly during infancy, because babies cannot survive without them. Infants seek not just figures who will feed them but "objects", mothers mostly, who make them feel protected and special. A close relationship with a reliable and nurturing caregiver is a necessary component of the child's development of a sense of self, a self that is initially embedded in the infant's experiences of oneness with an understanding "other." William Fairbairn[16] and Donald Winnicott,[17] major contributors to the object-relations movement in psychiatry, elaborate on that basic point by underscoring the importance of devoted maternal care in facilitating subsequent transitions in the development of the self. From an object-relations perspective one can begin to sketch out an alternative to Freud's analysis of Leonardo. In doing so, I will make use of the same information about Leonardo's youth that Freud cited in building his case for Leonardo's nearly total repression of sexual impulses and his pure and perfect sublimation of them to serve his intellect.

Freud reported that not much was known about Leonardo's childhood other than that he was born in the town of Vinci in 1452. He was the illegitimate child of Ser Piero da Vinci, a member of a prominent family in the region. His mother, Caterina, was probably a peasant girl. Ser Piero eventually married another woman, Donna Albiera, and they were childless. Sometime between the age of three and five, young Leonardo was taken from Caterina and brought to the home of his father and step-mother. The substance of Freud's analysis of Leonardo is based on this in-formation and on his interpretation of Leonardo's early fantasy in his crib.

Freud's major observations and inferences were as follows. Leonardo must have "spent the first critical years of his life not by the side of his fa-ther and stepmother, but with this poor, forsaken, real mother."[18] During this period Caterina compensated for her lack of a husband by caressing her son. "So, like all unsatisfied mothers, she took her little son in place of her husband and by the too early maturation of his erotism robbed him of his masculinity."[19] As a consequence, Leonardo suffered from his mother's "perverse" overstimulation. He interpreted the image of the bird in the dream that opened Leonardo's mouth and struck him many times with its tail against his lips as being derived from memories of "innumerable pas-sionate kisses" Caterina had pressed on his lips.[20] The bird symbolized Caterina and harkened back to Leonardo's "suckling" days, the "first source of pleasure in life," days that "doubtless remained printed" on him.[21] Had Leonardo's father been present during his formative years, he would have provided the kind of competition for Caterina's attention that ushers in the Oedipal dilemma that Freud believed was crucial for the sexual maturation of sons. Instead, Leonardo was left on his own to figure out how he had come into existence without a father. His partial solution to the problem was that his mother must have a penis, represented by the bird's tail, and, like the "vultures" of antiquity, had impregnated herself. Thus much of the damage had already been done when Ser Piero "tore"[22] Leonardo away from his mother. Caterina's image had been so thoroughly imprinted in his mind as an irreplaceable love object that normal sexual development was then and forever blocked.

Leonardo's longing for his mother and the restoration of early feelings of contentment when he had suckled at her breast and gazed into her lov-ing face came back to him when he began to work on a portrait of a Flo-rentine lady named Mona Lisa del Gioncondo. The features of her "un-fathomable smile" brought forth memories of the mother he had lost. The mysterious smile "awakened in him as a grown man the mother of his ear-liest childhood,"[23] and for several years he obsessed over that smile until he got it more or less right on canvas.

Freud could have stopped there. Leonardo missed his mother. Period. Ser Piero took his son away from his mother at a very bad time, at a junc-ture that was critical to Leonardo's psychological development. Freud's own dynamics may have gotten in the way of his exploring that possibility in greater depth, and here we return to Jones's comments regarding Freud's early relationship with his mother and the effects that relationship had on his sexual maturation.

Several writers[24] have observed that Freud was not insightful about his relationship with his mother and, in particular, failed to recognize his ambivalent feelings toward her. The gist of their combined arguments is this. Freud's mother, Amelia, was a far more powerful force in his life than his father. Ruth Abraham writes: "Freud's father was a somewhat passive, aging man who by the time Freud came to know him had failed at business and (had) largely retired from leadership in the family."[25] He is further described as mild, inept, and disappointing; hardly the image of a castrating Oedipal father. By contrast, Amelia was the "ruling figure" of the household. Several years younger than her husband, as Abraham describes her she was the "source of all nurturance and love" for Sigmund *and* "overwhelmingly powerful, sexual, and possessive."[26] The result was that Sigmund (Amelia called him "mein goldener Sigi") both adored and feared her. He adored her tenderness and feared her power. George Atwood and Robert Stolorow argue that Freud's internal representation of Amelia's loving qualities formed the foundation of an idealized image of mothers and their ties with their sons.[27] Repeating an earlier quotation, Freud described such ties as "altogether the most perfect, the most free from ambivalence, of all human relationships." Of course, any acknowledgment of the "unsafe, negative, and tyrannical" mother would have done irreparable harm to that idealized image.[28] Abraham joins others who have written on this topic by proposing that Freud avoided tarnishing his internalized image of the "good" Amelia by diverting the negative feelings inspired by her feared qualities onto his mild-mannered, passive father and slotting him into the role of the king whom Oedipus was destined to kill.

So the general consensus among the contemporary theorists just cited is that Sigmund's early relationship with Amelia was more problematic than he was able to admit to himself. He defended against acknowledging his contradictory feelings for her by separating the good feelings from the bad and projecting the latter onto his father in order to preserve his "most perfect" image of her. He went on to specialize in boys' relationships with their fathers and boldly used his observations as a springboard not only for delving into the psychodynamics of individuals but also for understanding the onset of human civilization[29] and one of its major by-products, religion.[30] By concentrating on this perspective, he diminished the influence of early mother-child ties and stopped short of considering the prospects of nonconscious yearnings to recover feelings engendered by them. I suggest that the anxiety evoked by the mixture of loving and fearful feelings toward Amelia acted as a barrier against recognizing how his observations regarding these "most perfect" ties pertained to his life.

This possibility brings us back to the issue of why Freud became so obsessed with completing his study of Leonardo. Again, following the leads provided by Elms, Freud's creativity had waned when he initiated his psychobiography of Leonardo. One could say that the process of sublimation that had fueled his work had begun to fail him and, in doing so, exposed the barrier that had sustained it. A crack in his psychological defenses threatened to release repressed conflicts that he had thus far been able to keep at bay. He taught us that repressed conflicts do not go away. They remain in the unconscious, imperishable, as fresh as the day they arrived. They continue to operate underground, influencing our judgment, distorting our perceptions, and shaping our ideas. All the unconscious wants, Freud pronounced on several occasions, is conscious recognition of its contents. But conscious awareness of a repressed conflict can be devastating. It can undermine the reality that a person has struggled so hard to secure. It can play havoc with one's worldview, with what a person most strenuously believes is true and not true. It can undermine the self.

So let us say that was the precarious condition Freud was in when he conducted his study of Leonardo. He had at his disposal a memory fragment and a few details about the early life of his subject. It is as though he had been handed a mostly blank TAT card and told to tell a story based on what he saw in the card. He turned the task into a hermeneutic exercise that entailed reading the "text" of Leonardo's early life. Since the TAT card held so few clues to what the story's main themes might be, his unconscious seized the opportunity to become the story's principle author. One could go so far as to suggest that Freud *unloaded* the contents of his unconscious into the story and structured it according to his own latent dynamics.

One of that story's main elements was the idea that the "innumerable passionate kisses" that Caterina applied to the lips of her son Leonardo were too much for him to bear. They were so overwhelming to the infant that he repressed his love for his mother and "preserved it in his unconscious and from then on remained faithful to her. While he seemed to pursue boys and to be their lover, he was in reality running away from other women who might cause him to be unfaithful."[31] Quickly now, back to Jones's statement that Freud's "mother's tenderness was fateful to him. . . . The violence of the caresses . . . established his sexual inactivity for the whole of his later life." Compare that observation about Freud's early relationship with his mother with Freud's inference regarding Caterina's relationship with Leonardo: "So like all unsatisfied mothers, she took her little son in place of her husband and by too early maturation of his eroticism robbed him of his masculinity." I submit that the shadow of Amelia looms large in that passage, and my odds-on favorite for the little son is "goldener Sigi."

Freud-bashing has become a cottage industry. *How Freud Got It Wrong* could be the lead title of a series of volumes containing collections of books, essays, and magazine articles that criticize his person and his ideas. I do not consider myself to be a member of the legions who discard his ideas and urge us to "move on." Neither this chapter nor this book

could be written without the benefits provided by Freud's insights into psychodynamic properties of human growth and development. I have no interest in throwing out the baby with the bath water; too many promising
babies would be lost.

In my analysis of Freud's interpretation of Leonardo's desire to fly, I
have done what Freud taught me to do. I have used the analytic tools he
provided and have applied them to his life. One of my purposes has been
to underscore the degree to which a psychobiographer's personal issues
can both invade and be used to structure his or her perceptions, observations, and conclusions about another person's life. My second purpose has
been to raise questions about Freud's conclusions about sexual instincts
and their being the force behind images of ascension in dreams and
fantasies.

I alert the reader (and myself) to the presence of a "straw man" strategy.[32] I have set Freud up and targeted him for criticism for concentrating
on sexual forces that drive the desire to fly. That, of course, is the main
thrust of his interpretation of Leonardo. But, along the way, he introduced
another interpretation: that Leonardo's efforts to recreate his mother's
smile in his portrait of Mona Lisa and several other maternal figures in
subsequent paintings were expressions of his desire to restore the feelings
of security and well-being that had been associated with her smile in the
early days of his existence. Freud may have confounded this observation
by infusing his theory of infantile sexuality into the case. Maybe not, but it
is bad science when an assumption is treated as "datum" that is then used
as a "fact" to support the theory from which the assumption was derived.
Be that as it may, Freud elaborated a good deal more on the idea that
dreams and fantasies of flying are inspired by the seepage of blocked
sexual instincts than he did on what may be a more direct interpretation:
Leonardo missed his mother.

Where might one go if one were to explore this alternative or, equally
likely, complementary hypothesis? How might it be extended to enlighten
us about Leonardo's attempts to design a workable flying machine, hoping
that some day it would assist him in his desire to fly? Simply put, how
could flying dreams and fantasies possibly be expressions of missing one's
mom? That is the primary mystery I seek to resolve. The initial step in for-
mulating that solution is to consider the first rendition of the trials of a Pan
called Peter and then to match Peter's dilemma with the underlying concerns of his creator, J. M. Barrie.

PART II *Lift-Off*

There are three reasons why it is necessary to weigh an infant as soon as possible after its birth. You know two of these reasons but perhaps have never been told the third. One is that birth weight provides important medical information. It establishes the reference point for assessing weight gain or loss over the first few critical days and weeks of the infant's life. A second reason is that knowing the weight of the child enables parents to answer the third in a series of three rapid-fire questions about the newborn asked by friends and relatives; the one that is asked after the sex and name of the child have been proudly announced. Finally, here is the reason most people don't know or, if they once knew, have forgotten. Babies have the ability to fly until they have been weighed. The law of gravity does not kick in until the moment that it is physically demonstrated that the dial on a weighing instrument moves when the infant is placed on it. J. M. Barrie is responsible for discovering and sharing this secret, and, of course, he was a specialist in such matters.

Barrie was the author of *Peter Pan*,[1] one of the most enduring books and plays of the twentieth century. Peter is the intrepid leader of the group of lost boys in Neverland, the quintessential youth who flatly refused to grow up, the boy who needed no magic dust to fly wherever he wished.

Recall the story. Peter's timing was perfect when he arrived at the Darling residence. Mr. and Mrs. Darling had gone out for the evening, leaving Wendy and her brothers, John and Michael, unattended. Normally, Nana, the family pet Newfoundland and faithful baby-sitter, would have chased Peter away; but on that particular evening, in a fit of frustrated rage, Mr. Darling had placed the beast outside, and the children were now quite on

45

their own. Being alone and feeling abandoned is a ripe condition for being transported to Neverland. We know that because we are informed that the boys in Neverland were there as a consequence of having been forgotten or neglected, sometimes having fallen out of baby carriages and been left unnoticed on the ground.

Peter's invitation to Wendy to accompany him to Neverland was inspired by his wish for her to read to him. In fact the original purpose of his entering the bedroom on that adventurous night was to retrieve the shadow that he had inadvertently left behind one evening when he had sat by the open window listening to Mrs. Darling read to her children. Curious creature, that Peter. He relished his freedom and yearned for a woman to read to him. So what will it be, Peter? Are you a bird or a child? The answer is both or neither, depending on one's perspective. Betwixt and between is a more accurate answer.

The preceding description of Peter's dilemma is revealed in a novel Barrie wrote before the more familiar one. *Peter Pan* is in fact a more polished version of a major subplot in the prior novel, *The Little White Bird*,[2] where the child-bird theme is first introduced. It is a captivating fantasy.

The opening chapters of *The Little White Bird* introduce the reader to the mysterious Captain W., a retired military officer in his midforties, and his six-year-old playmate, David. The Captain describes to David how it came to be that he had secretly paved the way for his mother, Mary, to wed his (David's) father. "You don't seem to understand, my boy," said the Captain, that had he not taken certain actions, "there would never have been a little boy called David." In response, David sparked up and asked whether that meant he would still be a bird flying about in Kensington Garden? David was already familiar with the fact that all children in his part of London had once been birds in the Garden. The purpose for placing bars on nursery windows and fenders by fireplaces was to prevent children who forgot that they had lost their wings from trying to fly away through the window or up the chimney.

It is reported in later passages that unfortunate women who have no children can be seen trying to nab birds by offering pieces of cake as bait. Birds are undecided about which is the better life. In an effort to find out if babyhood would suit them, they frequently can be observed landing on empty perambulators in the park and hopping about from pillow to blanket in a twitter of excitement and exploration.

Captain W. reports that the first time he saw David he was a thrush that was caught by the leg in some cunning contraption of strings and twigs. The Captain's story became David's story, and when he repeated it, something he did quite often, he rubbed the leg as if it still smarted. On one occasion, David's companion could see the treetops in David's eyes, indicating regret about having been born.

"Think of your mother," said the Captain severely, when he suspected what was on David's mind. David replied that if he did revert to his original form he would often fly back to see his mother, hop on the frilly things of her nightgown and peck at her mouth. But in the end, David acknowledged that his pecking would awaken his mother and she would find that she only had a bird instead of a boy.

Later in the novel, Captain W. points out the island in the Kensington Garden on which all the birds that become boys and girls are born. No one who is human can be on that island, except for one. The exception is Peter Pan, the forerunner of the Peter Pan familiar to us all. Peter can reside on the island because he is only part human. Peter is "ever so old" and "always the same age," and still possesses every one of his baby teeth. He was born long ago and is one week old, having never had a birthday, nor is there the slightest chance he will ever have one. The reason for this, one presumes, was parental carelessness. Adequate precautions had not been taken to prevent Peter from escaping through a window in his nursery and flying back to Kensington Garden.

Peter was an enigma on the island. Fairies ran away from him when he approached them. Birds ignored him, thinking him to be quite odd. Every living thing shunned him. He did not consider himself to be a bird for he had no feathers, only itchy places on his shoulders where his wings had once been attached. And not for a moment did he think himself to be human.

One friendship, however, did develop. That was with Solomon Caw, an old codger of a bird, whose primary responsibility was to direct birds to the mothers who were to rear them as children. Solomon referred to Peter as "poor little half-and-half." When Peter spoke of his urge to return to his mother, wise Solomon simply said "good-bye," words that brought to Peter's attention the fact that he had no means of returning. "You will never be able to fly again, not even on windy days. You must live here on the island always," Solomon informed Peter. "You will always be Betwixt-and-Between," Solomon said, and the narrator observes: "that is exactly as it turns out to be."

Solomon was wrong about one thing. In fact, for a time, Peter was able to fly again. The fairies warmed up to Peter in response to his providing them with some special service, and the Queen fairy granted him two wishes. His first wish was to go to his mother, but to return to the Garden if he found her disappointing. The Queen said that she could give him the ability to fly home but she couldn't open the door. Peter assured her that his mother always kept the window open in the hope that he would some-day return. Thereupon the fairies tickled him on his shoulder blades and rejuvenated his ability to fly. He intended to fly directly to his mother's home, but as he flew over the housetops, Crystal Palace, Regent's Park, and other notable landmarks, it occurred to him that his second wish might be to remain a bird. Upon ending the detour and reaching his home, Barrie writes:

> The window was wide open, just as he knew it would be, and in he fluttered, and there was his mother lying asleep. Peter alighted softly on the wooden rail at the foot of the bed and had a good look at her. She lay her head on her hand, and the hollow pillow was like a nest lined with her brown wavy hair. He remembered, though he had long forgotten, that she always gave her hair a holiday at night. How sweet the frills of her nightgown were. He was very glad she was such a pretty mother.
>
> But she looked sad, and he knew why she looked sad. One of her arms moved as if it wanted to go round something, and he knew what it wanted to go round.

As Peter fumbled through some of his old drawers, one of them creaked, and his mother woke up, and he thought she said his name. He determined that if she said "Peter" again he would cry "Mother" and run to her. But she spoke no more. She slept once again with tears on her face. Her sadness made Peter miserable. So, sitting on the rail at the foot of her bed, he played a lullaby on his pipe and he "never stopped playing until his mother looked happy."

Peter returned to his mother's bedside at night a few more times and played her a kiss on his pipe. In time, he decided against his second wish, to be forever a bird, and told the fairies "I wish now to go back to mother for ever and always." They tickled his shoulders and he flew directly to the window. But the window was closed. Bars had been placed on it. Peering in, he saw his mother sleeping peacefully with her arm around another little boy.

> Peter called, "Mother! mother!" but she heard him not; in vain he beat his little limbs against the iron bars. He had to fly back, sobbing, to Kensington Garden, and he never saw his dear again. What a glorious boy he had meant to be with her. Ah, Peter, we who have made the great mistake, how differently we should all act at the second chance. But Solomon was right; there is no second chance, not for most of us. When we reach the window it is Lock-out Time. The iron bars are up for life.

EIGHT *He Played until His Mother Looked Happy*

Recall Henry Murray's strategy for interpreting imaginative stories. It assumes that to a degree, and in some instances to a revealing degree, they are derived from the storyteller's own experiences. Some stories are the daytime equivalents of nighttime dreams, in that their manifest content can be products of forces operating beneath conscious awareness. Murray capitalized on that proposition and made storytelling an important component of his life study methods.

Now we are in a position to operate from that perspective by seeking possible parallels between the problems faced by Peter Pan in *The Little White Bird* and some personal experiences of its author, J. M. Barrie. We will find ourselves on firmer ground in locating the dots and connecting the lines between Barrie's experiences and Peter Pan's dilemma than Freud stood on when he based his interpretation of Leonardo's interests in flight on a single, mistranslated, partial memory of an early dream that Leonardo jotted down in the margin of a notebook. We are in better shape because Barrie did most of the work for us in a book he wrote about his mother, Margaret Ogilvy.

But before getting to that juncture, it is worth speculating what kind of information about Barrie's early experiences might be reflected in Captain W.'s description of Peter Pan's longing to return to his mother. What might these images suggest about Jamie Barrie's circumstances as a child? As a budding depth psychologist, one's initial hunch might be that Barrie, as a young lad, had been displaced by a new infant, a boy, who became the center of love and attention that previously had been showered upon him. His position in the family had been usurped, and Jamie Barrie hadn't taken well to having been replaced. His heart had been broken, and his suffering had festered for many years. The circumstances of his sadness are reiterated in the story of Peter Pan, a story that gives expression to his sense of betrayal.

This idea could be verified by locating birth-order information from records of the Barrie family that, with some digging, probably could be found. Early sibling rivalry, one might say. Pure and simple. Not the slightest bit complicated. Happens frequently in a lot of families. One can only marvel at the poetic way in which Barrie treated such a common experience. What an image! A little boy, pathetically beating at the window of his mother's bedroom, tries to return to the arms of a mother who now holds another child. It is a scene that is sure to resonate in the hearts of all whom a younger sibling had replaced. Psychobiography here we come. At the very outset, one is in the advantageous position of having a hypothesis to be confirmed or discomfirmed by family records.

But before even tracking down that information, information that most surely would confirm one's suspicion, one can proceed straight ahead and make another prediction. Jamie Barrie was probably between the ages of three and a half and five when his mother had another baby. That would place him in the midst of the Oedipal dilemma. It is during this period that the male child experiences a renewed interest in his mother, and this interest is now sexualized. It bothers him that the father has more access to the mother and, in this instance, just when Jamie is in the throes of fantasies of how best to get rid of the father, another child is born. As if competition with the father wasn't enough! Now he has to contend with a newborn sibling.

On a roll now, one can complete the Oedipal scenario. Where does Peter Pan desire to go? Into his mother's private chambers, which is nothing other than a symbol for her private parts. Since young Jamie is not fully aware of the sexual nature of his longing to return, his entire body is eroticized and made erect.[1] The localization of the sexual instinct in the region of his genitals is too threatening, so it is diffused throughout his body, and up it goes. That figure at the window pleading to come in is an eroticized, erect penis, barred from entering the mother's bedroom. Yes, one concludes, even in the absence of data, Freud was correct: "The wish to be able to fly is to be understood as nothing else than a longing to be capable of sexual performance."

This analytic strategy is riddled with problems. I present it as a mockery of the low standards that sometimes characterize psychobiographic studies. It is similar to Freud's analysis of Leonardo in that psychoanalytic inferences are transformed into "facts" that are doubled back to confirm a theory. Even if it turned out that Barrie's mother gave birth to another child when Jamie was around the age of three (in fact, she did, but it paled in significance in comparison to another event), the analysis is so driven by theoretical assumptions that there is a danger of missing more critical features of the case.

Instead of beginning from the top, from the higher reaches of theoretical abstractions, and having them dictate the kinds of information to seek, I will begin at the bottom by considering what is known about Barrie's childhood.

Jamie Barrie was born in 1860 in a small cottage in Kirriemuir, Scotland. For his first three years, Jamie was the youngest of seven living children. Two other children, both girls, had died early in their lives. His older brother, Alick, was attending Aberdeen University. Four sisters lived at home. Mary was fifteen, Jane Ann was thirteen, Sara was six, and Isabella was two. David, age seven, was sandwiched between the four daughters. Margaret, the final child in the family, was born three years after Jamie.

Jamie's father, David Barrie, was a weaver who was successful enough in the trade to provide for his large family. He had married his wife Margaret when he was twenty-seven and she was twenty-one. Eighteen years later, Jamie was born.

These and many other facts are easy to obtain because J. M. Barrie has been written about so extensively. He was one of the most successful literary figures in Great Britain at the turn of the twentieth century. He began his career as a journalist, writing daily columns for several newspapers. Gradually that routine was replaced by writing books and plays, many of which were staged in both London and New York. *Peter Pan*, the book and the play, brought him fame, but during his lifetime he was also well known for his other works.

One of his books was entitled *Margaret Ogilvy*.[2] This was his mother's name; it was customary in Scotland for wives to retain their maiden names. Ostensibly, yes, the book is about Barrie's mother, who had died one year before it was written, but its primary focus is on Barrie's relationship with his mother. It is as much autobiographic as biographic.

Barrie begins the book by reporting that a set of six new chairs arrived at the same time he was born. The chairs were a big investment for his mother, and he imagines her whispering to him that they are just the beginning. She had great things in mind: "what ambitions burned behind that face." In turn, Barrie imagines himself declaring that he was there to help. She was a happy woman in those days, "placed on earth by God to open minds of all who looked to beautiful thoughts." What he recalled of his first several years was all hearsay. Full consciousness of his mother did not arrive until he was six years old. It was then, in 1866, that news arrived that his brother David, seven years older than little Jamie and barely known to him, had been killed in a skating accident. Barrie wrote: "I knew my mother for ever now."

Margaret Ogilvy never recovered from the tragedy. Although she had several other children, David had been special. He was handsome and ruddy and possessed other qualities that brightened his mother's day, every day. Nobody could replace him. Margaret was bedridden after the accident for several months and remained sickly until her death twenty-nine years later. Jamie's oldest sister, Mary, stepped forward to nurse her grieving mother. One day, shortly after David's death, Mary went to Jamie, "with an anxious face and wringing her hands," and told him to go to his mother's bedside and tell her she still had another boy. Jamie entered the dark room and stood there frightened, as no sound came from the bed. Suddenly he heard a listless voice saying "Is that you?" The tone hurt Jamie, so he gave no reply. Again, "Is that you?" Convinced that she was speaking to her dead son, Jamie replied, "No, it's not him. It's just me." He heard his mother cry.

Over the ensuing days, weeks, and months (lifetime one could say), Jamie spent much of his time trying to make his mother forget about David. The statement quoted earlier from *The Little White Bird*—"So, sitting on the rail at the foot of her bed, [Peter Pan] played a lullaby on his pipe and he never stopped playing until his mother looked happy"—is transparently derived from this period in Barrie's life. He would do anything to make his mother look happy, then and much later: as he declares in the book, everything he ever wrote, all of it, was for his mother. He was always mindful of the prospects of gaining her approval, of bringing a smile to her lips, when she read his works.

But six-year-old Jamie wasn't writing yet. The way he tried to make her laugh was to go to her bedroom and reenact something that he had done elsewhere that had amused someone, hoping that his antics would lift his mother's spirits. Barrie wrote that she did laugh now and then. On such occasions he would rush to his sister and beg her to come and see the sight, but by the time she came "the soft face was wet again." He could remember only one time he made her laugh in the presence of a witness. The project was so important to him that he kept a paper and a pencil handy so he could keep a running account of the number of times he was able to amuse his mother.

Mary encouraged Jamie to try to talk with Margaret about David when she lay thinking of him. Frequently Margaret was willing to do that, so much so that he sometimes interrupted her stream of fond memories by crying out "Do you know nothing about me?"

Later a different strategy occurred to him. It was a strategy of more than passing significance. He endeavored to become so much like his brother that his mother would not notice the difference. The character he played was born from Margaret's nostalgic memories of her dead son. She spoke of David's cheery way of whistling and described to the child sitting at her bedside how David would stand with his legs apart and his hands in his pants pockets when he puckered up his lips. Thereupon, after Jamie perfected his own whistle, he disguised himself by slipping into David's ill-fitting clothes and entered his mother's room. "Listen!" he cried out tri-umphantly. He stretched out his legs, plunged his hands into the knicker-bocker trousers and began to whistle.

Jamie was so desperate to be accepted by his mother that he pre-tended to be someone else—his dead brother. Despite his heroic efforts then and throughout his mother's lifetime, he says, "I had not made her forget the bit of her that was dead; in those nine and twenty years he was not removed one day farther from her." Still struggling to remove the iron bars guarding the nursery, to obtain the unobtainable kiss that his mother hid from him, Jamie vowed to make his mother proud of him.

"Wait till I'm a man," Jamie said to his mother, "and you'll never have reason to greet again." ("Greet" being the Scottish word for "grieve").

The truth of the matter is that Barrie was terrified by the prospect of growing up. "The horror of my boyhood was that I knew a time would come when I would have to give up the games." Look at what happened to David when he grew up. He gave up more than games. But what Jamie feared most was that he would not be able to survive if he failed to remove those dreadful tears from his mother's face. The tears and enduring sad-ness became objective evidence that his mother was unavailable to vali-date his existence, to confirm that he was a person of worth. The prospect of growing up under the shadow of being unworthy of his mother's love was unthinkable.

Both Margaret and Jamie created a temporary solution to their prob-lems. Together, they discovered a way to periodically escape the emotional turmoil that had been triggered by the family tragedy. Throughout the many days that Jamie spent at his mother's bedside, an opening into a con-versational safety zone emerged that involved Margaret reminiscing about her childhood. These conversations lightened Margaret's spirits and of-fered Jamie an avenue for becoming engaged with his mother . . . or at least engaged in the life of a little girl who became his mother.

In addition to relishing and making full-color mental records of his mother's accounts of her childhood, Jamie became an avid reader of books and poetry. He was so consumed by this hobby that he began to collect photographs of poets. One day he showed his collection of pictures to an old tailor friend of his. On viewing the photographs, the tailor quoted these lines from Cowley:

> What can I do to be forever known,
> And make the age to come my own?

Inspired by the passage, Jamie hurried home, rushed his mother away from the company of some visitors who had dropped by, and repeated the lines. In jest, he asked her if that was the kind of person she would like to be. Margaret replied: "No, but I would be windy of being his mother." Hope at last. Knowing that he already could weave stories well enough to please her, the die was cast. Jamie was to be a writer. "I would be windy[3] of being his mother," she declared. Jamie interpreted that statement to mean I would be "windy" of being *your* mother if you were to become famous. A route to her heart had been discovered.

Barrie's pen replaced the pipe that Peter Pan used for the purpose of removing the sadness from his mother's forlorn face.

NINE *Outside Opinions*

The image of Peter Pan pounding on the window trying to get his mother's attention as her arms are wrapped around another child and Barrie's account of his childhood project of begging Margaret to answer the question "What about me?" are so clearly alternative versions of the same story that they require little comment.

At this juncture, however, objections can be raised about having located and latched onto a childhood memory that happens to coincide with a plot in a story and exaggerating it far beyond its true importance. I affirm that this is the kind of information I consider to be lucky to find, as it conforms with my inclination to believe that childhood experiences, particularly childhood experiences of such magnitude, can reverberate throughout one's lifetime. But how can I be assured, and, more important, how can the reader be assured, that I haven't simply strolled into the trap that Kenneth Gergen noted when he wrote about psychobiographers' dispositions to find evidence to confirm their "preformulated convictions"?[1] This raises the difficult question of validity. Did I merely find what I was looking for in a heap of other potential gems that I ignored or shoved aside with a thesis-preserving vengeance? Have I blindly followed Freud's precedent when he sifted through documents, artifacts, and closets left behind by Leonardo for the purpose of locating items of information that he could massage to fit the shape of his preformulated mold? This is what I have called the problem of "opinions without evidence" in psychobiography, tantamount to declaring that one memory or one episode stands supreme over all other memories and episodes in terms of shaping the life being studied . . . because I say so.[2]

In many instances there is no easy way out of this dilemma. One approach is to say, in effect, hear me out, read on, come to appreciate the logic behind my argument and, in the end, you will come to agree with my position. Another approach is to say that I am smarter than you, so you have no choice other than to trust my judgment. A less insulting form of the same line of thinking would be for me, in this instance, to claim that if you had studied everything by and about Barrie that I have mulled over, if you knew what I know, you would come to the same conclusion. But that would require a leap of faith that I would not request of the reader.

Another strategy is to argue that a memory is seminal if it fits some external criterion for that. Here, for example, it could be asked if the tragedy of David's death and the effect it had on Margaret's relationship with her son Jamie was of such significance that it etched an initial outline of a blueprint that gave shape to much of the remainder of Barrie's life. Of course, a question of that broad a scope is difficult to answer. However, it becomes more manageable when asked in the context of its fit with specifications of "prototypical scenes." Todd Schultz describes a prototypical scene as a scene that "anchors" a life for personological inquiry.[3] It is a scene that achieves a kind of "super-saliency" by virtue of its oft-told status, its repetitious embellishments, and its packaging of core themes that both characterize and unify a person's life. Several scholars have worked on establishing criteria for extracting prototypical scenes from biographies. These yeomen in the cause of personology include Irving Alexander[4] (1988), Alan Elms[5] (1994), and Jefferson Singer and Peter Salovey[6] (1993), all of whom have proposed useful guidelines. One area of agreement is that a prototypical scene is a fundamental (primal, if you will) scene that both sponsors and attracts other self-defining memories that cohere to its basic form. It encapsulates a summary of enduring personal concerns that marks it as a source of derivative themes and provides a nest for other memories that seek meaningful places in the individual's master story.

Another criterion for a prototypical scene is its inclusion of a condition of having been *thrown* into a situation not of one's own making, coupled with a sense of having little or no resources to effectively cope with the situation and/or its results. For example, Jamie had nothing to do with his brother's death. It just happened. Nor did he have any control over his mother's reaction. Margaret did what she did, and there stood her son, helpless in the face of his very existence being denied.

But again, even a positive outcome of a criteria-filling exercise is no guarantee that one scene is *the* scene of choice.

There is another strategy that can strengthen the assertion that a prototypical scene has been identified: soliciting the opinions of others, which was the purpose behind Murray's "diagnostic council," described in chapter 5, whose members were charged with the task of studying case materials and arriving at a consensus regarding critical components of a person's life. The focus of these investigations was the identification of a central theme, an organizing motif, or a "complex" (as in the Icarus complex) that would link the distant past with the present and anticipated future.[7] The discovery of a *unity thema* was the ultimate prize for these deliberations. Murray described unity thema as a "compound of interrelated needs" whose history could be traced to early childhood. He wrote that "whatever its nature and genesis, it repeats itself in many forms during later life."[8] The concept of the unity thema was the predecessor of today's somewhat more manageable ideas regarding prototypical scenes. No matter what it is called, it might be noted that Murray's group of seekers of "compounds of related needs" were members of Murray's "camp" and thereby had been indoctrinated into a shared perspective about how to study lives. Nonetheless, diagnostic councils served the important purpose of guarding against any one member from building a case based on a set themes that were more pertinent to his or her own character than to the concerns, conflicts, joys, struggles, hopes, ambitions, and the life experiences of the person under consideration.

A more powerful strategy for arguing one's case that a specific early scene continued to resonate throughout a lifetime is to consider the observations of individuals whose fields and areas of expertise are unrelated to personology. In a rough sort of way the strategy parallels procedures for validating a new measure for a "variable" for use in psychological tests by comparing the results of its administration to a group of individuals with the results of administrating preexisting measures of the same variable to the same sample of individuals. What one hopes to demonstrate is that the new measure "converges" well enough with old measures to justify its use as a stand-alone instrument. Not surprisingly, the procedures are referred to as attempts to determine an instrument's degree of *convergent validity*. Transporting that strategy to the identification of prototypical scenes, one can seek the opinions of "outsiders" and determine if their impressions converge or diverge with one's own. In other words, the idea of convergent validity applied to case studies asks the following question: To what extent do individuals who independently study the same individual arrive at the same conclusions about the identification of pivotal events in a person's life?

Fortuitously, an answer to this question is available in the case of Barrie. I will show that the "Jamie with his mother" scene has impressed others as much as it impresses me as a turning point in this life. None of these individuals are inclined to bother much about early recollections, and they would probably bristle at the word *personology*. And yet, for their own purposes and special reasons, all identified the same scene as central to the ultimate design of Barrie's life. So, without either their permission or knowledge, I welcome them as members of my temporary, ad hoc "diagnostic council."

The first to arrive at the place now familiar to us was Denis Mackail, who published an exhaustive biography of Barrie in 1941. Having been commissioned to be Barrie's official biographer at the request of two literary executors, Lady Cynthia Asquith and Peter Davies (a younger brother of George Davies, who had served as the model for the character of David in *The Little White Bird*), Mackail was granted access to all the information about Barrie that was retained after his death. These materials included large boxes containing Barrie's note pads, diaries, rough drafts and revised copies of his novels and plays, letters to his mother, correspondences with other authors, and the results of interviews with many people who had been personal and/or theatrical acquaintances of Barrie. Mackail organized this mass of information into a long, thorough, and sometimes tedious 719-page biography that, in addition to describing landmark events in Barrie's life, included such details as the scores of cricket games, opening and closing dates of plays, and who had been seen in Barrie's company at various social gatherings.[9]

Mackail identified a few themes to which he returned on numerous occasions throughout his biography. One was that Barrie was a short and often desperately lonely man. Barely five feet tall, Barrie was extremely sensitive about his size. He suffered prolonged bouts of depression throughout his life. Headaches were nearly daily occurrences, and he rarely missed a seasonal cold. Mackail consistently describes Barrie as moody and anxious. He could also be quite humorous, both in person and in his writings. He was a crowd pleaser, but shortly after the crowd was pleased he would retreat to his smoke-filled residence and pace the floors. Through it all, through the depression, headaches, and fevers, and particularly during his early to midadult years, Barrie applied himself to his trade.

Mackail attributes Barrie's devotion to his work to the aftermath of the shock of the death of Barrie's brother David. Mackail writes: "And Jamie would do anything—anything on Heaven and earth—to get that look off her face."[10] Mackail frequently returns to this episode in Jamie's life and refers to the ghost that haunted Margaret Ogilvy and her living son's vow that she must never again be disappointed. By refusing to forget the little boy who had gone, she "fanned a spark" in the son who remained. Jamie's attempts to brighten the mood of his mother marked the "beginning of 29 years of incessant and unalterable devotion."[11] Mackail repeats what Barrie himself had observed. Everything he wrote was for his mother, and the primary purpose behind his writing was to gain her approval, to become known by her, to be recognized by her, to be let in. Mackail observed, just as I have observed, that one way to be let in was to become someone else, to become the dead brother: a boy locked in time who never will have a birthday—part spirit, part boy, the figure who resided in the mind of his mother.

It may be useful to note that Mackail was no fan of psychoanalytic psychology. He made various "digs" at the discipline and dismissed it with disdain. I mention this to underscore the fact that Barrie's sense of having been abandoned by his mother as a consequence of his brother's death and his lifelong struggle to be accepted by her was such a powerful force in everything he did that even a dogmatic anti-Freudian identified the episode as the point around which so much else revolved.

Two other authors, quite independently, have written about Margaret Ogilvy's reaction to David's death and the lasting consequences it had for Jamie, the child, and J. M., the author. One is a prominent scientist and the other a literary scholar. First, the scientist, Robert Sapolski.

Sapolski, a professor of biological sciences and neuroscience at Stanford University, is one of the world's leading figures in the area of stress-related illnesses. It is common knowledge that stress can take a toll on physical health, but Sapolski understands stress/health connections in the context of what happens beneath the skin, at the level of brain centers, hormones, neurotransmitters, and enzymes. In addition to being an excellent scientist, Sapolski is adept at translating state-of-the-art developments in science into language understandable to the general public without sacrificing the integrity of his scientific discipline. One of the keys for doing that successfully is to provide familiar examples of topics under consideration. Sapolski refers to J. M. Barrie in this way in "Dwarfism and the Importance of Mothers," a chapter in the book *Why Zebras Don't Get Ulcers.*[12]

The chapter describes how growth can be inhibited during periods of stress. Sapolski gives examples of stunted growth of children who received adequate nutrition but inadequate handling in orphanages in Great Britain and elsewhere, particularly during major wars when there was an abundance of homeless children. In some institutions, the children were fed healthy diets but were rarely given the creature comfort of being picked up and caressed. Sapolski also writes that more severe conditions of child abuse leads in some cases to a condition called "stress dwarfism." In the context of describing that condition at the organic level, Sapolski mentions having run across occasional references to Peter Pan and Tinker Bell in books on growth endocrinology. Mystified by these references, he found an explanation buried in a textbook chapter on the topic of how severe psychological stress can trigger psychogenetic dwarfism. Sapolski writes that the chapter

> gave an example that occurred in a British Victorian family. A son, age thirteen, the beloved favorite of the mother is killed in a skating accident. The mother, despairing and bereaved, takes to her bed in grief for years afterward, utterly ignoring her other six-year-old son. Horrible scenes ensue. The boy, on one occasion, enters her darkened room; the mother, in her delusional state, briefly believes it is

the dead son — "David, is that you? Could that be you?" — before realizing: "Oh, it is only you." On the rare instances when the mother interacts with the younger son, she repeatedly expresses the same obses-
sive thought: the only solace that she feels is that David died when he
was still perfect, still a boy, never to be ruined by growing up and
growing away from his mother."[13]

Sapolski identifies the younger boy as J. M. Barrie. He describes him as
having seized on the idea that by remaining a boy forever, "by not growing
up, he will at least have some chance of pleasing his mother, winning her
love. Although there is no evidence of disease or malnutrition in the well-
to-do family, he ceases growing. As an adult, he is barely five feet in height,
and his marriage is unconsummated."[14] With this example in hand,
Sapolski describes the growth-stopping physiological mechanisms triggered by stress that can result in the rare condition of stress dwarfism.

A couple of comments. First, it is reassuring that Sapolski is on the
same page with regard to the momentous importance of J. M. having been
shut out of his mother's life and the consequences of the events surrounding David's death. It helps confirm that the episodes with which I have
been dealing have not been selected because they happen to correspond
to some themes in Barrie's literary works. On the contrary, Sapolski, building on his knowledge of endocrinology, lifts Barrie to the level of a proto-
type case of a person who suffered from traumatic experiences severe
enough to stunt his growth.

In the context of being pleased about securing outside independent
agreement about the importance of Jamie's early crisis, I do not believe
that there is sufficient information about the average heights of members
of the Barrie and Ogilvy families to allow one to firmly conclude that
J. M.'s small stature was the result of stress. The few photographs I have
seen of Margaret Ogilvy, for example, convey an image of a very tiny
woman. A genetic explanation of J. M.'s size is by no means out of the
question. But irrespective of how it came to be that J. M. remained so
small, both Sapolski and Mackail concur that Barrie was unhappy about
his size.

In passing, it might also be observed that Sapolski apparently based his
comments on a hand-me-down version of Barrie's story. He quotes Margaret Ogilvy as having said, "David, is that you? Could that be you?" when
Jamie entered his mother's room. Barrie's written version was somewhat
less poignant: Margaret asks, "Is that you?" and Jamie replies, "No, it's not
him, it's just me." This alteration of words is probably so inconsequential
that it is hardly worth noting, but the fact that Barrie did not say that his
mother called out for David leaves open the possibility that Jamie, on that
particular occasion, merely presumed that his mother had hoped he was
his brother.

Barrie and Margaret Ogilvy, 1893. From A. Birkin, *J. M. Barrie and the Lost Boys* (New York: Clarkson N. Porter, 1979). © Great Ormond Street Hospital Children's Charity, 1993.

Another minor piece of misinformation in the story that had been massaged and passed along in endocrinology textbooks was that J. M. was from a "well-to-do, British Victorian" family. Well, not quite, if that description conjures up an image of a family living on an estate in the rolling hills of England. That mental picture is a far cry from a tiny four-room cottage located in the little Scottish town of Kirriemuir that lies west of the Firth of Tay and five hundred miles from London. The two first-floor rooms held a weaving loom and supplies for the father's work. A small kitchen was on the second floor above the loom and also served as sleeping quarters for all of the children, except for the youngest, who slept in a crib next to Margaret's bed in the adjacent room. It is likely that the father usually slept next to his loom or in the supply room. So imagine a small, cozy two-story cottage, reduce its size by half, and you'll be in the range of representing Jamie's first home.

The third and final member of my panel of experts is Jackie Wullschlager. His book *Inventing Wonderland*[15] deals with the lives and literary works of several authors, Barrie included, whose books for children reflected changes in British culture that occurred as the Edwardian era gradually replaced the Victorian era in the late 1800s, up to 1914, when

World War I ushered in a new reality. The idealization of children marked the Victorian and Edwardian eras, and Barrie's portrayal of a lad who would never grow up was a perfect match for that venue. Barrie wrote about a Pan named Peter who handily defeated the bumbling Hook and called out "I'm youth, I'm joy, I'm a little bird who has broken out of the egg" as he did so. Barrie's observation that "nothing that happens after we are twelve matters very much" was in harmony with the themes of childhood adventures contained in *Treasure Island, Kidnapped, Tom Sawyer,* and other late ninteeenth-century novels that featured boy heroes who easily outwitted adults. Barrie's personal obsession with childhood and its fortuitous convergence with the Edwardian fascination with playful boys paid off handsomely for the son of Margaret Ogilvy.

At age sixty-two, in 1922, Barrie wrote: "It is as if long after writing Peter Pan its true meaning came to me—desperate to grow up but can't."[16] Wullschlager identifies the source of Barrie's ambivalence, the desire to grow up countered by a desire not to grow up, as the same episode spotted by Mackail and Sapolski. Sobbing on the stoop one day, he is sent to his mother's room by his sister Mary to console Margaret by reminding her that she has another son. "Is that you?" Margaret asks, in a listless voice, when Jamie enters her dark room. He gives no answer. Wullschlager quotes the full passage that I alluded to earlier:

> Then the voice said more anxiously, "Is that you?" again. I thought it
> was the dead boy she was speaking to, and I said in a little lonely
> voice, "No, it's no' him, it's just me." Then I heard a cry, and my
> mother turned in bed, and though it was dark I know she was holding
> out her arms.[17]

Wullschlager then makes reference to the various strategies Jamie subsequently used to take his mother's mind off David and bring a smile to her face. One of his strategies was to imitate the behaviors that Margaret described as so endearing about David. "He dressed in his (David's) clothes, learned his brother's way of whistling, and became fixated on the idea of always remaining a boy."[18] The other strategy was to listen intently to Margaret's stories of growing up. Barrie's reaction to the trauma of his childhood set the stage for literary creations that placed him at the heart of a transition from Victorian works depicting pure and innocent yet courageous little girls to Edwardian stories about fun-loving, boisterous, and fantasy-prone little boys. Looking back on that period, Barrie occupies a position in the literary landscape of English authors that brings him shoulder to shoulder with the likes of Lewis Carroll, Edward Lear, Kenneth Grahame, and A. A. Milne whose major works include such classics as *Alice in Wonderland* (Carroll), *The Owl and the Pussy Cat* (Lear), *The Wind in the Willows* (Grahame), and *Winnie-the-Pooh* (Milne). Add Peter

Pan to that list, and forty to fifty years of adventures in Wonderland is pretty well defined.

Now that the case has been made that the events surrounding David's death have not been magnified merely because they fit a "personological" perspective, I can thank and dismiss members of the ad hoc diagnostic council and move on to other matters. The issue that presses most strongly for attention is what Wullschlager refers to as Barrie's fixation on the idea of always wanting to remain a boy. How could a boy in a man's body ever achieve his ambitions to be known, "forever," as an author?

TEN *What Can I Do to Be*

Forever Known?

Think of your own childhood memories. What events come to mind? Where were you? If you were not alone, who was with you? I remember the day that Keith, a fellow second-grader, told me he was going to beat me up. Now if it had been his brother, Kenny, also in our class, I would not have been so panic-stricken. Kenny was about half the size of Keith, and I think I could have whomped him. The reason that Keith (aged nine) and Kenny (aged seven) were in the same class is Keith had been invited to remain in second grade, just as he had been invited to re-take first grade two years earlier. For that and probably other reasons, Keith was not happy about his situation and one day decided to vent his frustrations by tearing off one of my limbs. When Keith issued his warning, he told me where he would be waiting after school. My home was only a few blocks away from the school building, and prior to Keith's threat I had never imagined there were so many routes to my safe haven. Backyards I had never visited. Fences I had never climbed. Dogs that had never chased me. Unfamiliar paths around a hill that my parents had cautioned me to avoid. Never mind their warnings, my life was at stake. I took detours through woods, hid behind a counter at the local grocery store, and sometimes had to endure the humiliation of begging my older sister to wait for me after school. Weeks after Keith had most likely forgotten his intention to snuff me out, my class assignments continued to suffer from my inability to concentrate on anything other than inventing new ways to get home. There is no good ending to this memory, other than it taught me the extent to which a few words could affect the course of many days.

Another memory. I fell in love with Rebecca in the third grade. She was the new girl in school. Perfect in every way. Lovely pigtails. I knew she liked me because one day she hit me over the head with a geography book, a true sign that our romance was headed in the right direction. In order to seal our friendship, I decided to present her with some flowers. The problem became one of where to find the flowers. I scoured my immediate neighborhood and came up empty, so I had to broaden my area of coverage. Finally I found some wonderful flowers growing in an unfamiliar backyard some distance up a street called St. Clair Avenue. I steeled my courage, wormed my way under the fence, and picked a dozen or so beauties. A car pulled up just as I was making my marine crawl retreat back under the fence. Rebecca, lovely Rebecca, and her mother got out of the car, and the thief was nabbed. How was I to know that I had grabbed a bouquet from the prize-winning garden tended by the woman who had given birth to the girl of my youthful dreams? One of the aftermaths of that very difficult afternoon was that Rebecca ignored me for the remaining few weeks of school. When school resumed in the fall, I learned that she and her family had moved to Indiana. Good riddance.

These memories are just two of a great many Sawyeresque memories of my boyhood. Hero, victim, tough guy, coward, hay fever sufferer, and dreamer—they all pertain to my experiences, or at least what a sixty-year-old man thinking back reconstructs as his experiences.

Most of Barrie's recollections were of a quite different sort. As a journalist, his early writings of a child growing up in Scotland were not based on recollections and embellishments of his own experiences. He wrote about someone else's experiences: his mother's experiences. The most remarkable part of it was he wrote about her experiences as though they had been his experiences. This is how that came about.

Earlier I referred to the hours upon hours, days upon days during his youth when Jamie sat at the foot of his mother's bed as she regaled him with stories of her childhood. This had become her primary diversion from her dreadful sadness over David's death, a way to momentarily suspend the shock that the tragedy had delivered to her system. Margaret's stories offered an avenue of escape for Jamie as well because they took his mind away, far away, from the time his mother had brought David back in his coffin. Her stories were of a time twenty to thirty years before Jamie had been born.

Mackail writes that Jamie "feels safer in the past, where nothing like that [the tragedy and Jamie's sense of maternal abandonment], he feels, can ever happen. He doesn't only listen to her stories but. . . . he struggles to enter into them until he virtually succeeds."[1] The phrase "virtually succeeds" says it well and is elaborated on in the following passage:

The reason why my books deal with the past instead of with the life I myself have known is simply this, that I soon grow tired of writing tales unless I can see a little girl, of whom my mother has told me, wandering confidently through the pages. Such a grip has her memory of her childhood had upon me since I was a boy of six.[2]

Prominent among the memories Margaret described to her son was the death of her dear mother when she was a mere child of eight, and how it fell on her shoulders to cook, clean the house, mend the clothes, and manage the daily chores of a household that included herself and two Davids: her father and her younger brother. David Senior was a hardworking stonemason whose income relied on devotion to his work from dawn to dusk. One of Margaret's favorite and often-repeated memories involved carefully preparing and hand-delivering her father's dinner to him at his work in her white pinafore and magenta frock.

Many of Margaret's stories were told to Jamie within the walls of her darkened room. On her better days, days when she was strong enough to get out of bed and venture outside, she would take Jamie to the cottage of her youth and introduce him to the sights, sounds, buildings, sheds, streets, and paths that unleashed a host of seemingly endless memories. She spoke of her father's church and its ministers and parishioners, ushers and elders, and of social gatherings where legends of specters and spirits were passed along. Jamie learned a great deal from his mother about how his church was special, what distinguished it from at least three other splinter groups (all housed in different locations in the small town of Kirriemuir) that many years before had been united under the name of the Original Seceders. David Ogilvy's sect was known as the Auld Lichts (Old Lights), two words that would become well known in Great Britain near the turn of the twentieth century, as they were contained in the title of Barrie's first triumphant book.

Jamie did not listen passively to Margaret's stories. He lived them. He imagined himself to be the little girl in a clean and neatly mended frock skipping down the path with her father's lunch container grasped firmly in her hand. In his mind, he was the girl who took loving care of her brother and who listened to legends and wondered about specters that wandered through the hills and secretly performed miraculous services for people in dire conditions of pain or impoverishment.

At the age of thirty-six, Barrie wonders what memories may sustain him in his old age. He concludes that it will not be his life that comes sweeping back, but hers, "a little girl in a magenta frock and white pinafore . . . singing to herself, and carrying her father's dinner in a flagon."[3]

The stories Margaret Ogilvy related to her son over several years provided him with ideas that he would subsequently use as an initial answer to his question "What can I do to be forever known?" They escalated the career of a young, hardworking and often witty journalist to that of author of books that brought early fame.

The first indication of what was to come was a failed initiative. A year before he went to college, Barrie wrote the better part of a three-volume novel and sent it to a publisher. The fee for publishing the manuscript was much more than Barrie could afford. He was able to handle the disappointment and later expressed relief that the novel was never published, calling it exceedingly "dull."[4] More difficult to justify, although the comment should have come as no great surprise, was the publisher's statement of encouragement to the "clever lady" who had written it.

After obtaining a Master of Arts degree at the University of Edinburgh, Barrie was expected to move into a career in teaching, as his older brother Alick had done, or become a minister, a role the Barrie family believed David had been destined to fill. But J. M. never wavered from his promise to himself that he would become an author whose mother would be "windy" of his achievements. His college years at Edinburgh had been lonely ones, and the most frequent word in his daily journals was "grind, grind, grind." All the grinding and the enormous amount of energy that went into his writing provided him with the discipline needed to cope successfully with the pressure of producing a minimum of two articles a day in his first staff job with the Nottingham Journal.

Despite his celebrated shyness and the severity of his headaches, Barrie followed up on the recommendation of his sister, Jane Ann, by applying for the position of "leader writer" for the Nottingham Journal that she had spotted in an advertisement. Soon after his arrival in Nottingham, he began a routine of writing at least twelve hundred words of prose a day, every day, without a break, for eighteen months. Keeping his pledge to his mother with a vengeance, the industrious journalist wrote fiction under the name of Hippomenes every Monday, and a Modern Peripatetic authored Thursdays' columns.

During this period, acquaintances had to be careful about what they said in his presence lest their words and comments appear the next day in the Journal. Barrie needed material for his copy and could weave the most mundane happenings into a clever tale. Accuracy meant nothing to Barrie. Nor was he the slightest bit concerned about the sensitivities of people who triggered a story. It was the story that mattered, and the boundaries between actual events and what might have happened were never fixed.

After a year and a half devoted to writing fiction, commentaries, and book and play reviews, the twenty-four-year old Barrie was suddenly back in Kirriemuir. For cost savings reasons, the Nottingham Journal had released its ambitious staff writer.

An accomplished author now, with over a thousand articles in print but none credited to his name, J. M. Barrie remained unknown. He fought his loneliness, his headaches, his depression, and family suspicions that he would never become self-supporting in his chosen profession and continued to write, write, write. Most of his stories were composed as first-person accounts of events of some elderly character who was drawing on and sometimes mocking his own memories. He sent these works to newspaper and magazine editors and became accustomed to not hearing back.

The drought was broken on November 17, 1884, when he received word that *St. James's Gazette*, a prominent newspaper in London, had published one of his submissions. Payment would be forthcoming. The article was titled "An Auld Licht Community," an alteration of the title he had given it, and, of course, the author was not named. With his foot now in the door, Barrie sent other articles and stories to Greenwood, the editor of the *Gazette*. One that was rejected and returned contained a note from Greenwood saying: "But I liked that Scottish thing. Any more of those?"

There were a lot more of those. With the assistance of his mother, he restored her (and his) old memories, and his pen took charge of the rest. Soon afterward *An Auld Licht Funeral* was published. That was followed by *Auld Licht Courtship*. Then came *An Auld Licht Scandal, An Auld Licht Wedding*, and more, with the author's name now attached to each.

Despite Greenwood's preference for Barrie to mail the articles from Scotland, Barrie was convinced that residence in London was a prerequisite for fame. Margaret was worried about the decision because of the discrepancy between her son's physical appearance (reed thin, short, and younger than his actual age) and whatever one might imagine his appearance to be on the basis of his writings. Nonetheless, Barrie arrived in London in the spring of 1885. Undaunted by the curious looks of publishers as they gazed in wonder at the anxious young man who tormented them to read his copy, and refusing to accept no as the final word, Barrie kept returning to the doorsteps where his works had been rejected until some, and eventually quite a few, editors took interest in the often humorous works of the boyish man.

As Barrie crowded articles into several newspapers, he began to merge some Auld Licht stories that had been published in *St. James's Gazette* into a book titled *Auld Licht Idyls*. The book, released in 1888, was an immediate success. J. M. had taken a giant step in the direction of answering his question about how to become known. Within a year, a second novel (in all there would be four based on his Auld Licht "memories") was published. Titled *A Window on Thrums*, the book was hailed in a front-page review of the *National Observer as a* "book of genius." Less generous were the words of a critic who called Barrie "a man who would make copy of his grandmother's bones."[5]

No mention of Peter Pan yet. That was to come later. In the meantime, more books, hundreds of articles, and now even a few plays flowed forth from his ever-active imagination.

You and I know that these works were coauthored. Barrie, of course, deserved and received credit for authorship, but a little girl whose life his mother had described during the years of his youth had guided his prose. In their effort to temporarily escape the trauma of David's death, Barrie had entered the Wonderland of his mother's childhood. Just as he had briefly endeavored to become David so that Margaret might love him, he entered into the mind and body of the girl whose life was fashioned and re-fashioned by the memories of his mother. He saw the scenes and dramas described to him. In his mind, he met the characters who had shaped her life. He shared her experiences doing daily chores. He witnessed weddings and funerals, listened in on debates and feuds between different breakaway sects of the same church denomination. He imagined characters so vividly that he knew the lengths of their beards, their mannerisms, their quirks and foibles. He thought the thoughts of that little girl, traveled her paths, and shivered when she was cold. "I have seen many on-dings of snow," Barrie writes in *Margaret Ogilvy*, "but the one I seem to recall best occurred nearly twenty years before I was born."[6]

Barrie himself was quite aware of the matter of coauthorship. In *Margaret Ogilvy* he describes a morning when he is anxious to set about writing because he had an idea in his head, "which if it is of any value, has most certainly been put there by her."[7] Margaret was both his coauthor and internalized judge. After her death, he writes, "those eyes I cannot see until I was six years old have guided me through life, and I pray to God that they remain my only earthly judge to the last."[8]

After Barrie had run out of Auld Licht stories and broadened the scope of his creative and entertaining novels and plays, his mother made appearances in everything he wrote. The fact that she could be located in the pages of his works is both acknowledged and evident in the following passage in *Margaret Ogilvy*:

> When it was known that I had begun another story my mother might ask what it was about this time.
>
> "Fine we can guess who it is about," my sister would say pointedly.
>
> "Maybe you can guess, but it is beyond me," says my mother, with the meekness of one who knows that she is a dull person.
>
> My sister scorned her at such times, "What woman is in all his books?" she would demand.
>
> "I'm sure I canna say," replies my mother determinedly. "I thought the women were different every time."
>
> "Mother, I wonder you can be so audacious! Fine you know what woman I mean."
>
> "How can I know? What woman is it? You should bear in mind that I hinna your cleverness" (they were constantly giving each other little knocks).
>
> "I won't give you the satisfaction of saying her name. But this I will say, it is high time he was keeping her out of his books."

And then as usual my mother would give herself away unconsciously.

"That is what I tell him," she says chuckling, "and he tries to keep me out but he canna; it's more than he can do!"[9]

Despite Margaret's feigned objections, she relished her appearance in her son's writings. She treasured all of his books and the many articles that preceded them. She kept every one of the letters, numbering in the thousands, that arrived daily when he lived in London, always placing the latest under the sheets on her bed. The arm that wanted to go 'round something eventually went 'round her youngest son's letters.

Barrie had found a way to be accepted by his mother. Initially, he did so by internalizing her narratives and writing his early stories from her perspective. Later, he wrote stories that contained characters based on his mother, and all of his products met with her approval. Throughout it all, psychologically and by his own admission, he wanted to remain a boy, a boy who could bring a smile to his mother's face and seek refuge in her arms. But the pressure was always on. David was never far from her mind. The bars guarding her room were never completely disassembled. Her memories of David always remained insurmountable barriers to obtaining what Barrie was desperate to obtain, and as a consequence he remained betwixt and between.

Betwixt and between what? Betwixt and between being a bird and a boy, if we are to be literal about one of the plots in The Little White Bird. Betwixt and between a little boy craving his mother's attention, attempting to be reunited with her, and an adult capable of adult relationships is another way to look at it. Psychologically, Barrie could enter neither world. He could not return to a time of innocence before the tragedy hit the family. Nor could he psychologically remove himself from the tug to remain a child in order to move into the sphere of establishing mature relationships, particularly mature, intimate relationships with women. Just as Barrie did everything imaginable to obtain his mother's approval, he sought his mother in the guise of other women, and, as many women know, that can be a problem. It was in the context of Barrie coming to terms with that issue that Peter Pan made his first appearance. But before that curtain rises, the stage must be prepared. The following chapter on attachment and separation is one of the necessary props.

ELEVEN *Attachment and Separation*

The study of J. M. Barrie brings us face to face with an issue that confronts all human beings and is more problematic for some than for others. The matter involves the question of how can one be embedded in relationships (that is, connected with others) *and* construct a sense of identity that, in some respects, is independent of one's relationships. This chapter introduces some ideas pertaining to attachment and separation in a way that provides a general platform for the remaining chapters in part II. The platform will be disassembled in part III when I look at several parts of it in much greater detail.

TOGETHER AND APART

Prenatal life is lived in the condition of the fetus being an extension of the mother's body. Physical independence is gained the moment the umbilical cord is severed. But unlike colts that are up and running in a matter of hours, the human infant faces many years of gradual disengagement, both physical and psychological, from parental care. *Psychological* dependence and independence is my present topic.

The infant's first experiences of connectedness are typically and primarily with its mother. Some psychoanalytic theorists describe this earliest period in an infant's life as one of fusion wherein it has no sense of boundaries. In chapter 16 I will show how that description has been updated and modified, but not in ways that deny the existence of an inborn drive to connect.

There is also an inborn drive to disconnect, to separate, to become psychologically autonomous, to differentiate a growing sense of self from other selves. The tension between merger and independence is played out in every life. Witness a child who, in the course of exercising her autonomy, meets a stranger and immediately runs to clasp her arms around her mother's legs. Or the adolescent who in high school battles with his parents for independence, finally goes off to college or enters the armed services, and is homesick. Or a forty-five-year-old wife and mother who adores her family and treasures the thought of taking a trip to London or Paris . . . alone. Although there may be peak periods when the issue arises, the interplay between connecting and disconnecting, between assimilation and differentiation, never completely vanishes.

As Yogi Berra[1] could have put the matter, attachment and separation is not a problem unless it's a problem. For most people it is not a concern around which their lives revolve. However, it can become the dominating factor in some persons' lives, especially in instances when there are major disruptions in consistent caretaking in childhood. Fifty years ago, John Bowlby[2] proposed that infants are born with an "attachment system" that is the human version of imprinting systems in, for example, ducks. Moments after cracking through their shells, ducklings instinctively follow whatever moving object is in their visual field. There is a high probability that the object will be the mother duck, but if she has been eaten by a fox or swallowed by a muskie, the ducklings will lock onto and trail after whatever moving object is on the scene. The human attachment system proposed by Bowlby is much less severe, a good deal more flexible, and takes a much longer time to develop than imprinting mechanisms in other creatures.

Under normal conditions, a child's attachment system is quiescent. There is no need for it to be activated as long as the child experiences a sense of security. For the first few years of life, security is garnered by the physical proximity of the primary mothering figure. Periodic checking of the attachment figure's availability is an essential ingredient of play and exploration. As the child advances in age, the actual physical presence of an attachment figure becomes less important than the mental representation that the figure could be available if needed. Under the conditions of repeated "safe haven" experiences, the child creates internal working models in the form of mental images to forecast and anticipate the sorts of supportive interactions that will ensue when the caretaker returns. According to Bowlby and many others who have followed up on his ideas, early-formed working models of self and other interactions can set the tone and course for subsequent close relationships.

Problems arise when a child's self-with-other working models are suddenly disconfirmed by reality, particularly when the "other" person is the primary attachment figure. A profound disruption of learned expectations leads to anxiety, a sense of helplessness, even fear of not being able to survive, and that is when the attachment system goes into high gear. That is when the issue of attachment and separation becomes a problem. The panic of having lost a secure base and the desperate struggle to do something about it can initiate a dynamic that has the strong potential of repeating itself throughout the course of one's life. Its consequences are far-reaching in terms of the negative effects it has on establishing and securing a sense of identity and on the development of nurturing relationships in adulthood.

I will argue that flight fantasies emerge from the tension between connectedness and disconnectedness, dependence and independence, that is caused by a sudden loss of caregiver attention or a dramatic shift in the primary attachment figure's demeanor. Flight fantasies not only are expressions of the tension but also, in some instances, represent fantasy solutions to the tension—solutions that occasionally come down on the side of merger or fusion with another. On the surface, flying can be viewed as an unmatched symbol of freedom from attachments, a rising above and away from the social and material world. But it is also important to consider the final destinations of levitation fantasies and/or the means of conveyance. In later chapters I will discuss instances when flying away is a thinly veiled image of flying back to an earlier stage of self-and-other nondifferentiation. But that observation is getting ahead of the story, because the match between that formulation and the information about Barrie that I am dealing with is less than perfect.

Once again, recall the image of Peter Pan in *The Little White Bird* waving his little arms against the iron bars of his mother's bedroom window. He wanted in, he wanted to be held. But the mother was not available, as another baby rested in her arms. Bad mother. Bad Margaret. How could a mother be so cruel? Not so fast, I caution. To blame Margaret does not take into account Jamie's other vector, the vector away from interpersonal fusion. Jamie's desire to merge with Margaret, to form an inseparable union with her, was countered by a desire to distance himself from her. Jamie wanted in and did not want in. "Ah, Peter, we who have made the great mistake, how differently we should all act at a second chance." What could Jamie's great mistake have been? Had he been away too long? Did he believe that he had ignored his mother and now she was getting back at him? I have no solid answers to these questions other than to observe that separation issues are usually well on the road to having some semblance of a working solution before the age of six, and that David's death probably served to aggravate a preexisting, unresolved condition. Pure speculation on my part, but I suspect that for several years before David's skating accident, Jamie and Margaret had been engaged in an emotional tag game. The game was probably more significant to Jamie than it was to his mother, for she was a housewife with a load of other responsibilities. The

game, as I imagine it, was conducted in accordance with flexible guidelines, guidelines that granted each player some room for improvisation,
more so for Jamie than for Margaret. Let us say an episode is initiated by
Jamie who would act as though he did not need his mother. Exercising his
autonomy, he would become absorbed in activities that did not involve
her, perhaps even stretching the limits of independence. The next step in
the cycle involved Jamie seeking Margaret's direct attention in order to assure himself of her availability. Then, once again, off he would go, only to
return, teetering back and forth on the cusp of an approach-avoidance see-
saw. Then came the fateful day when Margaret no longer played her anticipated role. Jamie, in his confusion, may have feared that he had been
away too long when he saw her crying pitifully on her bed, and for the remainder of his life he struggled to make his mother's face fit the features
he had learned to anticipate so the separation/attachment game could proceed on its accustomed circular path. It is striking to me that Barrie stated
in *Margaret Ogilvy* "I knew my mother forever now," after she had become bedridden. Prior to becoming a distinct person, she had been a consistent player in Jamie's subjective world, able to provide external credibility to his internalized, "me-with-my-Mom," mental representation.

In any case, irrespective of the details of how it came about, Jamie as a
child and J. M. as an adult needed to keep the tension in place. He
needed Margaret to both accept and reject him. That pattern, now exacer-
bated by Margaret's sudden interruption of the "accept me" part of the
game, eventually resulted in a standoff, with the image of Peter Pan, neither male nor female, a sexless being, half bird/half child, suspended in
midair.

The accept me/reject me balancing act that Barrie perfected with
Margaret throughout his childhood continued to be played out during his
adult years. Freud's concept of "repetition compulsion" can be applied to
this phenomenon if we think of such compulsions in terms of repeating
variations of general patterns of behavior instead of replicating specific actions. These patterns are not random. Instead, they can be thought of as
being guided by *scripts.*

ELEMENTS OF TOMKINS'S SCRIPT THEORY

The idea that much of our lives are conducted according to scripts derived
from early-formed templates brings us into a fascinating territory mapped
out by Silvan Tomkins (1911–91), who was one of Henry Murray's early as-
sociates at the Harvard clinic in the 1930s. He shared Murray's interest in
human motivation but eventually became disillusioned with the idea that
a basic set of needs (recall that Murray listed twenty of them) would be sufficient to answer the questions he posed. Tomkins believed that the puzzle

of motivation would remain unresolved until *affects*, or feelings, were granted their proper place in shaping lives.[3] Affects are the hidden players in the game of motivation. Their ebb and flow is monitored inside our bodies, sometimes completely outside our awareness. As I will discuss in chapter 17, we know we exist not because we think but because we *feel*. Feelings function as the barometers of our existence. Tomkins argued that virtually everything we do is either directly or indirectly influenced by how we have learned to regulate our feelings.

Tomkins's advanced degree was in philosophy, but he had studied drama as an undergraduate and had written several plays in conjunction with his work. He brought his interest in how plays are constructed into the realm of affect and its control and proposed that emotions are regulated by scripts. Actors are provided with the words to say, when and how to deliver their lines, the places to occupy on the stage, and, importantly, are coached with regard to what emotions to display and/or withhold during a performance. Actors would be lost without a script and at sea without a director. Likewise, we (all of us off-stage performers) would be in a constant state of confusion were it not for the fact that we operate in a world of rules. For example, the rule for gassing up at a filling station in New Jersey is to drive up next to a pump and wait in the car for an attendant. Try to "self-serve" in New Jersey and see what happens. But my script for getting gas in New Jersey is ineffective at most gas stations across the border in Pennsylvania. The script of sitting in a car next to a pump doesn't work in Pennsylvania; you must exit the car, grasp the nozzle, and do something, which, for me, is always a challenge.

While others, particularly Erving Goffman,[4] elaborated on the stage-like quality of everyday life, Tomkins concentrated on scripts of a different sort; *personological scripts*, call them. Each person develops a set of unique scripts that are covered with its owner's fingerprints, and a life can be productively viewed as an interplay between externally imposed and internally created scripts.

Tomkins was impressed by how early in life some personal scripts are formed, particularly scripts that evolve from sudden shifts in scenes that are accompanied by emotions of the sort that deliver shock waves through the body and directly into the brain. That kind of critical episode in a person's life, particularly if it is experienced as a threat to survival, can provide the makings of a blueprint for a master script. Subsequent to its installation, it serves as the source of spinoff scripts that serve both to "amplify" and "magnify" the significance of the original scene.[5] Tomkins's ideas about this phenomenon lie at the heart of and add critical elements to the contemporary work on *prototypical scenes* I described in chapter 9.

A personal script can be thought of as analogous to a melody that is repeated throughout the course of a symphony. The sequence of notes and chords and what instruments play them vary according to the makeup of the orchestra, the talents of its members, the conductor's style, and the location of the performance. Sometimes the melody is in the foreground, and sometimes it retreats to a harmonic position where it waits for the time to rise again. No matter where it is as the piece is being played, it is always close by as a reference point for the piece.

Orchestra members require sheet music that shows what notes to play, when to pause, when to play softly, and when to participate in a crescendo. After the piece is mastered, there is considerable leeway in how it is played. No performances are exactly alike. Similarly, our performances are never quite the same.

Stretching the analogy between musical notations and scripts a bit further, the identifying feature of a good jazz performance is that the musicians begin with a familiar tune and proceed to improvise on it in ways that leave only subtle hints of where they began. One can think about a master script in a similar way. It begins with the rehearsal of a few simple chords. These well-learned chords form the base for improvisations, all of which, subtly or explicitly, carry the stamp of the scene that spawned the original notes.

The notes in the tune that Barrie learned to play with his mother contained variations of a few chords borne from his experience of being sealed off from her. "Love me as you did before" was the central theme. He was desperate to restore conditions that marked his felt sense of safety prior to his brother's death. Time and again, he rehearsed the music in her presence, and it became the source of numerous improvisations. What is most remarkable is that the music played on despite the fact (from the perspective of an outside observer anyway) that she eventually became "windy" of his accomplishments. Let's face it, a rejecting mother does not welcome and relish the constant companionship of her child and cherish every letter he sends to her when he is an adult.

By all appearances, the war was over, but the notes demanded to be repeated. The scene of Jamie's original trauma had to be replayed, and it left its mark on virtually everything he did. The internal tension created by the series of clashing, love-me/reject-me chords became his life's signature. Barrie's skills at improvisation made him special. As I will show in the next chapter, variations of the original notes can be found in his books and plays, where they are massaged into memorable stories. Without the tension in place, it is doubtful that James Barrie would have become a household name. Equally instructive to students in personality is the fact that the script played an important role in orchestrating his interpersonal relationships.

A well-learned script is not confined to the location where it was initially rehearsed. Eventually it is taken to different auditoriums and performed in front of new audiences. In Barrie's case, the composition containing the theme of attachment and the countertheme of separation was improvised in such a way that they became two separate melodies played in the company of two different women. He played his reject-me piece with his wife, Mary Ansell. His performance was so stirring that increasingly over their fifteen years of marriage she could hardly bear to even be in his company. By refusing or being unable to meet her needs, under Barrie's tutoring, Mary perfected the role of the rejecting mother.

The other melody was performed in the company of Sylvia Llewelyn Davies. The "love me as you would love a child" theme on the page of the original script was acceptable to her ears as she provided Barrie with the opportunity to play with her boys, as one of her boys, under the condition of there being no pressure to grow up.

TWELVE *Life at the Intersection*

Throughout his adult life, Barrie was never without a writing pad in his pocket for entering notes for plays and stories and for recording scraps of passing thoughts. Many of these notebooks were among the items made available to Mackail when he undertook the monumental task of writing The Story of JMB. One of the pads contained an entry where Barrie referred to "a little box inside me that nothing opened until later years it did of its own accord. Just trifles in it, but I made a game with them for many years."[1] That notation was entered in 1926, when Barrie was sixty-six years old. It was in reference to the arrival of Peter Pan twenty-five years earlier.

I doubt that the little box sprang open of its own accord. It had some assistance. We need to know about the circumstances of Barrie's life during his mid to late thirties and the personal issues he faced if we are to discover the keys to the box. It should come as no surprise that women were involved. They were Mary Ansell and Sylvia Llewelyn Davies, with Margaret Ogilvy, of course, always lurking about in Barrie's mind. I will begin this part of the story about eight or nine years before Mary enters J. M.'s life.

BARRIE ON THE PROWL

J. M. was tormented by lust when he was in his twenties. With some difficulty he had partially overcome the tendency for his tongue to become twisted in knots when he spoke to women. Helpful in this regard was the

fact that he was beginning to be well known in the London literary world
for having written several novels and some lightweight, funny plays. Since
he was involved in auditions and the productions of his plays, he became
acquainted with young, attractive actresses anxious for cast positions.
Bowled over by their beauty, he charmed them with his wit, praised them
for their good looks, and targeted some for sentimental letters. Recognizing the lovesick tone of these letters, only a few responded to his romantic
overtures. Those who did, those who came back to him to laugh at his antics and be amused by his stories and his curious way of speaking, became
puzzled by his sudden retreat into dark and distant thoughts. The discrepancy between the bold openness of his letters and his shutting down in
person was bewildering. In part, he retreated into concerns about his
mother and the roller-coaster condition of her health. Whenever one of
the daily letters he received from his sister, Jane Ann, mentioned a worsen-
ing in Margaret's condition, Barrie would drop his work and travel from
London to Kirriemuir to be at his mother's bedside. His devotion was so
complete that he would later boast in *Margaret Ogilvy*, "Everything I
could do for her in this life I have done since I was a boy: I look back
through the years and I cannot see the smallest thing undone." Margaret
still kept the pressure on by whispering David's name as she feel asleep
some nights. What more could he do to prove to his mother that she had
nothing to regret about her "other" son?

Barrie's preoccupation with Margaret's health is the explanation
MacKail gives for Barrie's withdrawing his attention from actresses who responded favorably to his sentimental letters, but that is an inset on a larger
map. As I am about to show, it was Barrie's style; young adult editions of
his approach-avoidance, love-me/back-off-woman conflict.

ENTER MARY ANSELL

Back in London after a prolonged visit with Margaret, Barrie, now thirty-
one years old, had nearly completed writing a play entitled *Walker, London*. A young, independent, ambitious, and, yes, very pretty actress named
Mary Ansell had attracted his attention for her performance in Wyndham's
revival of *Brighton*, and Barrie began to charm her. Mary, an inch or so
shorter than her suitor, responded to his wit. She liked him, and soon they
were constant companions, with Barrie keeping a watchful eye on potential competition to guard against the sting of jealousy. Miss Ansell, an accomplished actress, was hired as a member of the cast of *Walker, London*.
The play was a riotous success.

For the next two years, Mary was as determined as J. M. to deny rumors that the two of them were engaged. The relationship they billed as a
casual friendship, however, changed abruptly in the spring of 1894 when

Barrie at the time of his marriage. From A.
Birkin, *J. M. Barrie and the Lost Boys* (New York:
Clarkson N. Porter, 1979). © Great Ormond
Street Hospital Children's Charity, 1993.

Mary Ansell at the time of her marriage. From
A. Birkin, *J. M. Barrie and the Lost Boys* (New
York: Clarkson N. Porter, 1979). © Great
Ormond Street Hospital Children's Charity, 1993.

J. M. returned to Scotland for what he had intended to be a brief visit. While in Kirriemuir, Barrie caught a cold that worsened into pleurisy and then pneumonia. He fought for his life for several weeks.

Mary came north to assist in the battle, and slowly the tide receded. She stayed during the lengthy period of convalescence, and in mid-July Londoners were treated to an announcement that Miss Mary Ansell had married Mr. James M. Barrie on July 9 in a quiet ceremony in the home of the groom's parents. J. M. married the pretty woman who had come to nurse him. Perhaps exaggerating, perhaps not, Denis MacKail writes that if Mary had not gone to take care of J. M., "there would have been no more books and no more plays."[2]

The still sick man and his wife went to Switzerland for their honeymoon, an event that marked the beginning of a (probably) sexless marriage. Of course, only the couple knew if the fifteen-year marriage had been consummated. In chapter 9, I reported that Robert Sapolski declared that it had not, but citations are absent. Wullschlager expressed doubt that the couple ever had sex,[3] and Mackail hedged on the matter. As for me? Normally I would consider it to be none of my business (or yours, for that matter), but it is such an important chapter in J. M.'s life that the question cannot be avoided. So, reading between the lines of what Barrie wrote and directly from what has been written about him, I am led to conclude that there was not much action between the sheets that lay on Mr. and Mrs. Barrie's bed. We know from a note that J. M. scribbled in one of his tablets a few days prior to his wedding that he was worried about his ability to perform: "You are very ignorant. How? Must we instruct you in the mysteries of love making?" We could chalk this up to premarital jitters, were it not that he jotted down fragments of dialogue for a possible play during his honeymoon: "Wife: 'Have you given up on me? Have you nothing to do with me?' Husband calmly kind, no passion (a la self)."

The marriage ended in July 1909, when Mrs. Barrie's gardener reported to J. M. that Mrs. Barrie had been having an affair in their summer home with a Mr. Gilbert Cannan. Mary did not deny her infidelity when J. M. confronted her with the information. Probably relieved that her secret had been discovered, she declared her love for Cannan and requested an immediate divorce.

Barrie had nothing to offer the marriage other than occasional entertainment when he was in a good mood and a great deal of money, which Mary spent on lavish and tasteful remodeling projects in their various homes. Living with a flesh-and-blood woman was very different from his romantic fantasies. At first, what he wanted from Mary was what he had sought from Margaret—a mother whose acceptance of him was complete and unconditional. Mary was probably willing to do that, but she expected something in return: physical displays of affection would have helped. But sex was not part of J. M.'s utopian fantasies. One does not have sex with one's mother, not with one's caretaker. In addition, having sex acknowl-edges entry into adulthood, and Barrie would have none of that. He wanted to remain a lad and never have to give up his boyish ways. At age eighteen, he had jotted down a note that prophesied what was to come. "Greatest horror—dream I am married—wake up shrieking. . . . Grow up . . . awful thought."

Barrie was a role player, and being a husband was not in his repertory. Recall that he had imitated his dead brother. He rehearsed being other children and practiced being what he imagined Margaret to have been when she was child. "Look at me!" he complained to Margaret; "You know nothing of me!" His existence was confirmed only when he was someone else. He could imagine himself being all of the characters in his books and plays. It is reported that he sometimes injured himself when he enacted the role of a character he was in the process of developing for a story. As a celebrity, he could entertain members of social gatherings with hilarious third-person quips and stories, and then would retreat back into his gloomy soul or disappear into the night, leaving nothing of himself behind, for he had no self to offer.

Repeating what Barrie said so often, he did not want to grow up. More boldly, he said he *could not* grow up. This is not to say that he was oblivi-ous to Mary's needs. In fact he was well aware of what she wanted and was sympathetic with her desires. As a master role player, he could just as easily place himself in her shoes as he could in any other role. He knew she sought intimacy, wanted to be loved, and desired children. He proba-bly even "felt her pain." The problem was that he wanted her to be his mother. Mary wanted an adult relationship. Mary wanted emotional inti-macy. Barrie wanted a mother because he had no sense of possessing a self independent of the enactment of his child-with-mother script. He was the only person he could not imitate because there was nothing there to imi-tate. It was a terrible dilemma. On the one hand, he wanted to be engulfed in a relationship with a woman, to be consumed by her. Remove those iron bars and let me in. And yet if he were to be let in, whatever fragments of self that existed might crumble. So the next line was "Step back, woman, I am not to be touched." That was the script he was destined to follow for the purpose of psychic survival. It was a pre-Oedipal game that was played so intensely that sex was out of the question. Sex was irrelevant. Sexual maturation, the ability to offer sexual gratification, requires having something to give. Again, Barrie had nothing to give, and he worked hard to keep it that way. He worked hard at remaining a child, always vacillating between the competing tugs to reunite and separate, and any expressions of sexuality would propel him out of the cycle that gave meaning to his life. Call it sexual repression if you must, but I see few signs of unacknowl-edged unconscious forces in operation. Barrie was remarkably conscious about what he wanted from Mary and what Mary wanted from him. He was explicit about the conflict in much of what he wrote. Some examples follow.

Barrie freely attributed erotic desires to the women characters in the story of Peter Pan. Tiger Lily was shamelessly in love with Peter. Tinker Bell hated Wendy and was so jealous of her that she tricked the lost boys into trying to kill her by shooting her from the sky. Peter punished Tink for her silly envy. Wendy was also forthright about her intentions. On their return from Neverland, Wendy made the last of several attempts to locate a spark of romantic interest from Peter. "You don't feel you would like to say anything to my parents, Peter, about a very sweet subject?" she asks. "No Wendy," replies Peter. "About me, Peter?" "No," Peter responds, as he gets out his pipes and begins to play, which she knows is a very bad sign.

This theme reappears several years later in a play titled *When Wendy Grows Up: An Afterthought*. In it, Wendy, now an adult, speaks with her daughter, Jane, about Peter Pan. Jane is curious about flying and asks Wendy if she can still do it. Wendy is not sure she ever really did, but knows that only the young and innocent are capable of flight. Wendy then speaks with her daughter about the many years she sat by the window waiting for Peter to return. She reports to her daughter that one day he actually did return, but he was so self-absorbed that he took no notice that she was a grown woman. Blowing the dust from an old question, Wendy recalled asking "What am I to you, Peter?" The boy who had aged not one bit replied, "You are my mother."

Daughter Jane falls asleep near the end of her mother's report on days gone by, and, behold, Peter suddenly arrives again after many years of absence. It's spring cleaning time in Neverland, and Wendy is being called to duty.

> WENDY (*not knowing what to do*) Peter! Peter, do you know how long it is since you were here before?
> PETER It was yesterday.
> WENDY Oh! (*He feels her cheek*)
> PETER Why is there wetness on your face? (*She can't answer*) I know! It's 'cos you are so glad I've come for you.

Then Wendy informs Peter that she cannot fly back to Neverland, for she is now an adult with a child of her own. "Don't cheat me mother Wendy, I am only a little boy," says Peter. "Peter, what are your exact feelings for me?" asks Wendy. "Those of a devoted son, Wendy," replies Peter. Just then Jane wakes up and Peter asks *her* if she will be his mother. "Oh yes!" says Jane, and Peter is seen teaching Jane how to fly as the curtain falls on the final scene of the brief play.

The theme of wanting a mother and not a sexual partner is not restricted to the character of Peter Pan. In the middle years of his marriage, Barrie wrote a book entitled *Tommy and Grizel*,[4] a *roman à clef* that does

little to conceal its real-life characters. Tommy is a Scotsman and a successful writer. Grizel, a stand-in for Mary, marries Tommy, and later
laments the fact that her husband remained "a boy who could not with
years become a man." Regarding the question "Is it cruel to ask a boy to
love?" the answer provided is "He did not love her." Grizel then muses,
"Not as I love him. . . . Not as married people ought to love."

Andrew Birkin traces the theme of a standoffish male as the character
as it is developed in *Tommy and Grizel* and its forerunner, *Sentimental
Tommy.* Birkin notes that both books are ruthlessly biographic and self-
critical. Barrie, through the character Tommy, anguishes over his lack of
passion. Tommy loved Grizel in his mind, but Grizel is described as knowing that it is not done that way. In a telling deletion from the last page of
the manuscript of Tommy and Grizel made just prior to its publication,
Barrie crossed out the following two sentences:

> She lived so long after Tommy that she was almost a middle-aged
> woman when she died. What God will find hardest to forgive in him,
> I think, is that Grizel never had a child.[5]

If J. M. was so disinterested in intimacy with Mary, why had be been
so possessive of her during the two years of courtship? The frequency with
which Mackail refers to Barrie's premarital possessiveness of Mary suggests
that J. M. was not a victim of a garden-variety "Ah shucks, I hope she
doesn't leave me," condition of envy. Jealousy with the kind of intensity
Barrie experienced is a by-product of a person seeking to become "real"
via a particular "self-with-other" relationship. When a person fears a sense
of depletion outside a specific relationship, that person is desperate. Real
or imagined threats of abandonment evoke hollow feelings of not being
able to psychologically or even physically survive a termination of that
relationship.

Premarital possessiveness shifted to a different gear shortly after wedding vows were uttered. Reality replaced fantasy, and Barrie realized that
he could neither exist in or outside of his relationship with a woman. He
settled in residence at the intersection, where the vector to merge collided
with the vector to separate. "Ever so old and always the same age, still possessing every one of his baby teeth." A little boy, yearning to get in the window and making certain that the iron bars are up for life. That was Barrie's
personal script. Peter Pan, stuck in time, lingering at the window, part bird,
part human, one foot in the nest and one foot out—a perfect symbol of
Barrie's working solution to a dilemma that brought him wealth and fame.

No question about it—Barrie was a literary genius, a master of the art
of improvisation. He staged his personal drama in a way that thrilled audiences and enticed them to return year after year to holiday performances
of *Peter Pan.* The same theme penetrated his novels. *Farewell, Miss Julie
Logan* (1932), *Sentimental Tommy* (1919), *Tommy and Grizel* (1943), and

several other of his books and plays contain variations of his "come close/stay away" interpersonal script. His Auld Licht books, authored, as I have shown, by an internalized little girl, became a platform for Barrie to become a recognized author. He subsequently used that platform to create prose that recycled themes that pervaded his personal life. The stunning success of his works is not simply a product of his literary talent. As I pointed out earlier, the issues faced by Barrie are universal issues. How one can be in a relationship and simultaneously independent of that relationship is one of life's great challenges. Artistic renditions of these countervailing forces evoke a sense of recognition in us all.

Have you seen a performance of *Peter Pan*? What did you say when Peter asked the audience, "Do you believe in fairies?" Did you join most of the members of the audience who screamed "Yes! I believe in fairies!" Or were you a bump on a log that stubbornly refused to participate in such childishness?

I can assure you that Mary Ansell's enthusiasm about fairies decreased dramatically over the course of her marriage to J. M. She had firsthand knowledge of the barren interpersonal consequences of her husband's investment in nursery specters. The only thing the couple shared during their life as a couple was their mutual affection for a dog, a Saint Bernard named Porthos, that they had purchased in Lucerne during their honeymoon. The dog was at least as large or even larger than its master and mistress and the three became familiar figures strolling the paths of London's Kensington Gardens. Gradually the three figures were reduced to two, J. M. and Porthos, who attracted the attention of children, mostly boys, who frequented the park. Porthos, later to be immortalized as Nana, the Darling children's nursemaid, was loved for his gentle patience. Barrie was loved for the games he invented for the boys. In his midthirties, J. M. was the oldest boy and granted himself leading roles.

The latch on the little box was about to spring open.

ENTER SYLVIA AND HER BOYS

Second only to Margaret Ogilvy, Sylvia Llewelyn Davies was the most important woman in Barrie's life. Sylvia was the wife of a barrister and the daughter of the well-known du Mauriers. The couple had three boys—with two more to come—when J. M. met Sylvia at a New Year's Eve event in 1897. She was a beautiful woman, well liked for her intelligence, wit, and charm, and Barrie was drawn into her sphere. Sylvia openly adored her husband, Arthur, and thereby was a safe person for Barrie to befriend. Mary Ansell (Mrs. Barrie) had now been tucked away in J. M.'s mind as the bad, demanding mother who asked too much of him. But there were no prospects of Sylvia ever sexualizing her relationship with J. M., and he was free to play. In fact, J. M. had already played with Sylvia and Arthur's older two children, George and Jack, in Kensington Park prior to making his first acquaintance with their parents.

Soon the two couples became good friends. The colorful foursome were frequently witnessed together at formal social events. At a more casual level, J. M. in particular, was a frequent and welcome drop-in visitor to Sylvia's home. He was drawn to the environment Sylvia created for her boys, and Sylvia, unlike Mary, put no pressure on him to be anything other than one of the boys. She trusted him completely to accompany George and Jack, then Peter, and later Michael and Nicholas to Kensington Park. They played games in the Park nearly every weekend, with Porthos being one of the regulars. It was there that an invisible boy was invented. Although he was said to reside on a small, inaccessible island during daylight hours, the clever members of the gang found all sorts of evidence of his nighttime activities in the central grounds of the Park.

One summer, the evolving epic was taken to a new location for further development. The Barries owned a cottage on the pinewood shores of Black Lake. The Davieses rented a house nearby, and for six weeks, J. M., Porthos, and the boys all but vanished into the forest. Showing up only for occasional meals and bedtime rest, the adventurers quickly returned to their shipwrecked island, where they built a hut for shelter and survived the deadly peril of Indians and pirates.

Mary could not have been thrilled by J. M.'s daily absences, and Mackail reports that Arthur Davies, Sylvia's husband, had reservations about his children's inseparable connection with their adult companion. Sylvia, however, Sylvia the good mother, let the children play on—all of them, J. M. included. It was during this period that the lid on the little box that Barrie had carried inside him began to open. One of the "trifles" that emerged from the encasement was Peter Pan.

Peter Pan, born from Barrie's desire for eternal childhood, free to enact the script of wanting and resisting maternal care, an asexual figure playing his emotional tag game, seeking and being repelled by intimacy, free to fly away and be sad and lonely, only to recover and lead the boys into new arenas of adventure.

Barrie was the last to tire of the drama. It was his respite, his solution to his headaches, and his retreat from adult relationships. As George and Jack got older and no longer believed in Peter Pan, Peter Davies, Michael, and Nicholas took their places, and new chapters were added to the saga.

Peter Pan arose from the whirlpool of Barrie's ambivalence toward women. He was drawn to them as potential sources of devoted protection and repelled by the implications of his needs. Psychologically, he could not exist either in or outside a relationship with a mother figure. It took Barrie awhile to do it, but he managed to create space for Peter Pan's appearance in the wash of competing tides to connect and disconnect—

Sylvia Davies. From A. Birkin, *J. M. Barrie and the Lost Boys* (New York: Clarkson N. Porter, 1979). © Great Ormond Street Hospital Children's Charity, 1993.

connect with Sylvia where sex was forbidden and to disconnect with Mary, who wanted him to grow up. Barrie conducted his personal life betwixt and between these two forces that had originally been embodied in one figure.

A critical event, probably the critical event, that assured the survival and contributed to the actions of Peter Pan, was the death of Margaret Ogilvy. If I have the timing down correctly, and I believe I do, the following observations contribute to the credibility of the position I have taken on the connection between Peter Pan and his creator.

Barrie frequently interrupted his activities in London in order to travel to Kirriemuir to check on the condition of his mother. Soon after her death in 1899, Barrie memorialized her in the book *Margaret Ogilvy* (1901), His tears smudged the pages of drafts of the book as he mourned his mother's departure. But instead of closing an important chapter in his life, the book reiterated that chapter and kept it alive. Even though he had arranged things in London in a way that allowed him to express his competing dispositions through his relationships with Mary Ansell and Sylvia Davies, the source of these dispositions was gone. No longer could he return to his mother's bedside and view her facial expressions. The tension that had sustained his sense of being a person, the tension that inspired nearly all that he did, the tension that provided him with a steadfast purpose and made his life meaningful required a new outlet for expression. Hear the latch on the little box begin to loosen up. Watch as Peter Pan comes into view.

Peter Pan did not suddenly blast upon the scene, dressed as Mary Martin in a green hat with a feather stuffed into its band. He arrived in a much less dramatic form, as a character in a subplot in *The Little White Bird* (1902), which Barrie began writing as soon as he had completed the book that honored the memory of his mother. Prior to Margaret's death, there were no hints, no references, nothing at all in Barrie's voluminous writings that foretold the story of a half boy, half bird who lived on an island in Kensington Park. I referred to him earlier as "poor Peter" and gave an account of his fluttering back and forth to his mother's bedroom and eventually encountering bars on her windows and another child resting in her arms. Peter Pan was originally a phantom figure constructed as a symbolic carrier of his author's need for a mythic base to repeat the "in and out" cycle of his childhood. Peter Pan's early actions, his playing his flute hoping it would make his mother look happy, his nearly unbearable loneliness, his indecisiveness and ambivalence, and all the rest parallel the plight of a child named Jamie. After Peter Pan's initial arrival in *The Little White Bird*, his character was reworked and embellished throughout Barrie's years of intensive play with Sylvia's boys. Barrie and the Davies boys gradually added Captain Hook, Tinker Bell, Smee, Tiger Lily, and a host of other characters to the story. Finally, ten years after the debut of "poor Peter," a more confident and rambunctious Peter was ready to go on stage and cut the figure that made him famous. ㄴ 때문, 제것대로, 다를 수있는,

So there we have it. Peter Pan represents a prepubescent, asexual lad who has no desire to end the cycle of hovering in the general vicinity of maternal protection. It is a well-worn, practiced routine in which his yearning to unite with his mother is countered by a fear that his fragile psychic boundaries will be obliterated. Peter Pan, flying back and forth from the window of his nursery, not quite a bird and not yet a person, is an image that befits Barrie's dilemma. Early attachment and separation issues predate genital sexuality, and the onset of erotic feelings brings with them the frightening prospect of never being able to fly again. Sexual contact attaches a person to the material world and is a sign of maturation that finally results in death. Again, only the pure and innocent can fly. Lest you become as a little child, it is written, you will be unable to enter the kingdom of heaven.

I will be mindful of the circumstances surrounding the creation of

Peter Pan as I consider the lives of a few other individuals who were drawn to the skies. Before moving on, I want to briefly recount how it came to be that a life study of J. M. Barrie became such a prominent feature of this book, and to mention some of the events that scarred his remaining years.

When I began to think about the prospects of writing about flying fantasies as an approach to describing the advantages and problems of conducting case studies, I designed a rough outline of the major points I wanted to emphasize. The outline contained a note to myself: "Might mention Peter Pan. Who wrote the play? Check up on the author. Is anything known about him? Could be an interesting supplement." All I had in mind was a possible footnote or perhaps a few lines about Peter's relationship with Wendy as an example of imaginary flight and resistance to intimacy.

Plans change. Understanding J. M. Barrie became a mission that was nurtured by some similarities between the psychodynamic forces operating in his life and what I had observed in the lives of others who were on my writing agenda. This led to an upheaval of my preliminary ideas and resulted in a yearlong immersion in works by and about Barrie. The result is the preceding partial psychobiography, which I will use as a primary base of comparisons I will make with in subsequent chapters.

In chapter 6 I mentioned that one of Freud's rules for undertaking a psychobiographic study is not to idealize one's subject. No temptation here . . . with a few exceptions. When I spend a day struggling to write a paragraph that is likely to be shredded the next day, I admire J. M.'s proficiency with the pen. I laugh at his clever instructions to actors in his plays and appreciate other expressions of his journalistic talents. Other than that, there is very little for a fellow Scotsman to idealize.

I do, however, empathize with Barrie. I have come to see him as an acquaintance, a friend almost, whose life became unbearably tragic. The public Barrie was showered with honors. Royalties never ceased to line his bank accounts. His literary opinions could sanctify or bury books. "Barrie Says War Will Be Long" was one of many solicited pronouncements to receive press coverage. His endorsement of products prominently displayed on billboards guaranteed good sales. But behind the fame, behind the public notoriety, there was a lonely, heartbroken man. Readers who prefer happy endings may want to skip the rest of this chapter.

Arthur Davies, Sylvia's husband, died of jaw cancer in 1907. Barrie had grown close to Arthur during the final year of his deteriorating health and assured him of financial support of his family. Two years later, in 1909, Mary and J. M. were divorced, and Barrie devoted even more of his attention to the Davies family. In 1910, Sylvia died, and the five boys aged seven to seventeen, fell under Barrie's care. The man who would be forever known for creating a Pan who took care of a band of lost boys inherited a family of sons, thereby transforming a fantasy plot into chilling reality.

~~George~~ Davies, the oldest, on whom the character of David in *The Little White Bird* had been based, was killed in Flanders in 1915. Michael and his best friend drowned in 1921; he had become Barrie's favorite son. J. M. had hastened to Michael's bedside when he had nightmares of someone flying in his window to snatch him away. Barrie had written to Michael daily when he went to Eton in 1913, hoping that his letters would alleviate his adopted son's loneliness and lift his depression. When not in school, Michael had accompanied his guardian to rehearsals and while still a teenager had become Barrie's most trusted literary critic. The most talented of the sons, Michael had been most devastated by his parents' deaths, and Barrie was aware of rumors that Michael's drowning may have been intentional. It was openly speculated that it was the result of a suicide pact between two twenty-one-year-old males who were in love.

Barrie continued to write, but it was his earlier works that maintained his stature. He had many acquaintances and was an honored guest at palaces and presidential homes. But psychologically he remained an outsider, unable to develop deep and trusting friendships to sustain him in his later years.

James Barrie died at age seventy-seven and, at his request, was buried in Kirriemuir at the site occupied by the graves of his mother and father, his sister, Jane Ann, two other sisters who had died in infancy, and his brother . . . David.

In 1960, over a decade after Barrie's death, another tragedy struck the Davies family. Peter, the third of five children born to Sylvia, committed suicide in London by throwing himself beneath an oncoming train. "Suicide while the balance of his mind was disturbed" was the verdict of the coroner's jury. Peter was sixty-three years old when he died. He had been a major figure in London's publishing world, known as an artist among publishers. *Peter Pan Commits Suicide*, or variations of that theme, became the headlines in scores of newspapers on April 6, 1960, the day after Davies took his life. *The Boy Who Never Grew Up* read one of them. There is little doubt in Andrew Birkin's mind that the mass media's habit of referring to him by the name Peter Pan was a factor in "disturbing the balance of his mind." In the context of a newspaper interview about a completely different topic, conducted the day before Peter Davies leaped into the path of a train, he had been asked about Peter Pan. "Please forget about that," he had uttered.[6] Peter Davies had borne the brunt of the public's association of his name with Peter Pan. In fact, Barrie had settled on the name for the boy who could fly before he knew the "other" Peter. There is no question that Peter Davies contributed to the character of Peter Pan, but that was equally true of his brothers, in that Peter Pan was groomed by Barrie as an amalgam of the quirks, qualities, and clever statements of all the boys. But the public preferred to see it differently.

THIRTEEN *May the Force Be with You*

So far, my exploration of the puzzle of fantasies of flight has been focused primarily on understanding Peter Pan as an image that gave expression to the conflicts of its creator. Much of what I have written has
been centered on the traumatic disruption in the relationship between
Jamie and his mother and the lasting effects that disturbance had on subsequent relationships. Peter Pan symbolized the dilemma of being locked
into a pattern of simultaneously wanting to return to an early stage of security provided by a welcoming mother and knowing that things had been
forever changed. Psychologically, he was unable to move beyond that
issue. It operated like a magnetic force, a "strange attractor" if you will,
that confined him within its boundaries. In this regard, some progress has
been made with my topic, but a single case study will not resolve the problem it poses. The connections that have been made between Barrie's life
and his creation of a boy endowed with the ability to fly are a place to
begin, not a place to end.

A discussion of the ideas regarding flight fantasies offered by Carl Jung
provides a different perspective on the topic of levitation, and I will now
consider his thoughts on the matter. Jung was a Swiss psychiatrist who took
an immediate liking to Freud's book *The Interpretation of Dreams* and
sought to establish a personal friendship with his likeminded colleague in
Vienna. He and Freud wrote numerous letters to each other, and their
warm relationship developed to the point of Jung being appointed the first
president of the International Psychoanalytic Association. Shortly thereafter, Jung began to work on and eventually consolidate a perspective on
psychic development that was at odds with Freud's position. Freud was tol-

개정증 판정.

erant of theoretical innovations as long as they remained rooted in the primacy of sexual instincts. Jung refused to abide by such restrictions. Freud did not take well to defectors from the psychoanalytic camp, and the relationship was terminated. As was not unusual during those days, each viewed the other as an incurable neurotic. Jung was dismayed by Freud's obsession with the sexual drive, and Freud was appalled by Jung's romance with mysticism—a topic I will now consider.

In his autobiography, composed just before his death, Carl Jung wrote that throughout his life he had been "a solitary, because I know things and must hint at things which other people do not know, and usually do not even want to know."[1] A few years prior to writing those words, Jung had used that knowledge to interpret the message contained in objects that inexplicably appear in the sky. His views on the matter and how they reflect on matters of enduring personal concern to him warrant consideration in both this and the following chapter.

I begin by going back to the image of Peter Pan frantically flapping his arms against the barred window of his mother's bedroom. For Freud, the attempt to fly into the room is a disguised or sublimated expression of the child's desire to express his sexual impulses in the direction of the object most familiar to him—his mother. Jung would interpret the episode at the window differently. Peter Pan was not seeking an outlet for alleviating built-up sexual tensions. Instead, what he sought is what we all seek, according to Jung—to return to the source of his existence. But to restrict ourselves to thinking of the mother as the source of our lives, the person to whom we may wish to return, misses the mark, according to Jung. The mother is a physical representation of something far more enduring. The mother merely gives birth to the child. She too was once a child, and someone had given birth to her. Both the mother and the child and all who have preceded them and all who will be born in the future are products and carriers of a force that is so awesome, so powerful, so omnipresent and mysterious that it can barely be put into words. I am speaking of the *collective unconscious*. A substance that everyone shares, the collective unconscious is akin to a massive subterranean pool to which, know it or not, or like it or not, we are all attached. The collective unconscious is the source of our existences. It contains the raw materials of our personalities. It comprises physiological paths forged by continuous experience of human beings through past millenniums. Humankind, Jung writes, "depends on and is sustained by an entity he does not know, but which he has intimations that 'occurred' or—as we fitly say—revealed themselves to long forgotten forebears in the gray dawn of history."[2] To our detriment, what was revealed to our ancient forebears is no longer as directly available to us as it was to them. We have become "rootless intellectuals" whose identification with fleeting consciousness is so great that we have forgotten the timelessness of our psychic foundations. Our faith in the "Goddess of

Reason" has resulted in our imagining that only the things we are conscious of affect us, and "that for everything unknown there is some specialist whom has long since made a science of it."[3]

Our problem is greater than that. Even if one were to make it a lifetime mission to look deeply inside and discover the contents of the collective unconscious, much of the material in it could not be articulated. The collective unconscious is beyond words, language is incapable of describing its facets; a fact that makes the task of writing about it exceedingly difficult. That is probably one of the reasons why Jung wrote that he could only "hint" at its existence.

Instead of revealing its contents to us directly, they are expressed symbolically through images in dreams or spontaneously created forms. Most symbols are the results of the activity of archetypes, ageless predispositions that operate as corrective forces to psychic imbalances incurred by belief systems, rules of conduct, social pressures, and routinized ways of thinking that have taken us away from our true selves. Here is an example of how the collective unconscious operates. All men and all women have male and female components, and both components seek expression. A particularly tough male, a young man who takes pride in his strength, brags about his sexual conquests, and will not tolerate being "dissed," has a dream wherein an attractive woman he does not recognize comes toward him out of a mist. She motions to him to join her and endeavors to say something to him just as he stirs and awakens. According to Jung, the dream image goes much deeper than a typical wish-fulfilling boy-meets-girl scenario designed to give expression to sexual desires. Instead, the primary character in the dream represents the female component of the dreamer's own psyche seeking to be recognized. His anima, the unconscious female counterpart of his male persona (read mask), is asking to be let in, to be acknowledged as part of who he is, to be permitted to exercise an influence in his life. The energy he expends on maintaining his machismo persona is distorting his soul, his psyche. It is taking him away from who he really is, and the woman who appears in his dream serves as a reminder of the existence of underdeveloped aspects of himself. Properly interpreted, the dream image is inviting him to join her in the mist where she will assist him in recovering his soul.

The anima is one of many inherited archetypes contained in the collective unconscious. Archetypes react to the external facts of a person's life. They stir and endeavor to make themselves known when the psyche becomes too one-sided, too bent out of its natural shape. When energy flows in one direction only, pressure mounts to give expression to the force that opposes it. Since the opposite force is often unconscious, it can only express itself indirectly, that is to say symbolically.

Jung proposed that one of the archetypes is the Self (with a capital S). What typically comes to mind when we think about the self is the self with a small *s*, our everyday self, the "ego" that assists us in managing our worldly affairs, the "me" that gets us through the day and makes plans for tomorrow, the person who occupies this or that role—who pays the bills, cleans the house, argues with a neighbor, and has a favorite sports team. Jung observed that such matters are of great importance to our self-definitions. However, problems arise when we become attached to our roles, when we make the mistake of believing that the masks we are required to wear are who we really are. Matters that loom large in our minds, the impressions we desperately seek to make on others, the "stuff" we are driven to possess, in the end, are trivial in the larger scheme of things. Combined, they represent a tiny fragment of the potentials of the Self.

A common symbol of the Self is a sphere, a circle, something that wraps around itself like primitive drawings of a snake with its tail in its mouth. Wheels, the sun, anything round, including forming a circle around a campfire, can represent the Self. Some religious art works that decorate places of worship show circular forms like halos over the heads of angels, Jesus Christ, the Virgin Mary, or other holy figures. Jung referred to such images as *mandalas*—ancient symbols of wholeness, completion, and psychic totality. These images become prominent elements of dreams, paintings, jewelry, and other artifacts particularly during periods when persons are out of touch with the collective unconscious. They are reminders that the "ego" (the self with a small *s*) is not the real master of its home. The degree to which the archetypal Self is ignored, unrecognized, and unable to find expression is the degree to which it becomes energized and insists on recognition. It emerges from the depths of the human psyche in an effort to compensate for the energy that has been directed to outer matters, to the small, pedestrian things that dominate our attention, to the divisions that separate us from each other and ourselves.

It was in the context of describing fractured souls and splintered societies that Jung wrote about the appearance of unidentified flying objects (UFOs), which mainly take the form of dish-shaped, saucer-like circles—modern representations of mandalas. He viewed UFOs as products of the Self that are projected into the sky and are beseeching us to recognize our unfulfilled wholeness. He writes: "The message which the UFO brings . . . is a problem that concerns us all. The signs appear in the heavens so that everyone shall see them. They bid each of us to remember his own soul and his own wholeness."[4]

Jung appears to be intentionally ambiguous in regard to the question of the actual existence of flying saucers. Projections of mandalic forms may be so powerful that somehow they materialize in the sky. Or there may be debris that is always darting through the skies, but sightings of it are determined by the conditions of our psyches. We are more prone to see it when we are suffering from a false sense of security, from security promised to us by pledging allegiance to the flag of a state or a nation. Blind devotion to an earthly cause, adherence to a particular set of social norms or practices, eats away at our basic nature, and enhances the likelihood of our seeking symbols of the Self and its totality. "The plurality of UFOs," Jung writes, "is a projection of a number of psychic images of wholeness which appear in the sky because . . . they represent archetypes charged with energy."

Thus UFOs are reminders of what we have lost. Our attachment to things, to cars, houses, gadgets, or to this or that dogma, separates us from our humanity, and we seek to return to home base, to a place where we can once again commune with the world. Along with other spherical objects, UFOs are products of profound intuitions regarding the eternal continuity of all living things. A person is a temporary carrier of an immortal force that contains the residues of ancestral life. The collective unconscious is transpersonal and brings with it supernatural powers that are beyond our comprehension. It is simultaneously inviting and threatening.

It is inviting because at a nonconscious level we recognize that it is who we really are. We are fleeting personifications of a natural force, a timeless stream of energy. In effect, we are God. We are temporary physical manifestations of everything that ever was and ever will be, a passing collection of molecules that soon will be disbursed, only to be combined again and remanifested in new forms. In that way, we are immortal. Now *that* is inviting, *that* is attractive. Although our bodies will most certainly die and decompose, the spiritual force that is within us will continue on.

What is threatening about the Self archetype, what leads us to ignore or misinterpret the message it brings, is that it challenges virtually everything we consciously believe about who we are. Often brought to our attention by the anima (something of a workhorse of the collective unconscious), it threatens our self-boundaries, our sense of identity, and has the capacity of shattering our hard-won sense of having a self that is securely fastened to objects around us. Were we to suddenly recognize the Self and surrender to its force, our self, the person who we think we are and count upon to see us through the day, might suddenly evaporate. We would lose our bearings. The anchors that attach us to what we consider to be the real world would be severed, and we would be thrown into a state of utter disorientation and confusion. Jung warns us that a sudden shift caused by an influx of psychic energy can lead to feelings of pitiful insignificance for some people. A more dangerous outcome is "psychic inflation," which may manifest itself through feelings of superiority, godlikeness, or being an all-knowing emissary from outer space who has come to save the world. Such is the stuff of psychoses.

So the archetypal Self must be treated gingerly. Its energy must be allowed to arrive in small doses. Jung considered the goal of psychotherapy to be the full realization of the Self, and it takes time to do that. Archetypes, particularly the Self archetype, are not things to be taken lightly. We should let them in gradually and allow them to become integrated into our lives in a manner that does not deliver us into a state of serious unbalance. We need to be especially well prepared for the arrival of the Self in order not to be flooded by a potentially destructive sense of omnipotence. Years of therapy may not be sufficient to negotiate the merger of the self into the Self as the latter may announce its presence by way of dreams of flying through space, or sensations of being the sun, the moon, or at one with the Universe.

Thus, Jung's alternative to Freud's proposition regarding the meaning of flying fantasies is that they represent humankind's search for the soul, the true essence of the human being. Images of flying and symbols that we see in the sky signify that we have become disunited from the source of existence and also, when treated properly, invite us to become complete by realizing Wholeness. Wholeness can only be found by granting the collective unconscious its proper place in our lives; by knowing it, accepting it, and learning to trust its wisdom. Most certainly, Jung would endorse the phrase from *Star Wars*, "May the Force be with you." And most likely he would want to add: "and be careful how you let it in."

FOURTEEN *Carl Jung's Search for Permanence*

Y ou have a theory of personality. Virtually everyone has a theory of personality. Every time you think you know why a person, including yourself, acts in a certain way, you are drawing on some portion of your theory of human behavior. The major difference between you and, say, Carl Jung and a few dozen other people who have made it their life's work to explain behavior, is that your theory is implicit and theirs are explicit. You haven't taken the time that would be required to write your theory, to work out some of its details, to propose components of the psyche, energy sources, and external factors that combine in various ways to shape behavior. Were you to do that—were you to bring your implicit theory to the level of an explicit one—the results would not only describe how you think about various things but would also reveal a great deal about you, including your dominant drives, emotions, sentiments, conflicts, and personal scripts. In some respects, an explicit theory of personality can be thought of as a long story written to a full array of TAT cards. However, in this instance, the theorist selects the cards and determines which features in them deserve attention. The theorist's perceptions of what the cards contain and the story that is generated on that basis can be treated as an objective product that contains information about the subjective world of the author.

George Atwood and Robert Stolorow provide a more vivid analogy in the forward to their book *Faces in a Cloud*. There they quote the following passage written by Henry Murray:

> Man—the object of concern—is like an ever-varying cloud and psychologists are like people seeing faces in it. One psychologist per-

ceives along the upper margin the contours of a nose and lip, and then miraculously other portions of the cloud become so oriented in respect to these that the outline of a forward-looking superman appears. Another psychologist is attracted to a lower segment, sees an ear, a nose, a chin, and simultaneously the cloud takes on the aspect of a backward-looking Epimethean. Thus, for each perceiver every sector of the cloud has a different function, name and value—fixed by his initial bias. To be the founder of a school indeed it is only necessary to see a face along another margin.[1]

This perspective on theories of personality opens the prospect of entering a theorist's subjective experiences by way of his or her theory. It leads us back into familiar territory. I have addressed the question of what Peter Pan represented to his creator. Of course, Peter Pan was constructed as a character, not a theory. Carl Jung constructed a theory, not a character. Despite this major difference, it is possible to approach Jung's theory in a fashion that is similar to the way that I dealt with the relationship between Peter Pan and J. M. Barrie. In this instance, the strategy requires beginning with Jung's theory and then, by using information about the conditions of his life, investigating the possibility that his theory expresses, defends against, or tries to resolve matters of psychological importance to him.

That straightforward assignment begins to look like a nightmare of major proportions, however, when we settle down to undertake the task. Nearly ten thousand pages of Jung's books, essays, and articles are contained in the eighteen volumes of his _Collected Works_,[2] and that only includes what has been translated into English. Where do you suggest we start? His writings spanned many years and he covered so many topics during those years that the assignment takes on every appearance of being a punishing joke.

But the task is not as daunting as it may first appear to be. There is a persistent theme in Jung's writings, particularly in his later works, that, once identified, will be of help in penetrating to the personal foundations of his extraordinary quest. It is a fascinating story with numerous twists and turns culminating in a vision of flying in space "as though I were safe in the womb of the universe."[3] Jung's path from the womb of his mother to the womb of the universe was not direct. It involved over sixty years of shaping an object to serve as a substitute for one that had disappointed him.

My job is to extract a coherent short story from a story so long and involved that, fully told, it would result in a separate book. My intention is to resist the detours, no matter how inviting they are, and focus on the core of the story that led to Jung's vision of levitation. I am able to do that by taking advantage of the work of others. For instance, the analysis I offer benefits from the work of George Atwood and Robert Stolorow. Their book, *Faces in a Cloud,* consists of psychobiographies of four individuals who were important figures in personality psychology during its formative years. These theorists include Sigmund Freud, Wilhelm Reich, Otto Rank, and, to my good fortune, Carl Jung. The mission that Atwood and Stolorow set out to accomplish was to explore the ways that a theory of personality is influenced by the subjective world of its author, and that matches my present purpose precisely.

I also draw on Peter Homans's absorbing book *Jung in Context.*[4] The editors of the eighteen volumes of Jung's *Collected Works* organized his writings topically in a way that obscures the development of his thinking. Homans does a masterful job of aligning Jung's books and articles in accordance with separable phases of Jung's intellectual development in order to accomplish a mission similar to that of Atwood and Stolorow.

Both *Faces in the Cloud* and *Jung in Context* make extensive use of my other primary reference: Jung's autobiography, entitled *Memories, Dreams, Reflections.* These three works have served as my companions. They have deepened my understanding of the collective unconscious, why Jung needed to invent it, and how he worked on it until he got it right.

The first order of business is to describe the collective unconscious and discuss its hidden role in personality development. Following that, I will look into the conditions that led to Jung's "discovery" of the collective unconscious and how it slowly evolved as a potential healer of his fractured sense of self.

THE COLLECTIVE UNCONSCIOUS

The idea of a collective unconscious comprising inherited archetypes is Jung's most noted (and controversial) contribution to psychology. I have described it as indescribable, a force beyond words. It is an archaic source of energy that has no boundaries; a storehouse of inherited impersonal "memories" forged by the collective experiences of humankind throughout all time. But it is so deeply woven into the fabric of our lives, and so foreign to the conscious operations of adult minds, that we are seldom even aware of its existence. There are times when we may sense its presence or have intuitions that something is missing, but mostly we ignore it. In doing so, we have become alienated from the core of our existence. In that boxed-off condition, the collective unconscious sometimes speaks to us through the medium of symbols, attempting to remind us that we are subservient to an entity we do not know, that we are not masters of our own home.

Infants are in touch with the collective unconscious because a differentiated conscious ego has not yet developed.[5] But slowly and very surely in modern civilizations, the collective unconscious is repressed under the aegis of outside forces. This has resulted in our becoming severed from the source of our lives and has led to humankind's disjunctive relationship with Nature. We strive for what our cultures inform us is worth striving for. We internalize the values stressed in our homes, neighborhoods, and nations and learn which "personas" are most suited to our roles and positions. Jung recognized that social order requires us to structure our lives according to the expectations of others. Problems arise when we come to believe that we *are* our personas; that being an executive, an underling, a wife or a husband, a belle, a vagabond, or a member of a particular social network is all that counts. This problem is compounded when we identify with our pretenses and masks and, with pride or shame, hold them to represent the totality of our existences. The extent to which this happens, the extent to which mass-mindedness has a lock on how we construe and conduct our lives, is an indicator or the size of the gap between what we think matters and what *really* matters. We have become like trees that are unaware of their roots and the nutrients that sustain them. We live under conditions that grant so much importance to the external trappings of life that we have lost touch with a reality that represents our only hope of saving ourselves from ourselves and from each other.

 The disjunction between what we think is real and what *is* real, the juxtaposition of the forces of the ego and the forces of Nature, is such a prominent theme in Jung's writings that it must be placed at the center of our considerations.

SALVATION 구제, 구세득.

Jung had a solution to humankind's dilemma. Recall what he said about UFOs: they are mandalas that have been projected into the sky and serve as reminders that we have lost touch with our souls. In his book on flying saucers, and on many other occasions, he stressed that salvation depends on our willingness to loosen our attachment to our personas and reduce our preoccupation with worldly things. As our investment in consciousness weakens, the collective unconscious will seize on the opportunity to reveal itself to us. It seeks to do so by means of bringing our attention to archetypal images that introduce us to a forgotten reality. We must allow that to happen gradually because a sudden burst of energy from the collective unconscious could flood our egos and render them helpless in the face of an overwhelming force capable of eradicating our psychological boundaries and making us "mad." But if we are willing to engage in a more gradual, piecemeal process of becoming familiar with the contents of the collective unconscious and are able to tolerate the confusion caused by its interruption of normal "meaning-making" activities, a transformation will begin to take place whereby the self will be replaced by the Self and psychic "equilibrium" will prevail.

In order to establish a balanced relationship between the collective unconscious and consciousness, one must first experience a partial merger with the collective unconscious. From that base, the Self can begin the process of becoming "individuated" from the collective unconscious and progressively assimilate it into consciousness. The end result is full awareness and a balanced psyche.

To summarize, there are three steps in the process of realizing the Self, as follows.

1. Ease up on one's attachment to social definitions of the self by reducing one's investment in personas as carriers of life's meaning.
2. Become familiar with a force that has been there since the "gray dawn of history" by merging with it.
3. Achieve a balanced relationship between the true source of human life and reality as known by consciousness through the process of individuating a Self from its archaic foundations.

Although I have oversimplified his ideas, the summary I have just offered captures the essence of what Jung saw in the clouds and recorded in his theory. My task is to understand his theory from the perspective of enduring issues in his life and how his theory is both a statement of and solution to his dilemmas. I begin with information that Jung provides in his autobiography.

JUNG'S RETROSPECTIVE ACCOUNT OF HIS LIFE

Jung began his autobiography in 1957 when he was eighty-one years old. He enlisted the collaborative assistance of his colleague and friend, Aniela Jaffe, by having her take notes on the contents of regularly scheduled conversations he held with her. The book, *Dreams, Memories, Reflections,* was close to its final form four years later, shortly before Jung's death in 1961.

Most autobiographies follow a "this happened and then that happened" historical format. There are elements of that in *Memories, Dreams, Reflections,* but Jung was more invested in describing the effects that various events had on his internal world than on the sequence of events themselves. In what some scholars refer to as Jung's "automythology," he draws the reader's attention to his internal, subjective representations of seen and imagined forces, and the book thereby takes on the flavor of a fable. That is particularly evident in the first several chapters that contain detailed descriptions of his early memories.

Readers oriented to facts might question the accuracy of what a man in his eighties recalled about his childhood. Throughout our lives, we continue to revise our memories and shift them around in order to create coherent stories.[6] This is how memories operate, and often early recollections cannot be checked against objective information for verification. But memory modification is not a serious problem in this instance, because my focus is on Jung's *beliefs* about his childhood experiences rather than on the accuracy of his recollections. Frequently, firmly held beliefs about events, including the distortions they may carry with them, can exercise as much influence on psychological development as the raw facts of the events.

Jung was born in 1875. His father was a God-fearing, devout pastor in the Swiss Reformed Church, as were eight of his uncles. His mother was a housewife and was Carl's primary caretaker during his first three years. Being in her company was associated with Carl's feelings that the world was a very good place. Jung's first memory was of waking up in a pram under the shadow of a tree with a feeling of indescribable well-being. The blue sky held the sun that delivered its golden rays glistening through the dark green leaves, and everything was "wholly wonderful, colorful, and splendid." Equally pleasurable were his recollections of being perched in a highchair and becoming aware of the pleasant taste of warm milk and its inviting aroma. He recalled the inspiring sight of the Alps bathed in sunset reds glowing against snow-covered peaks, and sand being rippled by lakeshore waves splashed with sunlight. These "inconceivable pleasures" were among the "delicious memories" evoked in Jung's mind when he reflected on his childhood. His needs were well served as he feasted on Nature's glories and lived in harmony with Her.

Young Carl's pleasant world was shattered when, at age three, his mother was hospitalized for several months. This was a major episode in Jung's life. He attributed his suffering from an outbreak of general eczema to her departure. This inflammation of his skin was the first of several physical symptoms that characterized his childhood, giving him direct experience with what he would later interpret as physical reactions to psychological trauma in his work with neurotic patients. Jung reports the presence of hints ("dim intimations") that his mother's illness was related to marital difficulties, but neither that nor any other explanation could alleviate his misery. The point was his mother had vanished and he was deeply troubled by her absence. Even though he was placed under the care of a conscientious maid during his mother's stay in the hospital, a person of whom Jung retained fond memories, his mother's departure resulted in a decision Carl made that stuck with him throughout the remainder of his life. It was a remarkable decision. "From then on," he wrote, "I always felt distrustful when the word 'love' was spoken."[7] Imagine the far-reaching implications of that decision. Love was never to be trusted. Love was mercurial, slippery, here today and gone tomorrow, never a steady state, not to be counted on. For sure, he could no longer rely on his mother. Her departure, her temporary absence, shoved Carl into a new reality, the hard, cold reality of pain and impermanence. Nothing lasts. Love, the most basic of all emotions, is fleeting.

Jung writes about this pivotal event in his life in a manner that suggests that he experienced a second birth, only this time he was delivered into a world of suffering and death. His first birth, when he was physically dislodged from his mother's body, involved an easy transition from the safety of her womb to the security of her warm and caring arms. The carefree connectedness of being a part of her body as a fetus was replaced by a broader sense of unity with Nature. He described his first three years as living in a state of bliss.

His second birth was a psychological one. He was suddenly torn away from the person most vital to his existence. The end of a well-known nursery rhyme says it well. "The bough broke and down came the baby, cradle and all." Thud! Welcome to reality. Goodbye to the wonderful continuity of all things. Carl felt abandoned, psychologically shredded, and from then on mistrusted all of the trappings and pretenses of human relationships. When his mother departed, she took a piece, a vital piece, of her son with her. A central figure in his internal representation of living in a harmonious world had vanished from the physical world, and he could not envision a meaningful existence independent of the up-to-then reliable nurturance of the omnipotent mother. This first hideous taste of unreliability, of impermanence, contributed to Carl's growing "resistance to life in this world," as evidenced by a series of potentially fatal "accidents" suffered by him after his mother's return.

Barrie said: "Now I knew my mother forever" after she became mired in her sadness. Jung became conscious of his mother by virtue of her absence and rejected her. Both of them draw our attention to the idea that consciousness arrives when the external world fails to confirm a child's subjective representations of life as it has been and is expected to remain. When an important feature of the environment that is associated with a normal meaning-making routine is altered in a way that threatens a child's sense of security, especially when that alteration has real or imagined bearing on its psychological survival, an alarm is sounded that calls for actions intended to restore conditions associated with safety. If these actions fail to resurrect a world that matches internal images formed from repeated experiences with a person who is subjectively experienced as essential to the child's survival, the child lives at the edge of panic.

That is not an "in passing" comment; if we are to understand why Jamie was so obsessed with bringing a smile back to Margaret's face and why Carl was so devastated by his mother's sudden absence we have to comprehend the fact that these events signaled the collapse of their subjective worlds. When reality violated their implicit "pictures" of life being conducted in their mothers' reassuring company, they experienced *the end of their internal worlds* and scrambled to locate signs that held some promise of restituting the feeling tone of living in harmony with another person.

To that end, Barrie never gave up his project of getting Margaret to smile. Jung's problem was less tangible. His mother could shape her face any way she wished, but it wouldn't matter because he had given up on her altogether. Much of the rest of his life can be understood in light of his voyage to find something to heal his wounded sense of self. When his mother had deprived him of her company, she had shattered his "soul." Jung's solution to the problem was to attempt to fill the void with new companions, permanent companions, who would restore his earlier sense of omniscience. He sought companions with whom he could *merge*, but mostly they disappointed him. His ultimate solution was to invent a companion, and he called it the collective unconscious.

A BRIEF HISTORY OF ATTEMPTED MERGERS

Something was always tugging at Jung after the day he felt abandoned by his mother. He didn't know what it was but was determined to find out. It pulled at him so hard that he writes:: "I always knew I was two persons."[8] In his autobiography, he referred to them as Personality No. 1 and Personality No. 2. No. 1 was the son of his parents, the boy who went to school, was told to wash behind his ears, went to medical school, became a psychiatrist, had a family, and paid the bills.

We all have our versions of Jung's No. 1. Today, my No. 1 spoke to a student who was unhappy with her grade in my course. Replace "unhappy" with "outraged." She pulled no punches when she told No. 1 what she thought of it. After she slammed the door, it called the bus station to check on the cost of a round trip ticket to New York City. The line was busy. It called several more times and then realized that time was running out and rushed to attend a training session that covered information about how to use a new computerized statistics package. It became so confused halfway through the session that it wished it had not gone, but it stayed and faked its way through the final forty-five minutes. It even joined others and applauded the instructor. It spent most of the remainder of the day procrastinating before it finally got down to the business of writing about Jung's Nos. 1 and 2. I hope your No. 1 had a better day.

Jung's No. 2 was remote from his No. 1's participation in the realm of interpersonal relationships and worldly responsibilities. It drew its strength from, and in many respects was part of, a mysterious, unworldly force. The force was impossible to objectify so he variously spoke of it as Nature, the Cosmos, Creation, or God. Mostly he preferred to call it the Other.

Jung wrote that his entire life could be understood in terms of the play and counterplay between his two personalities. As No. 1 paraded through the course of the day, the magnetic force of the Other tugged at it, inviting him to "look down upon Creation simultaneously with God." Jung described this as a "terrible burden." Using psychoanalytic jargon, he spoke of it as an unending conflict between the "principle of the ego" and "the principle of instinct." The principle of the ego preserves the integrity of No. 1 by protecting its boundaries. The principle of instinct seeks to unite No. 2 with all things for all time, and in doing so threatens to disintegrate No. 1.

Hints of the Other's existence came shortly after Carl's mother packed her bags and entered a mental hospital. It came to him in various forms, but irrespective of its form, its central message always seems to have been some variation of *Merge with me and I will lead you to the Promised Land.*

The first messenger to announce the existence of the Other was a towering phallic figure that sat erect on a golden throne in a large underground chamber. It appeared in the earliest dream Jung could remember, a three-year-old's dream that he says preoccupied him throughout his life. The creature terrified him as he suspected that it might come down from the throne, move in his direction, and devour him.

Much later in life, Jung interpreted the image as his first encounter with God. He was impressed that God occupied a subterranean throne; so impressed, in fact, that he recalled the image whenever his father, Pastor Jung, spoke of a God above. Neither God the Father nor Jesus Christ were real to Carl after his encounter with the underground counterpart. Over time, Carl came to pity his father, believing that he had bought into a conventional, manmade construction of a God on high that bore no relationship with the truth. Carl's skepticism about his father's faith was consolidated when he was a teenager and had a vision of God sitting high about the world on his golden throne and dropping an enormous turd onto the gleaming new roof of a cathedral and breaking its walls asunder. (This is the only instance I have encountered in Jung's writings indicating that the Other had a sense of humor.)

Neither Pastor Jung nor his God could offer Carl the solace necessary to fill the emptiness he felt in his soul. Both were there and, in different ways, available to him as nurturing agents, but he perceived his father to be powerless (hardly an object for emulation) and his father's God to be wrongly conceived.

In the meantime, ambassadors of the Other kept on coming. During his early school years he experienced nocturnal visions and dreams that frightened him. Several times he saw an indistinct figure emerging from his mother's bedroom whose detached head floated in front of it in the air "like a little moon."9 He was also prone to anxiety dreams that were introduced by a tiny ball coming down from a long distance. It became monstrously large as it approached and he feared it might suffocate him. At other times, particularly when he suffered from what he labeled "pseudo-croup," he would wake up with coughing fits and see a glowing blue circle about the size of a full moon with glowing angels moving inside it. Added to the underground God he saw in his first dream, these images gave Carl his first inklings of the existence of the Other.

Establishing outside friendships can sometimes compensate for the feeling that something is absent in one's life. Chums can play important roles in prying children away from preoccupations with home life by offering all sorts of engaging diversions. That was an unappealing option for Carl. He hated competition, despised sports, and felt that he would alienate himself from himself if he surrendered to pressure to conform. He was onto the dangers of mass-mindedness even as a schoolboy, sensing that, given the opportunity, his peers would compel him to be different from what he thought he was. He felt their potential for splitting him apart and refused to don the personas or wear the masks of adolescence that would finish the job. In sum, his salvation was not to be found in the streets of his hometown of Laufen, Switzerland. As a consequence, he played alone. The mysterious Other guided his projects, and he became preoccupied with symbols of unity. Jung gives several examples of this genre of invented games, and I have selected two that take us directly to the heart of his concerns.

At age ten, he carved a manikin from a ruler and painted a small oblong stone with two colors; one color defined the upper half and the other defined the lower half. He placed the two objects, the manikin and the bi-colored stone, side by side, in a small case and hid it in the attic of his home. It comforted him to know the case was there and, under conditions of grave secrecy, he would visit these companions when his mother's illness and his father's irritability oppressed him. Whether or not it was his intention, Jung clarifies the symbolic meaning of his secret elsewhere in his autobiography when he writes about an intimate relationship he had with a large stone near his home. He reports that one of his favorite games was to sit on the stone and think, "I am sitting on top of this stone and it is underneath." Then he would imagine the stone, thinking, "I am lying here on this slope and he is sitting on top of me." Then the question arose: "Am I the one sitting on this stone or am I the stone on which he is sitting?" That memory sheds a great deal of light on the symbolic meaning of the objects tucked away in the attic. The manikin represented Carl in his fragmented condition next to the ying/yang oblong stone that symbolized a lost, but still hoped-for, sense of unity.

Remarkably, thirty years later, Jung returned to the slope where he had sat on his stone. He was married, had children, a house, a career, and a mind full of plans. The stone was still there, and he sat on it. Immediately his life (No. 1's life, that is) seemed alien to him. The tug by the Other was as strong as before, and he was reminded of its "eternal" existence. His activities in Zurich suddenly felt remote to him, and he recognized that he had fallen into a pattern of moving further and further away from Nature's truth. The pull to merge with the Other was so strong that he had to tear himself "violently from the spot in order not to lose hold of my future."

Jung's craving to form an alliance with a self-unifying force took a new turn in the first decade of the twentieth century. Dreams of underground gods, visions of angels circling above his head, and fantasies of stones gave way to a new object. This time it was a person and his name was Sigmund Freud.

Primitive fantasies went underground for a period of time during Jung's early adulthood. They allowed him to complete his medical training and obtain certification in the field of psychiatry. By age twenty-five, he was energetically engaged in research at a hospital in Zurich, as well as seeing patients. He published several papers on mainstream topics and kept abreast of the literature. He was particularly struck by some research on hypnosis in France that postulated two minds—a conscious mind and an unconscious mind—and wondered if the unconscious mind might be the container of repressed thoughts that Freud had written about in his 1900 masterpiece *The Interpretation of Dreams*. Freud had been disappointed by the reception of his book and welcomed the interest shown in it by a young psychiatrist from Switzerland. Jung's first visit with Freud resulted in a nonstop thirteen-hour conversation. Freud was impressed by his gifted and admiring visitor and swept him into his confidence.

Fifty-five years after their first meeting, Jung wrote: "Freud was the first man of real importance I had encountered; in my experience up to that time no one else could compare with him. I found him extremely intelligent, shrewd and altogether remarkable." This first impression was strong enough to survive the subsequent rift in their relationship, after which neither of them had kind words for each other. "Merger" is the term that Homans most frequently uses to describe the intellectual partnership that Jung and Freud developed during the first few years after their initial contact. Their letters to each other, published in 1974 by William McGuire,[10] are packed with expressions of mutual admiration. Freud sometimes took the leading role in articulating their oneness of mind. For example, in one early letter to Jung he wrote: "when you have injected your own personal leaven into the fermenting mass of my ideas, there will be no further difference between your achievement and mine."[11] In his turn, Jung wrote that his veneration of Freud had resulted in something akin to a "religious crush," and in a followup letter Freud wrote: "I am satisfied to feel at one with you and no longer fear that we might be torn apart."

But, of course, they were torn apart and became bitter enemies. Their early letters of mutual admiration became letters of insult later on, with each accusing the other of suffering from chronic neuroses. Freud came to

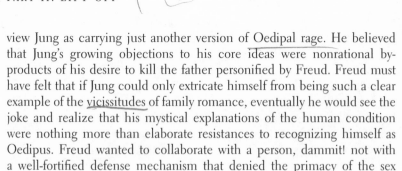

view Jung as carrying just another version of Oedipal rage. He believed that Jung's growing objections to his core ideas were nonrational by-products of his desire to kill the father personified by Freud. Freud must have felt that if Jung could only extricate himself from being such a clear example of the vicissitudes of family romance, eventually he would see the joke and realize that his mystical explanations of the human condition were nothing more than elaborate resistances to recognizing himself as Oedipus. Freud wanted to collaborate with a person, dammit! not with a well-fortified defense mechanism that denied the primacy of the sex instinct.

Of course, Jung thought differently about the matter. He believed that his work on himself and his treatment of patients had uncovered a phenomenon that had escaped Freud's attention. After repressed memories were uncovered, talked about, and worked through, after the unconscious had been cleansed of its contents, something else remained. This "something else" suggested to Jung that there were *two* unconscious minds. One of them was the Freudian unconscious, where a person's memories of fearsome experiences and anxious moments were cast and shielded from consciousness. Jung referred it as the *personal unconscious.* The other unconscious was impersonal and transcendental, having only tenuous connections with a person's life history. It sought to connect us with sacred truths, with knowledge so ineffable that it would not be put into words. Jung called it the *collective unconscious,* and here you and I can recognize that the Other had returned.

In some respects it can be said that Freud worked as hard to merge with Jung as Jung did with Freud. Initially, Freud had high expectations for his young colleague and believed that after he had grown out of his Oedipal condition or somehow had been cured from the grip it had on his life, sheer talent would be there for him to carry the banner of psychoanalytic theory well into the future. But there was a hitch in the operation for Jung. For a time, he idealized Freud and went so far as to suggest that his hero's ideas were nothing short of the base for a religion that would surpass and replace all other religions. However, over time, he developed some "yes, but" considerations about Freud's emphasis on the power of the sexual instinct. *Yes* the son's Oedipal relationship with the father assists in explaining many actions and fantasies, *but* what about nonsexual or pre-Oedipal issues? What parts do they play in shaping lives? Jung idealized the man but could not idealize his theory. Freud's theory did not address the Other that so haunted Jung, and since the man and his theory were inseparable, the would-be merger could not fill the empty space in him. Recognizing that neither Freud nor his theory could fill the void in his life, Jung looked elsewhere for a solution.

He turned to myths for the answer. He hoped that Freud would ultimately bless his work and not only see but also embrace its relevance to psychoanalytic theory. To that end, he voraciously read myths and legends from around the world and began his opus entitled *Symbols of Transformation*. Jung shared his enthusiasm about the project with Freud in his letters and asked him to read drafts of the work. Freud recognized that Jung had altered Freud's theory of libido, ripped it from its sexual roots, and, as Homans says, used it as a stimulus for a "full-scale, grandiose foray into myths, rituals, symbolism, and practices of Judaic, Christian, Hellenic, Eastern, and primitive cultures."[12]

Freud viewed the book, first published in 1912, as a five-hundred-page anti-Freudian manifesto that so distorted his libido theory that it was no longer recognizable. My first impression of the book was that it contains a very nearly incomprehensible hodgepodge of free associations. It appeared to be an attempt to reify Jung's private thoughts and personal fantasies by linking them to both well-known and obscure mythic characters and plot-lines. In short, I sensed that Jung had projected his fantasies onto the cosmos and had adjusted Nature to fit his design. A more patient, less cynical reading shows that much of the book is structured around the mythic voyages of legendary heroes. The prototypic hero first departs from the world as known. He soon encounters and subsequently defeats various mythic characters that guard his path. But these struggles are mere warmups for regressing to a primal relationship with the mother that, in the guise of the anima, threatens to devour him. He manages to avoid her consumption by extricating himself from the "libidinal" bond that connects them. This renunciation of their primal condition results in the ultimate sacrifice of relinquishing his "infantile personality" in order to become a distinctive person able to adapt to the world. That is salvation in a nutshell.

Yes, I know, summarizing the contents of five hundred pages of richly elaborated scholarship on the topic of myths, primitive rituals and religious legends from nearly all corners of the globe into five dry sentences is hardly fair. But it is my page-saving way of recognizing the three steps to salvation, already mentioned, as so lavishly embellished in *Symbols of Transformation*. First, drop the personas and depart from the world as known. Second, regress to a primal state and merge with the mother. Avoid being consumed by the libidinal bond with her, and progress to the third step of individuating a self—a full-bodied, unified Self, capable of coping with anything that comes its way.

Homans suggests that Jung's merger with myth was necessary to heal the wounds of the lost connection with Freud and the psychoanalytic movement.[13] It was an attempt at restituting a sense of self out of the rubble of disorientation. I agree with that assessment as far as it goes, but it does not go far enough. It is my sense that the disintegration of Jung's relationship with Freud reactivated the already existing feeling of emptiness that had its origins much earlier in his life when his mother deprived him of her company.

Jung intuited that psychic repair would require going back to a time prior to his original injury and restoring the "infantile personality" whose life had been cut short. That was the tug of the Other. Sometimes in words (nearly always spoken in a woman's voice)[14] and sometimes through images, the Other came to him to remind him of the existence of an "archaic" world from which his life had been severed. According to Jung's "projected" readings of myths, the anima awaits the hero. She invites him to fuse with her, and the hero wallows in his "newly won union with the fundamental source of life."[15] The longing to return, writes Jung, "is just as innate in every individual as the 'longing for the mother,' the nostalgia for the source from which we sprang."[16] Once there, the welcoming image instills a feeling of "absolute, binding, and indissoluble communion with the world," accompanied by a "profound intuition of the 'eternal' continuity of living."[17] Of course, residence inside the Cosmos must be temporary, lest one forget to eat and fail to participate in the everyday world as known by consciousness. But first things first. Before individuation can occur, there must be something to individuate from. And it was that something that had been removed from Jung's life upon his mother's sudden departure, and he sought ways to restore it.

He gave up on his mother as a restorative agent and attempted to recapture the feeling tone of their early relationship by merging with rocks, with Freud, with myths, or with anything else that might do the trick. What was the nature of the feelings he sought to restore? What feelings had been interrupted when he was deprived of his mother's presence? It must have been the feeling of "indescribable well-being" of life in a world that was "wholly wonderful, colorful, and splendid" that filled his recollections of the first three years of his childhood. It had to have something to do with the "inconceivable pleasures" that were among his "delicious memories" of the sweet aroma of warm milk and the sight of sun rays reflecting on rippled waves as they splashed gently on the shores of a lake. He called it "bliss."

GLORY IN THE HIGHEST

In 1944, at the age of sixty-nine, Jung had visions of himself flying in space. He was in a hospital recovering from a broken foot and a heart attack. Under those conditions, one could argue that the visions were products of a state of delirium. Jung claims otherwise. He was in space, flying, and the entire experience was real. He emphasized that point, writing: "It was not a product of imagination. The visions and experiences were utterly real; there was nothing subjective about them; they had the quality of absolute objectivity."[18] Here are some of the ways he described his feelings. See if you recognize their tone. He was "bathed in a glorious blue light" and experienced "the highest possible feeling of happiness." "This is eternal bliss." "This cannot be described; it is far too wonderful." The feelings were "fantastically beautiful," "ineffably joyful," "eternal," and "ecstatic." In his "primal form," he detected the "sweet smell" of the Holy Ghost. Finally, in his weightless, levitated condition, he felt "safe in the womb of the universe."

Again, Jung claimed that his experiences were real, and I believe they were. They were as real as the feelings that had accompanied his experiences prior to his mother's departure. He recognized the feelings because they contained traces of the feelings he experienced during the predawn of his *own* conscious history.

It was difficult for Jung to imagine returning from outer space to being confined in little boxes. He resisted the tug of gravity and wished to remain forever in a state of boundless union with the Other. But he recovered, and, quite remarkably, the restitution of his early feelings provided the cure that he had sought for much of his life. In the language of his theory, he emerged with a Self that was individuated from the "mother matrix," and he entered a period of great productivity. He writes: "After the illness a fruitful period of work began for me. A good many of my principle works were written only then." His visions had provided him with the "courage to undertake new formulations. I no longer attempted to put across my own opinion, but surrendered myself to the current of my thoughts. Thus one problem after the other revealed itself to me and took shape." He writes that he emerged from his visions with an "unconditional 'yes' to that which is," an "unconditional acceptance of the conditions of existence as I see them and understand them, (an) acceptance of my own nature, as I happen to be."[19]

Although it took him over sixty years, Jung accomplished what Barrie could not. Margaret never smiled, and the feelings of unity Barrie sought were never restored. At a very young age, Jung gave up on his mother as partner who could assist him in finding the missing piece of his psyche, and he looked far and wide for an alternative solution. As he looked into this and that cranny, he created a paper trail of ideas of lasting importance. For instance, his writings about psychological types (e.g., introverted feeling types, extroverted thinking types) has led to the development of a type-testing industry of considerable magnitude. He created a school of psychiatry called analytical psychology that has drawn the attention of thousands of practitioners. His understanding of symbols has had an enormous impact on the field of literary analysis, and his extensive writings about myths, legends, and religious texts have inspired the development of courses and lively debates in seminaries and religious training institutions around the world. Joseph Campbell's seminal book *The Hero with a Thousand Faces*[20] is entirely structured around the three steps to salvation that Jung found embedded in legendary stories . . . and the list goes on.

It verges on the incredible for me or anyone else to suggest that these magnificent accomplishments evolved from the mind of a man as by-products of a search he conducted to restore an earlier sense of self that had been badly damaged when, as a child, his mother had disappointed him. But that is precisely what the "data" embolden me to suggest.

What impresses me most about what I have discovered by studying the lives of both James Barrie and Carl Jung was their *persistence* in attempting to resolve a problem they were confronted with during their childhoods. Their persistence not only impresses me but also intrigues me. We have a firm grasp on *what* happened, because they told us: Margaret stopped smiling, and Carl's mother was confined to a hospital for a few months. But these two events do not explain *why* these events had such a dramatic influence on the course of these men's lives. Why did Jamie become "for-ever conscious" of his mother when she ceased to smile, and why did Carl say that his life was "forever changed" when his mother was hospitalized?

I have suggested already that, in both instances, an important process of "self"-development may have been interrupted. I think we should explore that idea in depth, because it may bear on the question of persistence.

Another question pertains to *how* the problem caused by a sense of having been abandoned remained such a constant issue in these men's lives. More specifically, can any mechanisms be identified that kept the problem in place? This may be the most difficult question to answer, but it is not a challenge completely beyond our reach. It requires us to cross a border and become acquainted with a field of study that remains relatively unknown to personality psychologists: neuroscience and the brain.

I will not dwell on the matter, but there are some active border guards on both sides of the boundaries I must breach in part III. For example, there are some materialists on one side and some animists on the other who get on each other's nerves. I will ignore their sniping and slip by their sentry posts to see if some progress can be made in answering my *why* and *how* questions.

Portions of some of the chapters in part III may test the patience of readers with distinctive "personological" preferences who, for example, may reject the idea that research in the areas of child development and brain development are relevant to my considerations. For these readers, the matters discussed in part III may represent an unnecessary and jarring interruption of the level of discourse established in part II. But it appears to me that we would do well to seize the opportunity to think about fan-tasies of flight from different perspectives and, in the process, loosen up or completely dislodge a few of the stones in the walls that separate disci-plines. Bear with me during this extended detour, and be assured that soon enough, we will discover some interesting new tools to continue the work. We will fly again in part IV.

PART III *Ground Maintenance*

and Theoretical

Adjustments

FIFTEEN *Attachment Revisited*

The disruption of Carl's relationship with his mother gives us a point of comparison between his experiences and the experiences of Jamie Barrie, whose relationship with his mother was transformed by her grief over the loss of her favorite son. It may be that these parallel experiences are not incidental to the creation of levitation fantasies. This chapter and the three that follow explore this possibility.

First, this chapter returns to some issues I raised in chapter 11 about childhood attachment. I will describe the origins of attachment theory and endeavor to explain the idea of internalized images or working models of the world. In chapter 16 I describe some of the work of Daniel Stern, whose groundbreaking treatment of working models in the context of early childhood development has greatly influenced the way I think about the concept of the "self." His model of the infant and child's evolving mind is mostly a product of what I call an "outside-in" approach to understanding self-development. It includes a number of logical and carefully stated positions regarding internal processes that are combined to explain numerous observations of the development and change in infants' relations to the worlds around them. Stern is a child psychoanalyst and an infant researcher who rejects certain longstanding psychoanalytic assumptions and revises others. But his theory about what occurs inside the infant's mind, by necessity, is a theory based on inferences about hidden or under-the-skin processes that operate in tandem with observed external behaviors. Other psychoanalytically oriented theorists make different inferences, so the question then becomes: How can it be determined whose inferences are to be preferred? In this instance, we can do better than throwing up our hands and declaring "Who knows?" because neuroscientists who study the brain's development from the "inside out" are providing information that can be brought to bear on the viability of various outside-in inferences.

Neuroscience is a burgeoning field that, for the most part, is populated by researchers who specialize in one or another sector of the brain, with some concentrating solely on the electrochemical properties and actions of small clusters of a dozen or so of the brain's billions of neurons. However, there are a few neurologists who take a more encompassing view of the brain and are willing to address the big questions; questions regarding the concept of "self" (what is it anyway?), the matter of consciousness (again, what's that?), and the relationship between self and consciousness. Antonio Damasio is one of the few neuroscientists who have demonstrated a willingness to take on these larger issues. In doing so, he has constructed a neurological model of self and consciousness that I will argue supports Stern's primary inferences. I present this case in chapter 17.

The title of this part of the book, "Ground Maintenance and Theoretical Adjustments," is meant to suggest an analogy to servicing an aircraft. In this instance, I will be doing more than towing an object into a hangar, changing the oil, checking the flaps, and vacuuming the aisle. My objective is to break down some of the main components of my emergent model of early social and mental development and determine how they work together in generating fantasies of flight. This is a challenge because it requires me to present some information that is beyond the level of general knowledge. The fact that this information is intrinsically fascinating works to my advantage. The fact that it is loaded up with various technical details is a disadvantage. My strategy for diminishing the disadvantage is to translate Stern's and Damasio's ideas, concepts, and theoretical formulations in ways that may violate the letter of their models but preserve the spirit of their insights.

I begin with a discussion of early childhood attachment behaviors.

ATTACHMENT AS A PRIMARY DRIVE

How did attachment theory emerge as a topic of special interest in psychology? For several decades in the early and middle portions of the twentieth century, it was believed that classical conditioning theory held the solution to why infants prefer to be in the company of their mothers rather than with other caretakers. It explained why infants cease to cry when held by their mothers, why they tend to smile when their mother comes into their visual fields, why only the mother can soothe the child in times of distress. The explanation offered by conditioning theory was an extension of the results of Ivan Pavlov's research with dogs around the turn of the century.[1] Pavlov, a Russian physiologist, demonstrated that dogs could be trained to salivate at the sound of a tone. The training involved presenting a tone immediately before giving a dog a whiff and taste of powdered meat. Repeated pairings of first the tone and then the food resulted in the animal associating the tone with food, as evidenced by the dog's reflexive drooling at the mere sound of the tone in the absence of morsels of food. It was a short step from Pavlov's experiments and the hundreds of others that followed them to the more general idea that family pets learn to "love" their masters not because they are such wonderful people but because their physical presence is so frequently paired with food.

What had been observed in laboratory studies of animals was then extended to account for human learning. For instance, Pavlov's observation was used to explain why infants go through a period of being more responsive to their mothers than to other people. The mechanistic reason offered was that infants are conditioned to associate the presence of their mothers with receiving nourishment. Food, after all, is the object of all creatures' "primary" drives, and anything that is associated with satisfying that life-sustaining drive is bound to be good. Therefore, repeated pairings of the mother and her offerings of the breast or bottle make her the object of a "secondary" drive that seeks reduction by merely being in her company. So much for that. Problem solved. From this hard-nosed, cut-the-lubby-dubby perspective, mothers are the human equivalents of Pavlov's tones.

These waters remained relatively undisturbed until Harry Harlow[2] challenged the assumption that infants' preferences for their mothers was the result of a spinoff secondary drive whose existence relied solely on its original association with the pleasurable sensations of alleviating hunger. Harlow issued his challenge on the basis of the results of his research with rhesus monkeys. His work consisted of variations of the following laboratory arrangement. Soon after birth, an infant monkey was removed from its mother and placed in a room that contained two surrogate mothers constructed of wire-mesh frames that approximated the size and shape of adult monkeys. Identical headlike forms, each with two eyes, were attached to each frame. One major difference between these mother substitutes was one was covered with cloth and the other was bare. The other important difference was a nursing bottle was fastened onto the unclad surrogate, and the cloth-covered "mother" provided no source of food.

Observations of the monkeys placed in the room showed that they preferred to cling to the cloth-covered surrogate, and made only brief visits to nurse from the nipple-capped bottle rigged onto the uncovered surrogate. After feeding, the monkey would typically climb down from the nursing frame and snuggle up with the softer one. Most striking was the fact that when the monkey was on the floor or elsewhere in the cage and something frightened it, it would scramble onto the *cloth* mother instead of seeking refuge with the food-providing object. On the basis of these results, Harlow proposed that there was nothing at all "secondary" about monkeys' comfort-seeking drives. Something other than food was involved in their actions, something in the order of cloth being a better substitute to satisfy inborn needs to seek safety by clinging to something furry, instead of something that offered food and no other creature comforts. An uncatchable hard line drive had been sent in the direction of the assumption that hunger was the animal's single most important drive and that all subsequent learning was built on that initial base. Harlow had identified another drive, a drive to become attached to a comforting figure that was separate from the instinctive urge to be fed.

The British psychoanalyst John Bowlby could not have been surprised by the results reported by Harlow. More than a decade before Harlow published his study, Bowlby[3] had written a report based on his observations of the home lives of forty-four institutionalized juvenile delinquents. Bowlby had been struck by the deviant parenting received by these children and made special note of them having experienced prolonged separations during childhood. Bowlby extended this work with the World Health Organization in the late 1940s and again noticed the profound effects of early separation on subsequent development.[4] Harlow's findings regarding the behavior of infant monkeys conformed nicely with Bowlby's conviction that the provision of mothering is as important to the (human) infants' development as proper diet and nutrition.

Bowlby eventually proposed an "attachment behavior system" to account for his observations.[5] He argued that this system had been retained through the evolutionary process of natural selection. Attachment systems are manufactured by copies of ancient genes that originally gave our primitive forebears an edge on survival. Following the course of natural selection, we continue to inherit the same genetically driven programs that millions of years ago afforded infants protection against being attacked by predators. He proposed that there is an instinctive quality to attachment systems that orient infants to seek to be in the proximity of nurturing figure and to reflexively protest when the figure is unavailable. Attachment systems originally played a vital role in keeping the organism alive long enough to do what genes require them to do, that is, to assure the genes' continued existence in the genetic pool by compelling the bodies they have created as their temporary carriers to pass them on to future generations. Infants born with defective attachment systems tended not to survive, and thereby the genes that resulted in their "unfitness" gradually disappeared. While human beings no longer need to be fearful of hungry beasts, our genes don't know that, and today's newborns are as urgently driven to seek objects that represent havens of protection as did the children of our distant ancestors who roamed the forests and prairies looking for food and shelter.

Bowlby's theoretical perspective and the books he wrote to elaborate on it captured the attention of many other scholars, to the point where his work had a dramatic impact in developmental psychology and related fields. A good deal of credit for bringing his ideas to United States and elsewhere is given to his Canadian colleague, Mary Ainsworth,[6] who established a now classic set of procedures for systematically studying different patterns of mother-child attachment behaviors in laboratory settings.

So the proposition that infants are born with attachment systems in place became the preferred way to understand why infants show signs of distress in the absence of their primary attachment figure. To drive this point home, many fathers can recall a period of time when they were frustrated by their inability to provide the kind of infant-comforting magic that appeared to be come about so naturally when their youngsters were being attended to by their mothers. There are times when only the attachment figure, and nobody else, can placate a troubled soul.

But the time comes in the lives of most children when they can endure long periods of not being in the proximity of the "mothering one." In fact, as children develop, there are occasions when offspring actively avoid the company of their mothers. How are we to understand this development? Does that mean the attachment systems shut down after they have provided their early service? The answer to the latter question is a resounding *no*, according to contemporary specialists on the matter. In fact, the operation of the attachment system becomes less observable. It goes underground, so to speak, and becomes much more sophisticated. Think about it this way. Children, particularly when they are up and running, do not require the actual physical presence of a caregiver *as long as they are convinced that she is available in the event that she is needed.* Separations can be tolerated when the prospects of reunions are assured. In other words, a child's mental "appraisal" of its mother's availability in her absence can become as important as her actual physical presence in times of need.

WORKING MODELS

How are such appraisals made? Bowlby offered the idea of "internal working models" as his answer to this question. The following visualization will help to make this concept understandable. Take a moment to form a mental image of a place other than the one you are now in. A bedroom that you occupied when you were in grammar school will do. Allow a picture of that room to come to mind and begin to explore it. Does it contain a desk? If so, where is it located? Do you see any objects like posters or banners hanging on the walls? What wall are they on and how are they arranged? Now explore the remainder of your room in as much detail as you can.

You have just gained conscious access to memories of your former bedroom. It is likely that your "mind's eye" enabled you to explore the various features of the space by first looking one way and then turning in a different direction to see the room from another angle. It may be that you didn't capture every detail of the room as it actually was, especially if it has been many years since you have been in it. So let us suppose that you were able to magically suspend time and physically return to the room, and further that it has been preserved unchanged from the time you last saw it. There would likely be some surprises. For example, the physical space might be much smaller than you had imagined it to be. There might be a crack in the ceiling that was missed in your mental image and you may have distorted some of the features in the pattern of the wallpaper. In those ways, the image you created may not have been fully accurate, but it was a good enough "working model" of the room for you to be able to recognize the room were you to see it again.

I doubt that you have thought much about your old bedroom before performing this exercise. Memories of it were conveniently tucked away in the circuitry of your brain so that they and the myriad other things stored there do not constantly divert your attention away from concentrating on matters at hand. Let us view such memories as normally preconscious but available to be organized as "pictures" when conscious attention is brought to them. 밀접한 관계가 있는.

More germane to this discussion than mental images of rooms are the internal representations we have of ourselves "when-with" specific other people. There is some literature on this topic, to which my colleague, Richard Ashmore, and I have made some contributions.[7] Here is one of the procedures we have devised. Think of someone who is important to you. Recall a situation when you were with that person. Focus in on a specific interactive episode with that person, throw the episode onto an internal screen, and review the scene carefully. Is the person acting the way he or she typically does, or is there something unusual about the person's behavior? You would not be able to answer that question if you did not have a working model of how that person normally is when he or she interacts with you. That is, you could not appraise the image unless you had something to contrast it with.

This exercise simply slows down what are normally high-speed, unconscious processes that enable us to recognize alterations in our environments. They occur outside of awareness and are incredibly efficient. One of the functions these beneath-the-surface working models serve is to assist us in making our interpersonal lives predictable. They summarize past experiences and enable us to know things like "Uncle Norman is moody and doesn't like to talk much, but he always brightens up when I talk with him about professional football" or "Cousin Bob is a character and it's always 'play time' when he's around. I've got some stuff for us to do when he comes tomorrow and he's going to get a real kick out of it." Working models allow us to anticipate events and to be prepared for sequences of actions and inform us about how to be and how not to be when-with particular others. Without these implicit expectations based on our history of interactions with various people in our lives, every encounter would be a new encounter, and we would have to start from scratch in the field of foreign others. Working models condense and organize an immense amount of historical information. They are the brain's way of assembling memories of the quality, tone, actions, and consequences of past interactions and informing us when deviations from the usual experiences arise.

In this way, working models conserve energy. They prevent us from having to engage in the mental work that otherwise would be required to figure out how to be and what to do in a relationship. They provide us with a compact history of past interactions that contributes to a sense of continuity. They serve as implicit guides that are informed by what we have learned to anticipate in our ongoing relationships with other people.

Small deviations between our working models and external events are usually easy to manage, requiring only slight, effortless modifications. In fact, we often find it interesting when our expectations are not entirely confirmed. Unanticipated changes in our surroundings can wake us up and provide some welcome novelty to our daily routines. Even infants show interest in familiar objects that are presented to them in slightly altered forms.

However, big surprises are less easy to manage. Imagine what it would be like if you had been married for several years and went home to a spouse who was suddenly so different, out of sorts perhaps, that you were unable to summon up a working model that came at all close to matching the new circumstance. First, there would be conscious recognition that something has changed. That would be followed by cognitive activities aimed at determining what had changed. After it was determined what had changed and some thought was given to the matter, decisions about what to do about the change would be required.

Up to this point, a critical ingredient has been left out; I have described working models as implicit guides to interactions that can be brought to consciousness by an act of will. That act of will comes about when a discrepancy arises between the predictions of the working model and what reality brings our way. The terms I have used are highly "mentalistic." Scattered throughout this discussion are words like "cognition," "thinking," and "decisions." These terms would be sufficient if our lives were conducted completely in the upper cortical regions of our brains. But alterations in our environment do more than activate mental algorithms that may be required to adjust the mind's pictures. Alterations in the environment affect the way we *feel*. Return for a moment to the example of a spouse who is suddenly so out of character that he or she falls completely outside any working model his or her mate can evoke. Such an event would not only result in a cognitive scramble to "process" the information. It would jolt the mate's *feelings*.

Much of chapter 17 will be devoted to the all-important topic of feelings; there and elsewhere, I observe that feelings are not incidental features of life. Systems of feelings and systems of thinking are not independent of each other. Working models are products of a shared mission to reduce risks to survival, and neither thinking nor feeling can accomplish the feat without the other. This observation allows us to understand why Jamie Barrie was so desperate to make his mother's face match the features of the face he associated with feelings of safety. Put briefly, Jamie experienced feelings that his survival was at risk when he could not observe a face that matched the face of his working model of a mother that was inextricably linked with his feeling of well-being. I will elaborate on this later.

Returning to the earlier observation that a time comes when the physical proximity of the mother becomes less important than the child's confidence that she will be available when needed, not right now, but soon enough, it is the child's internal me-with-mother working model that makes it possible for it to engage in all sorts of activities away from her immediate company. An important feature of a child's working model is its expectations about the mother's physical and emotional availability in the event that it needs reassurance.

A child's working model of self-with-mother (or other primary attachment figure) is flexible in that it condenses a great number of variations of typical scenes with her. Scripts of "how to be with Mom" that are contingent on "how she is being with me" are embedded in the model. These scripts are not rigid. There is a good deal of pliability around their edges that allows for on-the-spot improvisations. This notion is consistent with Daniel Stern's proposal that a child develops a "generalized" representation of the tone and quality of repeated interactions with objects around it, particularly the mother. Stern is a child psychiatrist and first-rate scientist whose ideas about working models, internal mental representations, and core self-development have not been granted the attention and credibility I believe they warrant. In the next chapter I present an overview of Stern's theory of early social development.

SIXTEEN *Stern's Outside-In Theory of Self-Development*

Core

There is a commonly held notion that infants begin life in a state of symbiotic fusion with the mother and that in many other ways they lack the ability to differentiate themselves from their surroundings. Daniel Stern disagrees. He observes that shortly after birth infants show clear evidence of possessing a self in the making.[1] He refers to it as the *emergent self.* Although it operates outside of awareness, Stern describes it as willful, coherent, and bounded. One can witness its presence when a baby shows preferences, actively seeks visual and auditory stimulation, attends to changes in its environment, and demonstrates mastery of simple cause-and-effect relationships. Within just a few months of developing proficiency with intentional movements, the infant enters the stage of *core self*-development. During this stage it gives evidence of knowing, moment by moment, that it is an organized invariant in the world of other objects. Of course, the baby does not yet "know" that it "knows." Its ability to know that it knows comes later.

Around the infant's sixth or seventh month of life, it is able to sense that other core entities exist whose actions alter its own core self. After this discovery has been made, the infant begins to recognize certain patterns of being regulated by core others. It experiences not only itself being regulated but also its capacity to regulate the other. As both selves (the infant's and the mother's) coregulate each other, internal representations of their interactions are formed in the minds of the two participants. These representations comprise *representations of interactions generalized* (RIGs). Stern writes: "A RIG [represents] something that has never happened before exactly that way, yet it takes into account nothing that did not actually

123

happen once."[2] In other words, it is a general summary, or an "active ex-emplar," of repeated episodes, none of which were exactly alike, that char-acterizes the child's self-with-specific-other experiences. A RIG is based on averaged experiences and is a kind of abstract representation that packages the actions, feelings, and sensations, as well as certain features of the envi-ronment, that have become associated with past experiences with a par-ticular other.[3]

Stern suggests that RIGs be considered the building blocks of working models. Repeated interactions with an object result in the aggregation of specific RIGs into an organized internal representation of one's past his-tory with that object. A particular working model can be evoked by inter-nal needs and/or by external cues. For example, let us say that a mother is fond of making playful gurgling sounds when she changes her infant's dia-per. The next time she gurgles, the sound operates as a cue for activating the infant's internal representation of "me-with-Mom-when-she-gurgles." Eventually, being placed on the diaper-changing surface can serve as a cue that evokes the joyful "been there, done that" RIG in the mind of the in-fant, who may initiate the Gurgle Game instead of waiting for its mother to signal that the game has begun.

These kinds of repetitive interactive experiences take on new mean-ings when the infant takes the "quantum leap" into a more advanced stage of self-development, a stage that Stern calls the *subjective self*. The subjec-tive self operates in the "domain of intersubjective relatedness." Stern writes: "At this stage, for the first time, one can attribute to the infant the capacity for psychic intimacy—the openness to disclosure, the perme-ability or interpenetrability that occurs between two people."[4] The infant has reached a stage where its self is sharable and capable of engaging in "intersubjective union" with another. Infants and their mothers are able now to read each others' faces and reach a level of affective harmony that provides them both with feelings of oneness with the other. This ascen-dance from the preceding stage of core self development marks the activa-tion of the infant's attachment system.

Finally, beginning around the age of eighteen months, the *verbal* self begins to emerge. The onset of the verbal self is both a blessing and a curse. It is a blessing because it signals entry into the distinctively human conceptual world, a world of symbols and categories. Words replace ges-tures and grunts. Internal states and external facts can now be talked about, discussed, and negotiated. Verbally coded memories are stored and are available to be recalled, built on, and modified in ways that provide the objective "me" with a sense of continuity. The downside of this develop-ment is that language causes a split in the experience of self. In Stern's words, "it moves relatedness onto an impersonal, abstract level intrinsic to language and away from the personal, immediate level of intrinsic do-mains of relatedness."[5] Although ultimately the verbal self may appear to be emancipated from the domains of self that preceded its development, Stern makes a strong case that the emergent, core, and subjective selves do not waste away. In fact, they continue to provide the (sometimes alienated) base on which the verbal self struggles to make sense of the world.

The following discussion describes Stern's theory in more detail. Stern's view about the time of life when the attachment system initially becomes active may surprise you if you were taught that the system kicks in at the moment of birth. "Bring me my baby so we can bond!" or words to that effect are commonly heard directives from mothers who have recently given birth. It is likely that the original bonding process is psychologically more important to the mother than to her infant. But *bonding*, whatever it is, is not the same as *attachment*. As I said previously, Stern takes a strong position against the notion that infants are born selfless. The belief that the first order of business for a newborn is to become symbiotically fused with the mother is hard to break. The idea that babies emerge from the womb in an undifferentiated, open-system state of confusion has been promulgated in psychoanalytic literature for quite some time. In declaring his opposition to that position, Stern writes that infants "never experience a period of total self/other undifferentiation."[6] Instead, at almost the very outset of life, an infant operates with the nonreflective awareness that it is a bounded entity that is in the process of experiencing emerging internal organization.

As this process continues, the baby experiences itself as an invariant in its small universe where many things around it are in various states of flux. Faces appear as people look into the crib. Then they disappear. One's diaper gets changed, mobiles get dangled above one's head, sounds like "goo-goo" come and go, and all kinds of other things occur in one's transient surroundings. As these changes occur, the infant experiences itself as remaining pretty much the same. In that way, the child is said to experience a sense of invariance (or relative sameness), and the consolidation of that sense is said to lead to a nonconscious awareness of a *core* self. The sense of core self and experiences of its relative separateness from other objects develops in conjunction with the growing recognition that other core selves exist—not inside the infant, because it has never been confused about whose body its core self occupies, but out there—in the mother for instance. This sets the stage for the important discovery on the part of the infant that core others have the capacity to alter the state of its own core self. The infant "notices" the conjunctions between the actions of other core selves and the alterations that occur in its own experiences of self, particularly at the level of alterations of feelings. In addition, the baby becomes more aware that its own actions alter the state of the other. In other words, not only can the other regulate the infant's core self but it can regulate the core self of the other. In fact, they can coregulate each other.

After this groundwork has been established, the infant enters a new domain of development that Stern calls the _subjective_ self. The subjective self is formed by way of repeated experiences that feelings can be importantly changed during the course of interactions with another person, or in Stern's language, with a "self-regulating other." Now the infant and its mother can play the Gurgle Game, play peek-a-boo, and participate full out in a host of intersubjective activities and have a grand time in the process.

These activities are most prevalent between the ages of seven and fifteen months. It is throughout this period that the phenomenon of attachment arrives front and center. Two subjective selves, the mother's and her child's, unite as one. These experiences of togetherness, of "intersubjective union," give the child its first sense of psychic intimacy. Although its sense of core self remains steadfast throughout, the child's subjective sense of self becomes partly embedded in its relationship with the mother. Mom does this and I do that and we are quite a pair. Episodes of emotional "attunement" are particularly relished. The baby smiles and the mother smiles back. The child pumps its legs and the mother sways her arms or upper body at more or less the same beat. The child reaches its arms forward and the mother picks it up.

Unlike the child's earlier core self experiences of existing as a bounded and separate entity, its subjective sense of self is permeable, and the mother becomes an indispensable part of it. The infant's experiences of its subjective self become represented internally as moment-by-moment accounts of "when-with-Mom" episodes. These records of felt experiences and the conditions in which they occur become amalgamated with other similar me-with episodes into a RIG. When cues that are appropriate to the activation of that RIG are present, the RIG operates as a guide for how to be and what to anticipate in the impending episode with the mother. Over the course of repeated episodes, this RIG becomes elaborated and perhaps forms company with other RIGs in ways that generate a more global me-with-Mom working model of actions that are associated with the quality, tone, and feelings engendered during periods of intersubjective relatedness.

I make special note of the following. If the child's me-with working model is to provide its intended service, it must be validated from time to time. It makes no sense to create a working model that doesn't work. Both partners in me-with episodes are expected to behave in ways that roughly conform to the model. Not all of the time, but at least some of the time. Let us say that the mother comes into the baby's room when it begins to stir from a nap. Her arrival serves as a cue that activates the infant's working model of "me-with-Mom when I wake up." But in this instance "Mom" is preoccupied by other things and doesn't behave in her accustomed way. What that means is their intersubjective "dance" will not take place this time, but it is likely to occur at some other time—the sooner the better, as far as the infant is concerned. The absence of a match between the child's working model and a vital element of it (in this instance, the mom who is not playing her anticipated part) can be distressing to the child. But if the overall quality of attachment is good, a mismatch between the model and what actually occurs at a particular moment is likely to be experienced as a minor glitch in normal operations, and no permanent damage to the child's subjective sense of self will be done. In fact, "Mom" might occasionally violate a particular working model frequently enough that a parallel working model is created that informs the child about how to be and what feelings are likely to arise in episodes with Mom when she is not in a mood to play.

In general, there is support for the idea that "good mothering" engenders trust on the part of the child. Good mothering (and good fathering as well) includes enjoying the child, providing structure that is conducive to its safety, being attentive to its cues, mirroring its affects and action, and an unabashed willingness to take time out to play. The kind of play that fosters secure attachment involves the repetition of familiar "been there, done that" games. Such games for a child at the intersubjective stage of self-development evoke sense of "psychic merger" with the love object.

What are the sensations or feelings that an infant might experience during episodes of "being one" with the mother? *Utter contentment* comes to mind when I attempt to think of words that could aptly convey the wordless feelings that one supposes accompany the infant's experiences of interpersonal oneness. *Euphoria* is another possibility. Harry Stack Sullivan[7] used that word and contrasted it with experiences of absolute tension. We conduct most of our lives somewhere between the opposing poles of that dimension. "Pure bliss" is what Carl Jung called it when he wrote about the conditions that surrounded the first three years of his life. It could be that residues of early sensations of oneness are what are partially recovered during moments of so-called peak experiences in adulthood. Abraham Maslow described such moments as ones where suddenly everything is right with the world.[8] Everything has its proper place in the universe, and it could be no other way. For an all-too-fleeting moment one's usual sense of reality is suspended, and one is flooded with feelings of wordless well-being.   해복감 됨김   ) 다시없는 기쁨, 행복.

"Utter contentment," "euphoria," "pure bliss"—what other words are available to describe the phenomenon? An acquaintance of Sigmund Freud called it an "oceanic feeling," and that's not a bad concept to add to our vocabulary of words to converse about difficult-to-nail-down sensations that accompany feelings of oneness.[9]

In most instances, the object associated with these difficult-to-label feelings is the child's mother. Mental representations of such "safe haven" experiences with her are aggregated into "indelible prints" of past pleasurable interactive episodes. In the beginning, these imprints provide the background for working models used in guiding everyday, "real," moment-to-moment interpersonal relationships with the "actual" caregiver. Then an important development takes place. Self-with-attachment-figure representations remain in place as working models that are accessible for playback and rehearsal during times when the attachment figure is not physically present. In this fully installed condition, the object can now be carried about in the child's mind and consulted as a source of on-the-spot assurance of the mentally depicted emotional availability of the attachment figure. Periodically the child will touch base with the attachment figure as a reality check to confirm the accuracy of its mental image. Then gradually the child can confidently endure longer periods of separation, assured that its survival is in the good hands of its internal companion.

In sum, a great deal of nonconscious self-development occurs before the child becomes *consciously* aware that it is a unique, stand-alone person who bears a name. I had the good fortune of observing an instance when not knowing that one knows became full-fledged knowledge. One day when my son Sam was eighteen months old, he was standing on a couch looking at his image in a mirror. Standard stuff, nothing unusual. He looked away and suddenly looked back at his reflection. With an expression of utter amazement, he pointed to the mirror and shouted, "That's Sam!" It was as though a longstanding mystery had been solved. It was a profound and wonderfully exciting "Aha!" experience for him. If he had known the word, doubtless he would have screamed, "Eureka!" This phenomenon has been demonstrated in laboratory studies with children conducted by Michael Lewis and Jeanne Brooks-Gunn.[10] The procedures involve placing rouge on the tips of toddlers' noses and having them look at themselves in a mirror. Typically, children under eighteen months of age attempt to wipe the rouge off the image in the mirror. Slightly older children immediately bring a hand to their own nose and attempt to wipe off the reddish coloring.

The self that is recognized by children around eighteen months becomes the early precursor of the *verbal self*, according to Stern. That is the self that is most familiar to us. It's the one we talk about. We fill our brains with information about it. It is the key player in our autobiographic memories. Our extended consciousness is built around the verbal self. It is the "me" division of the self that William James separated from the "I."[11] James referred to the "I" as the internal stream of consciousness; similar to the idea of moment-to-moment, constantly-on-the-move, running accounts of what is happening. It never stands still long enough for us to capture more than a fleeting glimpse of passing images. The verbal self, the "me," is different in that regard. We can bring the "me" to mind as an object. We can create mental pictures of its numerous versions and hold them still long enough for them to be examined, judged and evaluated, praised, admonished, or envisioned in terms of their destinies.

What happens to the other domains of self—the emerging self, the core self, and the subjective self—after the verbal self is in place? Are they like early space rockets whose booster stages fell uselessly to the sea after they have propelled the payload into its orbit? In other words, do they vanish after their work is done, leaving the verbal self autonomous from its origins? Stern's emphatic answer of *no* to this question is accompanied by the illustration shown here, which depicts the continued existence and ongoing interpenetration of these domains of self throughout the years of a person's life.

If the emergent self ceased to exist, there would be no running accounts of the condition of the body. There would be no recognition of being alive. The absence of a core self would result in the lack of a sense of self-coherence and feelings of self-agency. The same is so for the subjective self. For a while the subjective self carries the burden of survival, and as far as "it" is concerned, it still does. I suspect that subjective self-experiences, particularly in the domain of intersubjective (self/other) relationships, are the strongest candidates for entry into that portion of the psyche that Freud identified as the "unconscious." They consist of verbally *uncoded* images and memories that continue to influence our passions and desires. They are our hidden or implicit working models of how things should be. They enable us to recognize conditions that threaten the survival of our subjective self. They are the primary sources of idealized relationships and urge us to seek relationships according to their designs. They also have their own special ways of signaling discomfort when reality does not match their implicit standards. Most important to the topic of this book, they don't go away. For some people more than others, they remain

From *The Interpersonal World of the Infant* by Daniel N. Stern. Copyright © 1987 by Basic Books, Inc. Reprinted by permission of Basic Books, a member of Perseus Books, L.L.C.

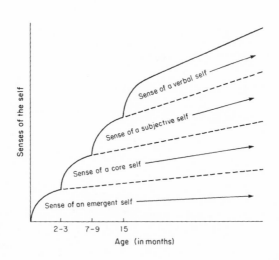

embedded in the brain as gardens of retreat that offer solace when life becomes hard and loneliness feels unbearable. During such dire times, previous experiences of being "one" with another, though not consciously recalled, offer themselves up as havens of felt security. They are the source of unspoken fantasies that if only we could reconstruct some elements of those previous experiences—feelings of what it was like, for example—then all of the elements of conditions under which our survival seemed assured might magically return.

These notions are important components of our "ground maintenance" work. However, we need to think further about some of the additional parts while we are still in the hangar. Then, we will see how well it flies.

Stern's theory of self-development is based on his own research and a comprehensive compilation of observational and experimental studies of infants and children conducted by others. His theory embraces an organized set of inferences about what occurs in the minds of children, based on studies of multitudes of youngsters over many years. However, there is always the chance, and in some instances a very good chance, that prominent constructs in a theory are aligned in a fashion that makes it an excellent stand-alone story but one that fails to relate to anything other than itself. Working models? Fine. Internal representations? RIGs? Okay, if you say so. It "feels" right, but is there any other evidence from a difference perspective on development that can be viewed as support for the main features of the theory? My affirmative answer to that question requires me to take a brief excursion into a portion of the burgeoning field of brain research from which we will emerge with a better understanding of Barrie's struggle to get his mother to smile and the nature of the void Jung sought to fill with his invention of the collective unconscious.

SEVENTEEN *Damasio's Inside-Out Theory of Self-Development*

Recently an unfamiliar sound jolted me from a nap. For a couple of moments, I was completely disoriented. I had no idea what time of day or night it was, where I was, or what in the world I was doing wherever I was. However, I knew I existed. The instant I stirred, there was never any confusion about who didn't know where he was. It was I. I recall a similar episode when I was much younger. I had dozed off, and the telephone rang. I dashed to the phone, picked up the receiver, and didn't know what to do with the strange object in my hand. Saying "hello" didn't occur to me, so I blew into it. My mother was on the other end of the line and suggested that I wake up. Once again, I was not the slightest bit confused about who it was who did not know what to do with the object in his hand.

It did not take more than a few seconds for me to recall where I was in the first instance and what to do with the phone in the second instance. My *extended consciousness* was quick to return. Extended consciousness enables us to locate ourselves in space and time, to recognize where we are, to access autobiographic memories, to think, to plan, to make decisions (like saying "Hello"), and do the myriad other things that we associate with wakeful consciousness. During the few seconds it took for my extended consciousness to return, my sense that I existed was based on the wordless knowledge that my body was still functioning.

That "knowledge" is grounded in an ongoing flow of background feelings. Antonio Damasio is a specialist on background feelings and much more. In his book *Descartes' Error*,[1] Damasio effectively challenges Descartes's famous dictum *Cogito ergo sum* ("I think, therefore I am"). In my episode with a telephone receiver, for a few seconds I had no access to my thoughts, but I knew I existed. How did I know that? According to Damasio, I knew that I was because I was nonconsciously aware that I *felt*. We *feel*, therefore we are.

Damasio is a researcher and scholar on the topic of the human brain; he is a neurologist at the University of Iowa who maintains an affiliation with the Salk Institute for Biological Studies in La Jolla, California. In a second book, *The Feeling of What Happens*, he provides inside-out support for several of Sterns's key outside-in observations of self development of children. It should be pointed out, however, that Damasio did not write the book for the purpose of adding neurological substance to Stern's theory. He acknowledges passing awareness of Stern's work[2] and credits others for bringing to his attention potential overlaps between his theory and Stern's, but pursuing areas of possible convergence was outside the scope of his book.

There are more than mere hints of connections between their theories. It is my impression that both scholars, operating from vastly different perspectives and building on hundreds of investigations of others in their respective fields, bring us to a tantalizing point in at least beginning to make progress in understanding the most difficult of all problems in philosophy and psychology : the problem of self and consciousness. Both researchers have phrased their insights in the languages of their specialized disciplines. Stern speaks of RIGs and working models. Damasio writes about primary and secondary circuits in the brain. Stern is fluent with psychoanalytic terms and has an extensive vocabulary grounded in the area of infant and child development. Damasio speaks of subcortical connections, cingulates, amygdalae, pons, tectums, and lobes. But in many respects, both scholars address the same phenomenon. I have an image of their two theories residing on two single-stranded chromosomes of a DNA molecule, seeking partners. But unlike genes that automatically find their matching partners when single-stranded chromosomes come together and create a single-celled organism, the kind of partnering I envision will require the work of humans to tie the strands together. The fit will not be perfect, but the reward for that kind of dedicated and innovative work is potentially enormous, in terms of leading to empirically sound and testable models of the interface between self and consciousness.

In the remainder of this chapter I take some initial steps toward fashioning such a model. My specific aim is to then show how a few pieces of this interlocking puzzle can be positioned in ways that account for J. M. Barrie's lifelong struggle to bring a smile to his mother's face, Carl Jung's need to locate a mother substitute, and in the process of doing both to create a more general template for understanding fantasies of flying. I am also addressing two other "side" issues. First, I want to encourage self psychologists to relinquish the belief that neuroscientists have nothing to offer, that the mind can be fully known outside any consideration of the brain. Although their numbers are still small, several neuroscientists are addressing matters of the self at the organic level, and ignorance of their contributions does not serve the field of personality psychology. I have selected Damasio's theory as a case in point, but there are other brain scientists whose research into and speculations about neurological foundations of subjective self experiences, or "subcortical cores of being," draw my attention.[3] Second, I agree with others who have observed the limitations of purely computational models of consciousness.[4] Mechanistic or digital simulations of the brain's cortical circuitry that treat emotions as "noise" and ignore the subcortical, affective base of a sense of "I"-ness, will fail to do the job that their sponsors so ambitiously pursue.

Damasio's theory of self and consciousness is built on his own and other neurologists' observations of the behavioral and cognitive effects of damage to specific regions of the brain. Some of these impairments are caused by accidents, others by lesions, tumors, diseases, or birth defects. Following the tradition of compassionate and lucid writing about neurological disorders established by Oliver Sacks,[5] Damasio creates a model of "normal" brain development that is based on studies of individuals whose brains have been compromised by damage.

Recall Stern's emphasis on the infant never experiencing a sense of confusion about whose body it occupies. Stern describes the self at birth, the emergent self, as a bounded entity that operates with the nonreflected awareness of its internal organization. Damasio gives a different label, the protoself, to what Stern calls the emergent self. Damasio defines the protoself as "a coherent collection of neural patterns which map, moment by moment, the state of the physical structure of the organism in its many dimensions."[6] My protoself arrived with me at birth. So did yours.

Like all living organisms, the body is designed to survive. Survival, at its most basic level, means that the internal milieu of the organism must remain within a narrow range of parameters. The heart must keep beating, the blood must keep flowing, the internal temperature must remain within a few degrees of normalcy; food must be converted to glucose, stored, and then reconverted into energy providing sugar; solid and liquid waste materials must be eliminated and other substances consumed to replace them, and so on. The aim is to maintain a condition of homeostasis, a safe degree of balance within a narrow range of set-point boundaries. Specific portions of the brain automatically regulate these sorts of functions and respond to signals from the body that indicate that its homeostatic condition has changed. The main areas of the brain that regulate and monitor these operations are located in and around the brain stem, commonly called the hindbrain. Our species is very much like other mammalian species in regard to the brain stem's design. The makeup and organization of brain stems across species is remarkably similar. Why is that? It is because over millions of years of evolution, "nature" settled on an exquisite, one-design-fits-all brain stem that serves the fundamental survival needs of a host of species.[7] Just like rodents, chimpanzees, warthogs, and whales, human beings are endowed with subcortical equipment located in a complex region deep inside the brain that is responsive to changes in the internal condition of the body. In sum, the protoself is not species specific.

A phenomenon that Damasio refers to as *core consciousness* arrives in early infancy as an extension of the protoself. Feelings are critical components of core consciousness. Nothing like core consciousness is possible without feelings, because feelings are the vehicles for communicating to the brain that the internal milieu has been altered. Core consciousness not only monitors the internal condition of the body but also provides running record accounts of any objects that alter its preferred homeostatic condition. In other words, core consciousness faces in two directions, both inward and outward, and coordinates information arriving from both locations. It simultaneously creates a running record of the feelings that emanate from the body (which, as you will recall, must operate within the range of narrow boundaries) *and* a running record account of any object that alters those feelings. This is Damasio's version of William James's "I," or stream of consciousness.[8] It consists of moment-to-moment wordless knowledge based on background feelings that includes images of objects that are associated with changes in those feelings.

One way to think about the brain is as retaining an archaeological record of its history of evolution. No parts have been deleted. What has worked, in terms of the species survival, has been kept.[9] Brains of higher order species are differentiated from the brains of lower order species by the *addition* of neural layers on the primitive brain stem. Primates have a more elaborate midbrain structure than do reptiles, and it is believed that the evolution of the subcortical components of the midbrain enable organisms to be more emotionally responsive to nuances in the environment and thereby better learners. Then, again over millions of years of evolution, an incredibly complex structure called the cerebral cortex was gradually added, layer on layer, to the midbrain. Bring to mind an image of the human brain. Chances are that image contains a picture of a grayish-white, convoluted, folded, and creased object that you have seen in a picture or in a jar in a museum. That is the outer layer of the cerebral cortex. It is about three times larger than the cortices of our closest primate relatives. It is also thicker, in that there are several inches between the outer layer and various components of the midbrain.

The size of our cerebral cortices enables us to proudly declare our *sapient* ("wise") status. We like to think of ourselves as nested at the top of the evolutionary tree. In fact, big brains have an enormous bearing on survival capabilities. Instead of filling this and many other pages by cataloguing the many benefits of large brains, I want to focus on one of the effects of the "big brain" in early childhood. Recall Damasio's emphasis that the organism has a moment-to-moment account of the condition of its internal milieu *and* an account of any objects that alter its condition. Rats do it, and so do infants. Rats do it instinctively, and that probably characterizes a newborn infant as well. But very soon afterward, as the neurons in the infant's brain find their proper locations, the baby is able to do it much more masterfully than any rat ever will, in terms of noticing and monitoring the effects of an object on its internal condition. One important advantage the baby's larger brain affords it is a *feeling of knowing* that something has changed and an enhanced image of the object that is linked with the alteration. This "knowledge" is wordless knowledge that is based on running imaged accounts of the alterations.

The next development is monumental: the ability to *rerepresent* running record imaged accounts of the relationship between changes in one's internal state and the objects associated with those changes. This is a step that distinguishes us from other primates; they are not bereft of this ability, but humans do it on a grander scale. Damasio describes this development as follows.

As the infant's brain continues to mature, a core sense of self is built on the substrates of the protoself. (Note that Damasio and Stern converge on the same label to refer this early stage of self.) Core self experiences are the results of the infant's more advanced ability to represent moment-to-moment, always-on-the-move, running imaged accounts of the condition of the body in conjunction with external events. Images of what is happening "now," both internally and externally, are constantly being replaced by other wordless images of what is happening "now." The previous now is history, and the now "now" will be over in a flash. As this process continues, changes in the environment that alter the condition of the body bring about a sense of awareness, delightfully described by Damasio as the self being caught in the act of knowing that something has changed.

The act of knowing that feelings have changed can result in the activation of previous imaged accounts of similar situations that are essential for *appraising* the present situation. Appraising is one of the functions of the various interlocking systems within the cerebral cortex. The process can be thought of as one that upgrades the status of previously recorded running accounts of similar situations by casting a summary of these accounts onto an internal "screen" for the purpose of comparing that display with the present configurations of external stimuli and internal states. My cinematic analogy is not likely to receive Damasio's full endorsement, but it is close enough for us to get an idea of what is involved in "secondary processing"; the act of representing and then rerepresenting images.

One of Damasio's most important observations is that meaningful "secondary" processing is impossible without a sense of self. He writes: "It is as if, without a sense of self in the act of knowing, the thoughts one generates go unclaimed because their rightful owner is missing. The self-impoverished organism is at a loss as to whom these thoughts belong"[10]—and, I would add, to whom *experiences* belong. In other words, without a core sense of self, the individual might still be able to generate running imaged accounts of whatever is happening, but no happenings would alter the individual's feelings, and as a consequence no external events would have any personal meaning. A good example of this, is the character of Chauncy Gardner, played by Peter Sellers in the film *Being There*. Chauncy's affective states never vary, and his steadiness through thick and thin, through high times and low times, bring him the respect and admiration of the entire nation—so much so that by the end of the movie, he is considered as a candidate for the presidency. The irony of all this, of course, is that he does not feel. Nothing means anything to him, and he comes off looking like a genius.

Since film examples only work for people who have seen the film under discussion (and there is nothing more tedious for me than to read about the plot of a film that someone else has enjoyed), I will spare the reader any further description of *Being There* and take up another example. Create a mental image of your place of residence. Look at your residence from the outside, and then go indoors and admire your possessions; your treasured family photograph album, the clothes in your closet, the bedroom set you recently purchased, and other items that are personally meaningful to you. Now imagine that you are coming home, and the entire place is burned to the ground. How would you feel were you to witness your home and all of your possession turned to ashes? More in line with the present discussion is How would your feelings be altered by the horrible sight? Without a doubt, your internal milieu would be pushed beyond acceptable boundaries. Signals of an internal state of imbalance would be delivered throughout your body, and most definitely you would be "caught in the act of knowing" that your feelings had changed. Your state of extreme disturbance would turn to panic once you realized that Ruffles, your blind cocker spaniel and closest companion, was missing. But if you had no core self that provided the critical link between alterations of feelings and knowing that feelings had changed, you would look at the rubble that once had been your home and simply notice that your residence was gone. That's it. What was, no longer exists. Same with Ruffles, the missing pet. Oh well, easy come, easy go. Bye-bye, old Ruffs—ta-ta. A different "now" has replaced a former "now," and since there is no self to be altered, nothing that happens makes much of a difference.

Of course, that is not how we conduct our daily lives. When an internal or external event alters our background feelings, a running imaged account of the alteration automatically takes place. When the alteration is strong enough to make us aware that our feelings have changed, the running account is then rerepresented in the brain, and *that* is what Damasio calls consciousness. It is an act of knowing that we know. It is based on the brain's "second-order" processing of an event that has impinged on one's core sense of self.

Take a moment to think about this phenomenon. Think of the countless things that occur around you in your daily life. In an active day, you are surrounded by innumerable objects and features in your surroundings. You may pass hundreds of people on the streets. Kids running around, hot dog vendors, cars zipping by. In the midst of all that, what catches your attention? It could be an acquaintance you see coming toward you or the former boss who fired you several years ago. Extrapolating from Damasio's model, a primary source of your selecting one person to recognize out of hundreds of other possibilities is the way the mere witnessing of that person alters your feelings, for better or worse. For better, if it is someone who generates feelings of warmth or fondness; for worse, if it is someone you are uncomfortable with and would just as soon avoid.

Let's go with the person who alters your feelings in a positive direction. There's Mary. Haven't seen her since she moved out of the neighborhood last year. Big grin. Hi, Mary. Great to see you! How have you been? Your me-with-Mary working model predicts that Mary will be equally happy to see you. However, Mary gives you a nasty look, mumbles "Fine," and coldly passes you by. The event disturbs you. It is unsettling because Mary had been an important person in your life. The two of you used to exchange secret recipes, drive each other's kids to school, and openly converse about various family matters. Now you can't get Mary off your mind. You wonder if you have done something that annoyed her. Maybe it was a Mary look-alike. No, it was definitely Mary. No other potential look-alike could possibly have a mole smack dab on the center of her chin like Mary. Your mental representation of the event and your awareness of the discomfiting feelings it engendered stay with you. You place a phone call to a friend to tell her about the incident, you talk about it at the dinner table, and you privately ruminate about the experience for several days thereafter. Why? Because Mary has altered your feelings in an unanticipated way, and your sense of self has been affected as well. It would help if someone you spoke with about the event said something like "Oh, don't worry about it. Mary is an odd duck. I thought you knew that." But nobody says anything even close to that, and you remain stuck.

You would not be "stuck" had Mary been pleasant to you. Encountering her would have been an unremarkable event had she smiled and reciprocated your greetings. But her actions did not fit your picture. They violated any and all me-with-Mary RIGs formed during past episodes involving Mary. That's from Stern. From Damasio, your feelings were altered by the encounter with Mary, your internal milieu was thrown out of balance, and suddenly you became aware that something was amiss. It is at this level—at the level of RIGs, working models, imaged representations, and rerepresented images—that Stern's outside-in observations join Damasio's inside-out observations.

I want next to focus on a piece of the intersection of the two models of core self-development during infancy and tie together a few of the strands. This requires going back to Stern's notion of the subjective sense of self. That is the self that engages in the "domain of intersubjective relatedness." To repeat an earlier quotation, Stern writes: "At this stage, for the first time, one can attribute to the infant the capacity for psychic intimacy— the openness to disclosure, the permeability of interpenetrability of boundaries that occurs between two people."[11] This is the same stage of self-development when, according to Damasio, the infant's brain has achieved the capacity of imaging changes in its life-regulatory processes in the course of interacting with an external object. At this point, it doesn't matter whose language we use. RIGs, *running imaged accounts, internal representations,* or *working models;* any or all of these terms refer to variations of the same phenomenon of the infant recording instances when its feelings are changed when-with another person.

It is important to remember that these developments take place in childhood *before* the arrival of the verbal self. The verbal self (a self that Damasio calls the *extended* self) is the objective, empirical, stand-alone self—the "me" who is writing these words as he envisions other "mes" reading them. Before that "me" emerges—before Sam recognized Sam in the mirror—the infant's subjective self is experienced primarily by virtue of feelings that are altered during interactions with others. This is particularly so throughout the stage of infant attachment. It is a stage of "interaffectivity," in Stern's language.[12] It is a stage when mother and infant share affective states, dance their harmonious dances, and relish each other's company. *It is also a stage when the infant has no sense of subjective self outside its relationships.* A subjective self that is never altered does not exist. It resides solely in the domain of relatedness and thrives during periods of involvement in cocreating mutual experiences with the love object. For the child, inner experiences of security and well-being accompany the merger of two subjective selves, its own and that of its primary caretaker. As Stern describes the situation, "it is only with the advent of intersubjectivity that anything like the joining of subjective experience can actually occur."[13]

As I discussed earlier, the security associated with episodes of experiences of oneness with the mother need not be restricted to times when she is in the child's presence. Memories of past self-with-mother episodes of oneness can be evoked in her absence. RIGs, in Stern's language, or *imaged representations,* in Damasio's, are available as running record accounts of being-with mother. They can be evoked at will. In fact, they may arrive on their own accord without any effort on the part of the child. The spontaneous retrieval of memories that carry with them feelings of inner peace and harmony makes it possible for the child to never feel alone. In other words, gratifying past self-with experiences are "internalized," making it possible for the child to endure periods when the (subjective) self-sustaining object is not physically present.

Such internalized working models that summarize past experiences of psychic wholeness with a nurturing figure, particularly an attachment object, require reinforcement from time to time. As I said earlier, it makes no sense to retain a working model that doesn't work—a working model that no longer pertains to anything "real." The child's recalled running record account of past episodes of "safe haven" experiences, an account that includes the major features of the external environment and the feelings of security that accompany them, periodically must be confirmed. The child anticipates confirmation on a regular basis because that has been more or less the case throughout the mounting months of its existence.

But what happens when reality no longer confirms a working model? Consider the following example. When I go to my car, place the key in the ignition, and turn the switch, I expect the engine to turn on. My implicit working model of that process dictates that that is how it will be. This working model of what it takes to start my car has been confirmed so many times, thousands of times, that it guides my actions automatically and enables me to think not about this but about anything that is currently on my mind when I enter the vehicle. But then a time comes when my working model is not confirmed. The engine does not engage, and the car won't start. That is when I become conscious of my working model of how to start my car and the discrepancy between its instructions and what just happened. Am I in the right car? Yes, it's my car. I check to see if I inserted the correct key. No problem with the key. Maybe the steering wheel is locked. I jiggle it, but it's already loose. That initiates a process familiar to many drivers. It is annoying and it may even end up being costly. The main thing I want is for my car to fit my picture of one that starts. However, I know I am going to survive in the face of it all. It might take several days of diagnostics and repair work to get my car back into shape, or I may even have to scrap it because the 250,000 miles of service it has provided me has brought it to its doom. Again, although my car might not make it, I will. The sense of "self" that extends into my possessions may be slightly frustrated and tarnished, but it will recover, and the day that my car didn't start will become a bland, inconsequential memory that, given some time, will lose any remnants of its original affective charge.

The discrepancy between my working model of a car that starts and the clunker that did not behave according to my prediction is trivial compared to the experiences of a child whose self-with-mother working model fails to predict reality. Working models derived from episodes of intersubjective relatedness are essential for the maintenance of the child's subjective self. The survival of Stern's subjective self, or Damasio's core self, can be experienced as being at risk when there is a sudden and persistent failure of reality to match primary features of the internal working models of the subjective self in good hands. Remember, this domain of self precedes the verbal or extended self, the stand-alone, individuated "me." Generally speaking, there are only hints of an individuated "me" in the works during the phase of subjective self-development. During that phase the child *is* its subjective self. It *is* the self—embedded in its relationships. That self can survive for some period of time by means of the child privately recalling previous experiences of intimate interactions if, and only if, the self-with working model is periodically validated. By that I mean that the features of the "real" environment must conform sufficiently well with the features of the internalized model at least some of the time in order to assure the survival of the model—but, more than that, the survival of the subjective self. If the model begins to collapse, if the "toolbox"[14] of affective consciousness is damaged, the sense of self-coherence will be placed at risk. As I said earlier, these events signal the potential end of an organized internal world, and feelings of utter panic take over.

What can a child do under such dire circumstances? One thing it can do is to attempt to change the environment into a configuration that comes closer to matching internal images of scenes that accompanied feelings associated with safety, of times when the child was experiencing no risk to its well-being. If reality can be transformed in a way that more accurately fits the child's internalized picture, then, once again, all will be right with the world, the internal milieu can relax, and the subjective self will survive. Another strategy is to create an imaginary world and reify it as a source of restorative power. Both options involve the fantasy that if the feelings associated with previous experiences of oneness—previous experiences of unity or psychic fusion with a love object—then the subjective self will resume its proper place of residence.

In the next chapter, I will demonstrate how these ideas enrich our understanding of the panic experienced by Jamie Barrie when his mother no longer smiled in the way that had previously served as a primary cue for the activation of feelings associated with the survival of his subjective sense of self. I will also apply them to the consternation experienced by Carl Jung when his mother suddenly vanished and for a period of time was not available as a reassuring presence to validate his sense of self. A major difference between Barrie and Jung was that Barrie never gave up on the prospects of restoring an earlier sense of self that had been contingent on a smile on his mother's face and the feelings of security that smile had once brought about. Jung went in another direction. Figuring that his unreliable mother would never again play her part in ways that fit his internal picture of a partner in pleasurable self-other coregulations, he invented another mother, an all-encompassing, life-sustaining, self-sustaining mother, for the purpose of replenishing his subjective sense of self. Fantasies of flight—the ethereal sense of weightlessness, for Jung; the ability attributed to Peter Pan to wing his way back to his mother's bedroom, for Barrie— were derivatives of desperate efforts to restore experiences of oneness, of psychic experiences of boundless merger to which the law of gravity does not apply. If the feelings associated with being lifted into a mother's loving arms, of sleeping comfortably on her shoulder, of the elation that once accompanied experiences of intersubjective harmony could be recovered, then time could be suspended, and all of the elements contained in previous running record imaged accounts of a thriving subjective self might magically be restored.

EIGHTEEN *What's Missing from this Picture?*

I have now introduced new tools for understanding why Jamie Barrie, the child, and J. M. Barrie, the adult, was so obsessed with bringing a smile to Margaret Ogilvy's face, and why Carl Jung reacted so strongly to his mother's absence. Both of them, at critical times in their development, experienced such traumatic discrepancies between their internal self-with-mother representations and what reality suddenly presented them that they scrambled to somehow restore conditions (or cues) that had previously evoked a sense of (subjective) self-continuity and thereby calm disturbances in their internal milieus. In both cases, the most familiar, prominent, and reassuring cue associated with core self safety was the mother. In Jamie's case, Margaret continued to be a physical presence in the family home, but the former Margaret—the smiling, cheerful, comforting Margaret—had taken a permanent leave of absence. Three-year-old Carl's mother simply vanished. Although her departure lasted only a few months, he made a critical decision during that interval. He decided to never trust either his mother or any other person to serve as a reliable coregulating partner capable of providing him with a sense of self-unity. Restorative efforts were required on the parts of both young boys, and Jung had to look outside his home.

In the previous chapter, I described three restorative strategies. One is to endeavor to get the external world to adjust itself in ways that conform to one's internal pictures of a safe environment. J. M. Barrie specialized in that choice. Another avenue for restoring earlier conditions of intersubjective harmony involves giving up all hope of getting the "real world" to behave itself and instead inventing an "imaginary world" that would do the

trick. Carl Jung selected that path. A third option, one that is not neces-
sarily independent of the other two, is based on the nonconscious fantasy
that if one were to succeed in recreating the feelings of earlier sensations
of oneness, new life would magically be brought to the imprints etched
into working models of former glorious times. This chapter begins with a
discussion of the first strategy: the attempt to modify features of the external world in ways that fit previously encoded internal pictures.

SMILE, DAMN IT, SMILE

There are places in my psychobiography of Barrie where I suggested that
he had no self to bring into the world. That was misleading. Of course he
had a self. He had a name and he used that name. He had an identity—
several identities, in fact. He was an author of articles, books, and plays.
He was a man from Scotland, a man short in stature, and an avid cricket
fan. He owned a dog and owned a house (several of them). He was a married man for fifteen years. He had an immense influence on literature at
the turn of the twentieth century. He was well traveled, a sought-after guest
of world leaders. He was referred to as *Sir* James Barrie after he received
his nation's highest honor. It is absurd to say that he had no self.

Now that a distinction has been made between the verbal self (the empirical self, the "me") and the subjective self, my exploration can be more
focused. It was at the level of a *subjective* sense of self that Barrie suffered.
Recall that the empirical self (Stern's verbal self, Damasio's extended self)
is progressively layered on the intersubjective core self that predates its development. That does not mean that the empirical self replaces or takes
over the functions of the core subjective self. Core consciousness still
monitors the internal condition of the body. It remains faithful to its duties
to manage and seek to stabilize alterations in preferred states of balance.
Under the condition of a pronounced threat to core self-survival it never
ceases its attempts to fix the problem. Much of Barrie's life can be understood in terms of his various efforts to repair a nonverbal self that could not
be fixed. Ironically, had he been able to heal his wounds and restore a
sense of inner harmony, I doubt that Peter Pan would have ever flown into
existence.

Barrie described his mother as a "happy" woman "placed on earth by
God to open minds of all who looked to beautiful thoughts." She had descended from Heaven to look after him. He counted on her to "be-with"
him, to comfort him, and to provide a secure intersubjective base for his
core self-development. Then her son, David, died from a head injury, and
Margaret was never the same as before. The formerly "happy" woman was
consumed by sadness. She became a morose figure, preoccupied with
grief over the loss of her beloved son. Barrie wrote: "I knew my mother for-

ever now." What did he mean by that? I believe that Damasio's theory of consciousness may assist us in answering that question. Consciousness, according to Damasio, arrives when we "know" that we "know" that something has been altered. The "something" that was most dramatically altered was Margaret. She was literally transformed, then and forever more, when David died. Another important alteration took place in reaction to Margaret's grief. That alteration occurred inside Jamie, whose feelings were altered when he observed unfamiliar expressions on her face and heard moans emanating from her bed. Following Damasio's lead, one could say that Jamie's awareness that his feelings had changed led to his conscious recognition that an important component of the external world had been altered.

A prerequisite for the onset of awareness that something in the external world has changed is a shift in feelings, and if that shift is sufficiently pronounced, there is a good chance that the alteration will be consciously registered. This formulation makes for interesting lunchtime discussions. But it is much more than a topic of stimulating intellectual play when a person's ongoing subjective sense of existence is called into question by the conscious recognition that something has changed. Jamie's sense of subjective selfhood depended on Margaret being a certain way. His attachment to his mother had been particularly strong—peculiarly strong, one could say, in light of the fact that he was six years old when David died. Under normal circumstances, six-year-old children have established a degree of separateness from their parents. They remain reliant on them for food, shelter, reassurance, and guidance, but their lives have expanded in ways that expose them to other relationships that take the heat off the one or two primary relationships. New players (siblings, other relatives, neighborhood children) who are ready and willing to engage in "coregulating" activities become available. Most children are able to establish new friendships, to seek and find new "objects" with whom they can dance on the stage of shared emotional involvements before the age of six.[1]

But, as noted in chapter 11, attachment is not a problem unless it's a problem. For Jamie Barrie, attachment was a problem. When Barrie was in his sixties, he wrote: "I could not grow up." That statement can be understood in the context of his repetitious efforts to secure an overall sense of self that, prior to its demise, had been experienced as organized, coherent, and stable. Until some semblance of order could be recovered, he could not grow up because there was no credible foundation for future self-development. What had been had disappeared, and he was desperate to bring it back. It suffered its demise when Margaret's physical reaction to David's death resulted in her no longer being available to validate Jamie's internal working model of conditions surrounding experiences of intersubjective union with her. His me-with-Mom internal representation of previous merger experiences collapsed like a house of cards, taking his sense of subjective self along with it. In his scramble to resurrect experiences of felt safety, he fastened his attention to one feature of his surroundings, a "linked companion," in Stern's words, that earlier had been a key element associated with feelings of intersubjective harmony. That one feature was Margaret's smile. If he could get that smile back onto her face, his intersubjective self could make a joyous return. Margaret's smile had become the primary visual cue associated with her emotional availability. It had become a prominent feature of his running record imaged account of a welcoming mother whose internalized presence had provided him with on-the-spot comfort and the reassuring confidence that enabled him to explore the world outside of her immediate company. The self-validating smile that validated Jamie's self, and all that had come with it, had to return. It was Jamie's only hope for recovering a coherent sense of self.

"So, sitting on the rail at the foot of her bed, [Peter Pan] played a lullaby on this pipe and he never stopped playing until his mother looked happy," Barrie wrote in *The Little White Bird*. This literary scene brilliantly captures what Jamie tried to do at this mother's bedside. Denis Mackail, Barrie's biographer, writes: "And Jamie would do anything— anything on Heaven or earth—to get that look off her face."[2] The look Mackail refers to was the look of pain and sadness that had supplanted her smile. Of course, Jamie wanted to remove that look because he wanted his mother to feel better. He loved her and he wanted her to recover her ability to enjoy life. It is called compassion. But compassion for his mother was not the sole source of his concern. Margaret's feelings had been permanently altered by David's death, and her consternation reverberated into the core of her younger son's existence. Just as David had been shut out of her life, she shut Jamie out of hers. "What about me?" he called out, "Do you no longer care about me?" We can now think of that "me" as his subjective sense of self. All of the cues he had counted on to evoke a sense of well-being had vanished. David had died, and psychologically Jamie died as a result. So he set to work in the project of getting Margaret to smile. On the rare occasions he succeeded, he ran to his sister so she could witness the miracle. But when they got to Margaret's bedroom, her face would be wet again and she would call out for David. Jamie carried a pad and pencil with him to keep a record of the number of times Margaret smiled. Days went by when no marks were placed on a page.

In a moment of inspiration, Jamie decided that if it is David you want, it will be David you get. So he practiced being David. He worked on replicating the way David used to stand with his legs apart and his hands in his pockets, and rehearsed his cheery whistle. On the day of his performance, he donned his brother's clothes and entered his mother's dark room. Barrie did not report on Margaret's reaction, but if it brightened her mood, the cure had no lasting effect. However, the idea of being someone else stayed with Jamie. Perhaps he could fill the vacancy caused by the disap-

pearance of his intersubjective self by internalizing another person's subjective experiences. A borrowed or hand-me-down subjective self is better
than none at all. Here is an example of a borrowed one. Barrie recalled a
time when a friend of his was so distraught about a death in his family that
he didn't feel up to participating in outdoor games. Jamie volunteered to
grieve for his friend, to take on his sadness, and thereby enable his companion to play in a trouble-free state of mind. So Jamie sat on the sidelines
crying as his friend ran about with other children.

As remarkable as that was, it was merely a tune-up for an even more
remarkable exercise of Jamie's imitative skills. Over the course of many
days, weeks, months, and years, he sat by his mother's bedside as she regaled him with stories of her childhood. Mackail writes that Jamie "doesn't
only listen to her stories but . . . he struggles to enter into them until he
virtually succeeds."[3] As Margaret related her childhood memories to her
son, Jamie imagined what it would have been like to be the little girl who
had become his mother. As a rule, we generate running imaged accounts
of our own experiences. In this instance, it appears that Jamie created running imaged accounts of his mother's "secondary" (talked-about) running
record imaged accounts of her experiences. Margaret's hand-me-down
subjective self served as an internalized substitute for thoughts whose
"rightful owner was missing."[4] Jamie's mental images of the girl his mother
described to him were so vivid that he became acquainted with and developed personal relationships with characters who had been prominent for
his mother during her early years. He imagined himself as the "little girl in
a magenta frock and white pinafore dress . . . singing to herself, carrying
her father's flagon." He sat in on religious debates of the village elders, and
"witnessed" history-making storms that had heaped snow against doorways
many years before his birth. "I have seen many on-dings of snow, but the
one I seem to recall best occurred nearly twenty years before my birth."[5]

To borrow Barrie's term for a moment, I have never encountered a
more "on-ding" example of a person internalizing the subjective self of another person and making it his own. One might say that Jamie "incorpo-
rated" his mother's memories of her childhood in an effort to fill the
vacancy caused by the destruction of his core sense of self. Some psychoanalytic psychologists refer to this process as "swallowing the object," but
that idea strikes me as an unfortunate and obscure summary of the
gradual, day-by-day process of Jamie imagining what it would be like to
have been the child his mother described to him and then becoming that
child. Margaret, or, more accurately, a subjective Margaret whom Jamie
had never known, was internally installed, piece by piece, story by story, as
the next best option in the face of his failed attempts to get her to smile.
The "new" subjective self acted as a replacement part that served Barrie
reasonably well. Although it had no capacity to coregulate his feelings, it
did a good job as coauthor of his books. In the end, of course, it was a poor

substitute for the "old" self that had been lost. His internal working model of earlier times when the now vanquished subjective self had once flourished in the flow of its merger with Margaret never gave up. Jamie the child and James the adult continued to return to Margaret's bedside for the purpose of checking to see if the smile had returned. Until the very end of Margaret's life, Barrie never ceased his efforts to bring his subjective self back to life and make it resume its proper position. It seemed that the only way that could happen was to restore cues that evoked feelings of being united with the "object" that had been essential to core self-survival.

Of course, there was no hope of getting Margaret to smile after her death. One would think that the game was finished. Fortunately for the generations of children (and adults for that matter) who have enjoyed Peter Pan, Margaret's death resulted in a fantasy enactment of the script that had taken Barrie back to her bedside for twenty-nine years. One year after Margaret was buried, Peter Pan, half human, half bird, was released from the "little box" inside his creator. His first mission was to fly to his mother's bedroom to check on the expression of her face. Peter Pan came into existence as a new edition of Barrie's mission to restore a sense of self. Although Peter could not provide a solution to the problem of restoring a sense of self, he did provide a base for Barrie's involvement with Sylvia's boys, as well as a character for later elaboration in a story and a play that made Sir James a wealthy man.

THE COLLECTIVE UNCONSCIOUS AS A SUBSTITUTE MOTHER

James Barrie's lifetime project was to reconstitute his sense of subjective self by getting his mother's face to fit the picture of the face that had been etched into his childhood working model as the primary cue that all was well. Carl Jung charted a different course. He not only cleared the path for himself, but he did it for countless others who seek to unite with a force reminiscent of something residing in the shadows of a former life. That something is a feeling, a feeling of being connected to a life-sustaining substance. Objectively, it is impossible to pin down. Subjectively, one senses, it is real.

Carl gave up on his mother. When she packed her bags and stepped off the porch, she took a part of her son with her. In the language I have been using to describe this phenomenon, one could say his mother had been so embedded in his working model of conditions surrounding an intersubjective sense of wellness that his running-record-imaged-account "blissful" states of internal homeostasis were jolted into consciousness. What was missing in that picture was not a smile but an entire person. Even though she eventually returned, the damage was done.

Jung was propelled into a lifelong search for an entity that could restore his shaky sense of subjective existence. He found it. Hints of its presence came to him in a childhood dream when it appeared as an underground God seated on a throne. He feared that it might devour him, and still he was drawn to it. It continued to return in other guises and other forms as reminders that his socially constructed, empirical "me" (Personality No. 1) was living a rootless existence. However, if he surrendered to the seductive force of the Other and permitted Personality No. 2 to merge with it, No. 1 would have no resources to cope with reality.

As I discussed at considerable length in chapter 16, Jung's quest to revitalize a sense of self that once existed by virtue of its coexistence with another object was partially realized during a series of visions wherein he was flooded with inspiring sensations of being lifted up, of flying above the world, and being able to look down on the world from the position of the sun, the moon, and the stars. Now tell me, after all that, who needs a mother?

This concludes my application of my recovery-of-early-feelings theory of levitation fantasies to the lives of Barrie and Jung. The reader may have noticed some circularity to this undertaking, in that I derived the theory, in part, from studying these two men, and then I doubled back in order to show how well the theory fit them. This pattern of circular reasoning can be partially broken by applying the theory to different cases. I will deal with none of the case studies or the few incidental phenomena I will touch on in the final part of book in as much detail as I have with Barrie and Jung. Instead, I will now explore the question of whether there is sufficient evidence that the effort to restore an early sense of intersubjective harmony with a maternal figure is a theme that cuts across an array of expressions of the wish to fly.

PART IV *Variations*

on a Theme

NINETEEN *Dumbo*

Academic psychologists take their work very seriously. Science requires discipline, attention to details, and a ruthless dedication to a set of rigorous standards for confirming or disconfirming propositions. Normally, I pledge my allegiance to these standards and promote in my courses the importance of learning about methods for investigating psychological phenomena. But I also feel an obligation to keep the students in my courses awake. Relying on a belief that it is okay to have fun at work, I occasionally refer to fairy tales in my lectures. "Our Lady's Child," contained in a volume of the Grimm brothers' collections of German lore, is one of my favorites.[1] Its rich symbolism makes it a delightful text on which students can exercise their skills in interpreting prose from different theoretical perspectives. Sometimes word slips out that Ogilvie is doing it again, and some of my most valued colleagues openly mourn the disservice I am doing both to the discipline of psychology and to the minds of the three to four hundred students in an auditorium. I defend my habit by asserting that it is only an illustrative ploy. My "I'll keep their interests up and then you can train them" response to their objections does little to alleviate their concerns.

In this chapter I continue my habit of illustrating a set of ideas by applying them to a story: a modern fairy tale called *Dumbo, the Flying Elephant*. The following notations on some of the main elements in this well-known story provide a venue for my reiteration of the observations I have made earlier about the coincidence of imaginary flight and maternal separation. This analysis of the story is not offered as "proof" of anything that has been said. Regard it as an exercise, a way to consolidate some gains, or a vehicle of transition from the realm of theory to the realm of application.

The original story of Dumbo, written by Helen Aberson and Harold Pearl, was further developed by five writers for an animated film that was produced by the Walt Disney Studios in 1941. The fact that the movie and the children's book printed under the same title were scripted by a *group* of writers and further embellished by cartoonists precludes any attempt to link the fantasy to a constellation of concerns of any one person as I did with Peter Pan and J. M. Barrie. Instead, I will stay within the boundaries of the story per se and see if there are some familiar elements in it. My assumption is that the writers and animators employed by Disney to make money for his company managed to package a product that provided auditory and visual expressions of some experiences and concerns of generations of children. Had the movie not struck such chords, it would have been a flop.

In the Disney version, Dumbo's troubles began at the very outset of the story. The stork that had delivered a large number of babies to the circus animals lost count, and for a day it appeared that Mrs. Jumbo would be childless. Finally the errant stork got things straightened out, and Dumbo was delivered to his proud mother. "So cute!" declared the other elephants, until little Dumbo sneezed and revealed his abnormally large ears. "Freak!" shouted the women who seconds before had praised his appearance.

The ridicule heaped on Dumbo served to redouble the strength of Mrs. Jumbo's love and devotion to her child. She protected him by shutting the partition of her section of a railroad car so that Dumbo could not be seen, and thereafter did everything she could to keep him out of harm's way. In fact, it was her overzealous protection of him that forced them to part company. That occurred in the aftermath of Dumbo stumbling on his oversized ears during the traditional parade announcing the circus's arrival into a town. A boy in the crowd seized on that opportunity to taunt the baby elephant. In a fit of maternal rage, Mrs. Jumbo grabbed the boy by her trunk and lifted the frightened youth into the air. She returned him safely to the ground, but her actions were sufficient for her to be declared mad. The awful consequence was that she was isolated from the rest of the circus animals, including Dumbo, and imprisoned in a cage with heavy chains attached to her legs. Dumbo was now forced to cope on his own with a world of rejecting others. There were no elephant child labor laws to protect him from the abuse that ensued.

Circus officials tried various ways to incorporate Dumbo into circus acts, but his youth, his incompetence, and especially his pathetically large ears prevented him from fitting in. One humiliation followed another until finally Dumbo's clumsiness resulted in the grand collapse of the Big Top tent. The tragedy was the source of such embarrassment to the rest of the elephants that they took the solemn vow that Dumbo would no longer be considered to be an elephant. To be mocked about one's appearance and awkwardness is one thing, but to be excluded from one's own species is quite another. The icing on that cake, as if it needed any icing, was the fact that Dumbo had no one to turn to for comfort. Like Peter Pan's mother, Mrs. Dumbo was behind bars, albeit a quite different set of bars.

Another torture was in store for Dumbo after various failed attempts to integrate him into elephant acts. It was an "Icarian" torture, in that it contained the four main elements of the myth: rising, fire, falling, and water. He was forced into a company of clowns who invented a crowd-pleasing skit that took advantage of and further mocked his odd appearance. Dumbo was painted as a clown and placed on the top floor of a building that was set on fire. Clowns pretended to try to put the fire out, but, in accordance with the script, they were unable to extinguish the flames. As a consequence, every performance reached its climax when Dumbo had to jump from a tower into a safety net. Of course, the net was porous and barely broke Dumbo's fall into a tub of water that was hidden beneath it. As the roaring laughter of the audience continued, a wet, lonely, and abandoned elephant child went his dispirited way.

What Dumbo needed was a companion, a chum who would serve not only as a friend but also as a guide. Timothy, a vagabond mouse, enters as the unlikely guru to fill that role. This is the story's first indication that Dumbo was destined to become a hero. Timothy issued what Joseph Campbell[2] terms a "call to adventure" that Dumbo did not refuse. Less heroic elephants would have not been able to resist their "instinctive" aversion to the tiny rodent, but Dumbo was desperate for some kind, any kind, of relationship.

The first stage of the adventure involved a trip to his mother's cage. It was a risky trek because all were aware visiting Mrs. Jumbo was not allowed. Despite the heavy odds of being caught for violating this rock-hard circus rule, Timothy arranged for Dumbo to temporarily visit his imprisoned mom in the dark of night. The tone of this heartrending, tearful reunion was set when Mrs. Jumbo managed to drag the metal balls chained to her legs across the floor so that she could get close enough to the bars to stick out her trunk and gently lift and rock her lonely and emotionally destitute son for a few brief moments. These moments were precious ones, however, because (one might speculate) they reminded Dumbo of the feelings of weightlessness that had been associated with his mother's care.

Timothy interrupts the ecstasy by reminding Dumbo that it was time to go, lest he be caught and punished by the authorities. When Timothy and Dumbo leave, they pass a tent occupied by the clowns, who are engaged in a drunken celebration over the success of their outrageous skit. At Timothy's suggestion, both he and Dumbo secretly sample some alcohol that had spilled from beneath the tent's flap. The next morning, after an elaborate dream in which all sorts of creatures fly, Dumbo awakens in the branches of a tree.

How had he managed to get there? The leader of a gang of crows speculated that he must have flown by flapping his ears. But everyone, including Dumbo, knows that elephants can't fly; everyone, that is, except Timothy and the crows. To replicate his nighttime feat, all Dumbo needed was confidence. To that end, they give him a feather to hold in his trunk. The feather served as a Supernatural Aid for his aerial voyages. Without its magical powers, he believed he could not become and remain airborne.

Soon the time arrived for another show, and Dumbo was prepared to reap his revenge. Dressed and painted as a clown, he was placed on his perch. The routine fire was started, the hoses were shown to be ineffective, and Dumbo was instructed to leap into the net. The feather amulet slipped from his trunk just as he began his descent, but quick-thinking Timothy, who was riding on his back, told him it was merely a crutch and he could fly on his own. Thereby, to the amazement of a stunned audience, Dumbo flew around the inside of the tent, dive-bombed the clowns, and sent others who had tormented him for cover. His aerial feats made him an instant local hero and soon thereafter an international star.

The moral of the story is things work out well for those who find ways to make use of their inborn capacities. Instead of lamenting your imperfections and surrendering to the forces of shame, ignore the taunts and transform those so-called defects into astonishing abilities that no others can match. That, I suspect, is the primary message of the story. It is intended to exorcise the ugly duckling feelings that erode the confidence of children and to replace despair with hope.

But there is another feature of the story that I want to comment on. At the end, Mrs. Jumbo returns . There she is, seated in the back of the train, pleased as punch, as she witnesses her baby flying overhead. Flight did the trick. It brought Dumbo's mother back to him. He regained her full attention, as well as gaining the attention of all who gazed upon him. He had entered a state of pure Being and, in doing so, recaptured the aura of having once been "so cute." Through flight, he reinstated the "epiphanal" moment of birth when others glorified his presence. Writing about Grope, Henry Murray called it "cynosural narcissism," the desire to attract and enchant all eyes.[3] Rising "like a star in the firmament" approximates the feelings of being lifted up and held as an object of glowing wonderment for others to behold.

I doubt that the authors of Dumbo had this latent theme in mind when they wrote the story. It may have been a matter of simple convenience or literary happenstance that Dumbo's mother materialized after he realized his ability to fly. But the threads are there for tying, and the convergence of crosscutting themes that I visited in previous chapters are too enticing to let them pass by unnoticed.

The next chapter expands on the theme of flight as a means of going back to better times. A young man I have named Larry replaces the fictional Dumbo in a story of nighttime voyages into the sky.

TWENTY *Larry, a Lonely Long-Distance Runner*

To recapitulate my working theory regarding the genesis of flying fantasies: it is postulated that imaginary flight originates from a desire to recapture feelings of being the object of the devoted care and attention of the mother. These images are expressions of latent, impossible-to-verbalize yearnings for the reestablishment of a subjective sense of self that was acquired during a period of core-relatedness with a devoted caretaker before trouble set in. The "trouble" encountered thus far in this exploration is a sense of maternal abandonment at a time when the child's "experience of being" still hinges on the mother's willingness and ability to provide the physical and emotional security that matches what the child has learned to anticipate from being connected with a secure environment. Mrs. Jumbo could no longer provide her protective services when she was jailed. Nor could Carl Jung's mother when she was hospitalized. And Jamie Barrie failed in his efforts to restore Margaret Ogilvy's smile, which he had subjectively associated with being a person of worth prior to David's death. These growth-stopping events led Jung, Barrie, and the fictional Dumbo to attempt to restore the feelings of spiritual togetherness that had been such a natural part of their lives before they were forced to surrender to the weight of Earth's gravity. Life became hard after the smooth quality of their relationships was disrupted. A critical chunk of how they had come to know the world and its consistency was suddenly missing, and they wanted it back. They sought to recapture the sensations that had accompanied feelings of being in a dyad relationship with the mother. I suggest that imaginary flight comes about as part of an attempt to restore sensations of being lifted up, of rising effortlessly and being securely carried about in the arms of an adoring caregiver. Goodness, a sense of well-being, and feelings of timeless continuity that counteracts the demise of intersubjective coexistence is to be found "up there." If one could fly, life's pains could be left behind and a magical kingdom of pleasurable body sensations associated with infancy would be resurrected. As written in the psalm: "Oh that I had wings like a dove, for then I would fly away and be at rest."

That's where my theory now stands, and it needs to be held in a manner that does not preclude alternative perspectives, because in the process of seeking evidence for this or any other theory there is a temptation to select information that supports it and to ignore information that contradicts it. In fact, the situation is trickier than that. People want to be right about their ideas. I want to show that the emergent theory of dreams and fantasies of levitation has the power to provide insight into the phenomenon. I want my argument to be convincing, lest I become the laughing-stock of colleagues who have wondered what in the world I have been doing during the period when dust was building up in my lab. I want to demonstrate that I have uncovered a fundamental truth about the latent source of imaginary flight, and in the process of doing so, there is the danger of my having set up a straw man named Sigmund Freud for the purpose of showing that my theory of the latent meanings of levitation fantasies carries more explanatory power than his.

Under such conditions, one can be blindsided by being so committed to a theory or a set of beliefs that one sets about picking and choosing information that can be shaped and molded into a hardened form. This is the major drawback of idiographic studies. Just as one can locate passages in the Bible or other religious texts that seem to support one's beliefs, it is nearly always possible to pore over case study materials and find something close to what you are looking for.

In this instance, I am now on the alert for information that confirms a growing conviction that a disruption of maternal care is a core ingredient for giving birth to imaginary flight. The problem is that it is possible to find evidence that virtually every person has experienced less than fully harmonious interpersonal relationships with their primary caregivers. In other words, if an investigator wants to score a victory by documenting that a case study research "subject" had at one or another time been disappointed by his or her mother, the victory is guaranteed. Statements to that effect can be pried out of most respondents as a last resort, in the absence of conforming autobiographic memories or a theme in a spontaneous story told to a TAT card or other data gathering-devices.

That is one of the reasons why psychobiographical studies are viewed with such suspicion in the field of psychology. Nothing can be proven. Two investigators who study the life of the same individual can create two quite different, equally plausible accounts of that person's life. The winner is likely to be the one who creates the most appealing package. This dilemma can be avoided by studying variables instead of people. Variables can be measured by rating scales or other standard devices. Measurements are converted to scores, hard numbers, which are then compared with other scores, other hard numbers, and the complexities of human behavior are thereby reduced to statistical results that are potentially replicable by anyone who follows the same procedures. In several respects, this is an enlightened alternative to the nearly unsolvable quandary of how to validate the results of case studies. The problem with the alternative is that it places restrictions on the kinds of phenomena that can be studied. The field of personality psychology is loaded up with facts about what traits tend to go together, how extroverts differ from introverts, how stereotypes are formed and what functions they serve, and hundreds of other "in general" or "on average" pieces of useful information. But the objectivity that is required for accruing this knowledge about human behavior is unsuited to the task of understanding the internal worlds of swarming subjective experiences where so much of our meaning-making activity takes place. I have granted myself a temporary license to enter this cavern of subjectivity and to drag some others with me to see if these chambers contain some worthwhile secrets. In doing so, I need to be aware of the prospect of finding only what I seek and exaggerating it to the point of taking it as proof of my preconceived interpretation.

THE CASE OF LARRY

There is no danger of having to comb through the information Larry told me about himself to see if a time could be discovered when his relationship with his mother was disrupted. She committed suicide when he was four years old. Larry was the oldest of four children, and his mother was pregnant with a fifth child when she took her life. The family lived in Texas near the border with Mexico. Larry's father was Spanish and his mother was Caucasian. His father worked on an oil rig and was away from home for several weeks at a time. After Larry's mother discovered that she was again pregnant, she desperately sought to have the fetus aborted. Larry's father was strongly opposed to the idea and solicited the assistance of the local Catholic priest and several members of his extended family to persuade her to keep the baby. A brother-in-law, whom Larry's father had asked to keep an eye on his wife while he was at sea, found the mother's lifeless body in her bedroom; she had taken an overdose.

Twelve years later, Larry lived in New Jersey with his six siblings, his father, and his stepmother. Although the family had moved several times, Larry had maintained commendable grade point averages in the various high schools he had attended. He was "college material," according to his school counselor, who also knew that Larry's above-average long-distance running skills could feasibly position him for a scholarship. However, Larry's track coach became concerned about him. His running times were up (up is bad in this instance) from his junior year, and he had begun to skip some practices. His tendency to keep to himself had become even more noticeable, and the school counselor attributed his condition to depression. Larry attributed it to a "heavy load of loneliness."

An acquaintance of mine who knew Larry's family asked me if I could speak with him about his college options. It is assumed that professors, even those who have no college admissions experiences, know about such things. Begging limited knowledge about what Larry's options might be, I agreed to speak with him anyway. But Larry didn't want to talk about college when he came to my office to see me. He wanted to talk about something else. First, however, he wanted assurance that I was not a therapist. I told him that I was interested in a field that was close to clinical psychology, but I did not have the credentials necessary to conduct therapy. He was relieved to hear that and asked about the kinds of things I did. I gave him a brief tour of my "lab," which at the time consisted of a large table with piles of paper on it, a couple of chairs, and a folding easy chair that I told him I used to take secret ten-minute naps. He thought that was pretty funny, and went on to tell me that he was having trouble sleeping. New editions of an old dream kept waking him up. He was so tired during the day that he did not have the energy to run. He felt guilty about letting down his coach, but he saw no alternative.

It turned out that Larry wanted to talk, and he did so for several hours. He also wanted to come back under what I suspected was a pretense of learning more about what I did. How could an advocate of case studies close the door to that kind of opportunity? Particularly after Larry had informed me that the new edition of past recurring dream involved flying. The following is a summary of what I learned about the latent meaning of dreams of flying from Larry.

At age four, after his mother's tragic death, Larry began to have nightmares. In his words:

> What's interesting is that it was always the same dream and I still remember it vividly. I am soaring through the sky like a bird looking for something, and I have no control over myself. I climb to terrific heights and drop like a dive-bomber. It's scary but I'm all right until, on the last dive, I look down and see a telephone pole right in my path and I can't get out of the way. I would usually wake up screaming.

His nightmare continued for over a year, as far as he could recall, and occurred during a period of time when his vision deteriorated. He said that everything became cloudy and he could only clearly see objects a foot or two from his eyes. After around six months, normal vision was restored, and by age six his nightmares had subsided. Now he was worried by the fact that images of himself flying had returned to disturb his sleep. Brick buildings and other hard, immovable objects had replaced the telephone poles that had previously gotten into his path.

I took Larry's interest in my work to heart and showed him a few tools of the life study trade. He showed special interest in the TAT cards I handed him and looked through the entire set of twenty pictures. I asked him to select a few cards that captured his fancy and to tell me a story to each one. He granted me permission to tape-record the six stories he told. The first card he selected was number 11. It depicts a road skirting a deep chasm between high cliffs. On the road in the distance are obscure figures. Protruding form the rocky wall on one side is a long head and neck of a dragon. Larry omitted any mention of the dragon in his story, a long story that warrants careful reading. The following is a transcript of it.

> Well, this is an archaeologist sort of type and he's made a discovery. One summer he was working in Peru, in the Andes, and he was going along the footpaths on the top of the Andes. And he made this wrong turn so to speak. He just sort of got a little lost. And he thrashed into the underbrush and he came upon what seemed to be a narrow stone paved road. He started to follow it and decided to come back later and follow it. He was in no condition to explore it now. When he did come back [it was] with a full expedition, equipped to spend several weeks out in the underbrush in the foothills of the Andes. And a . . . well it was a very small party, he really only had a couple of people with him. He wasn't sure what he would find but he remembered something in the researches he had done on some of the ancient tales of ancient walled fortresses. Yes, that's it, ancient walled fortresses. And he started. It took him a while to find [big sigh], a long, long time to find the place where he had wandered off the normal trails. And he started hunting and he just kept going further and further into the heart of the Andes, into the foothills.

At this point Larry had become intensively involved in his story. He closed his eyes and began to whisper the rest:

> And he started seeing that his trail was extremely well kept. The roads were in fantastic condition and there were some amazing footbridges and places where the road had been built up and strengthened to fight off the torrential rains. The scenery became even more magnificent as he went further and further along the road. The climbing became rougher and rougher but the road stayed in good condition even in the steepest part. He was going up and up but he really wasn't aware of how long he'd been climbing because it was just so fantastic and magnificent. He knew he was about to find what he had been

searching for as an archaeologist. All the tall trees and the steep rocks rising on either side, almost straight up, just seemed to climb. Everything was just so steep. And there he saw it ahead. He couldn't believe it but he had made it. The road sort of went into a cave . . . sort of a black space surrounded by trees and he just knew deep, deep down inside of himself that this is what he had been looking for all this time. Another half hour's climb and he was there and all of a sudden it become warm and dark. The trees were closing overhead like a cathedral. It became very still. Even though here were a lot of trees outside there didn't seem to be any birds inside and he was a little surprised. He then emerged into a dark clearing and he realized that he had climbed to the top. He saw this tremendous . . . this tremendous wall made of huge stone blocks that had been dragged there centuries before by these Spaniards. That convinced him even more that he was in the right place. He just sat there, tremendously happy. It was nice, more than nice, sort of like paradise.

I am a fisherman. I know what it is like to cast my line from a jetty or troll hours in a boat and catch nothing. Then, suddenly out of the depths a striper or a bluefish takes my bait and runs with it. That's what keeps me going back. The excitement is memorable. I know the familiar statement that it's just being in the fresh air and witnessing the marvels of nature that counts. Catching a fish is simply an extra. I have expressed similar sentiments myself, but I don't believe them for a moment. It is the same with reading TAT stories. I can read dozens of them and enjoy myself while doing so. However, most of them are routine, and one gets the impression that they are variations of culturally shared scripts. Then, again from the depths, comes an attention-grabbing whopper that provides me with a glimpse of hidden cravings that momentarily burst into view.

Larry was eighteen years old. He had never taken a course in psychology and had never been exposed to the idea that we possess two minds: one conscious and the other unconscious. The story could not have been the result of an attempt to demonstrate his sophistication about such things. It is my impression that after the first third or so of his story, when he began to whisper, his unconscious mind had seized an opportunity to take control over it and dictated the remainder of the plot. He became so engrossed in the story that it appeared to me that he had forgotten that I was in the room with him. It was as close to witnessing a person having a waking dream as I can recall.

We don't have to be very clever to interpret this story. To put it bluntly, at the end of the story, the hero managed to arrive in a womb-like cavern of safety. To review some of the central features of the story: an archaeologist exploring the Andes stumbles onto a narrow paved road. He senses a great discovery but returns for more supplies. He builds up his courage and sets out again on his voyage. After some difficulty, he locates the place where he had "wandered off the normal trails" and senses a protective fortress high up on a mountaintop as his ultimate destination. He finds the path to be in surprisingly good condition as he climbs upward. It is strong enough to survive torrential rains (read urination?). The higher he climbs, the more fantastic and magnificent the view becomes. Suddenly, above him in the distance, he sees a cave, "sort of a black space surrounded by trees," and he knows that this is what he has been looking for. When he enters this "warm and dark" enclosure, the trees close over him "like a cathedral." He is surprised that there are no birds. Moving further into the cave, he finds a clearing surrounded by a wall made of stones dragged there by ancient Spaniards. That "convinces him even more that he had found the right place," the correct womb that had been frequented by his father, a Spaniard.

The symbols in Larry's waking dream are unmistakable. The message is clear. What is up there is the warm, safe, shelter—a metaphoric womb. He had attempted to fly to that place after his mother died. He failed, of course, on each occasion and rapidly descended back to earth, nearly crashing into telephone poles. The nightmare continued almost nightly for a year after his mother took her life. He believed that it subsided at about the time he began to feel comfortable around his new stepmother.

Thirteen years later, when he was facing a major transition (graduating from high school and unsure about his future), the dream had returned. That context was ripe for the awakening of residues of past longings, and once again he sought the solace of nearly forgotten times. Buildings had replaced telephone poles in the new edition of the dream, but either image did the job of representing the hardness of reality. Larry's confusion and lack of direction activated his yearnings to return to a time before the wind blew, the bough broke, and the cradle containing the baby fell.

Finally, in a "let no stone be uncovered" spirit, a bit of speculation to wrap up this interpretation. Larry mentioned that the archaeologist was surprised that there were no birds in the cave. That may at first look like irrelevant addition to the story, but perhaps it was not. Recall that Larry's mother was pregnant when she committed suicide and Larry may have heard a Barrie-like fable that babies are birds before they are born, or he may have filled the gap with one or another version of a stork theory of birth. That would explain the archaeologist expecting to find at least one bird residing in the aerial womb.

Larry contacted me a few months later and reported that he was about to graduate from high school. He had done "okay" during the track season but overall was disappointed that he had been unable to match his previous times. He had not applied to any colleges because his family was going to move to another state. Nor had he contacted any of the several therapists I had recommended to him. He said that he might try to find a coun-selor after the family was relocated, but first he would have to get a job to pay the fees because his father was opposed to "voodooism," particularly if it cut into the family's limited income.

The next chapter is not a pretty story. It involves some of the details of the life of a murderer. It is one of several "variation on a theme" examples offered in part IV, and for those who would prefer, no harm will be done by skipping it and moving on to less violent examples.

TWENTY-ONE *Perry Smith*

Larry's dreams of levitation featured solo flights. He soared alone, just as his fictional archaeologist at the end of his TAT story was unaccompanied when he made his fabulous discovery. Perry Smith needed assistance in his imaginary voyages through the sky, and that came in the form of a large bird that appeared in his dreams and rescued him from life's hardships by carrying him to heaven. Charged, found guilty, and subsequently executed for his participation in the murder of four members of the Clutter family in Holcomb, Kansas, Perry was the lead character in Truman Capote's "nonfiction novel" *In Cold Blood.*

In his one-of-a-kind project of investigative reporting, Capote interviewed scores of people living in the farming community of Holcomb. They included close friends and relatives of the murdered family, present and past hired hands, farming neighbors, shopkeepers, local and state officials involved in identifying, capturing, and prosecuting the perpetuators of the crime, and many others whose lives were disrupted by the ruthless slayings.

Herbert Clutter, the head of the household, had been a prosperous rancher, a self-made man who was a highly respected figure in the agricultural community. Members of his household on the terrible night of November 13, 1959, included his wife, Bonnie, an invalid, his son, Kenyon, age fifteen, and his sixteen-year-old daughter, Nancy, considered to be the town's "darling." Capote's vivid descriptions of these four people, how they had fashioned their lives, their love for each other, their devotion to their church, and their involvement in all sorts of community activities personalized the crime by making the victims recognizable — exemplars of people any Midwesterner might have known in the 1950s. The manner in which Capote conveys the everyday activities, hopes, plans, and concerns of the family members made them real, not simply faceless objects of a hideous crime. In this way, he underscores the dreadful nature of the murders, the senselessness of the slayings, the deeply felt sense of loss on the parts of people who knew the family, and the fear and suspicions the incident left in its wake. Within that context, Copote blends information about the two men who were sentenced to death for the murder. Perry Smith and Richard Hickock, both in their late twenties, were arrested in Las Vegas six months after they had fled from the crime scene. They had driven through numerous states after the crime, had lived for a while in Mexico, had traveled to Florida, and, after a series of foolish decisions, had reappeared in a few of their old haunts and were eventually captured.

As he had done with the members of the Clutter family, Capote delved into the lives of Smith and Hickock and got to know them well by way of interviewing them on many occasions as they remained alive for nearly five years in prison waiting to be executed.

Hickock was more of an enigma than Smith, in that there was nothing in his background that foretold a criminal career. He was the only child of a poor but intact and relatively comfortable Kansas family. He had been an above-average student in high school and a star athlete on several teams. He had been married twice, both times to sixteen-year-olds, and he was an absent father of three sons; bad checks had been his original downfall and prison time the consequence.

Perry's life had been different, and through Capote's lengthy descriptions of him, a character emerges that evokes a sense of compassion for the slayer that nearly matches compassion for the slain. Capote never questioned Perry's guilt yet seemed to hold the opinion that the harsh conditions of Perry's upbringing contributed to his deadly actions. Had this information been allowed by the judge to be part of the trial, Capote believed it could have been a factor that might have mitigated against the judicial decision to hang him.

Over the course of many long interviews and conversations with Perry during the nearly two thousand days that Perry was confined in the death row section of the Kansas State Penitentiary, Capote developed a close relationship with the man. He learned about Perry's childhood, the various tragedies that had befallen him, his sense of emptiness, the vagabond quality of much of his life, his experiences in the merchant marines and the U.S. army, the criminal activities that led to his many incarcerations, his love of music and poetry, and his hair-trigger temper, over which he exercised no control. Capote confirmed many of Perry's personal statements by interviewing people who had known him, by personally retracing some of his wandering tracks, and by reviewing letters and other documents that verified the accuracy of his memories. The companionship between

Smith and Capote grew to the point that April 14, 1965, the day that Perry was taken to the gallows, marked the onset of deep mourning for Capote. He had lost a close friend.

This chapter continues my inquiry into the meaning of fantasized flight by considering the need-fulfilling role of the imaginary bird that made frequent appearances in Perry's dreams. Capote writes of Perry:

> Through his life—as a child, poor and meanly treated, as a foot-loose youth, as an imprisoned man—the yellow bird, huge and parrot-faced, had soared across Perry's dreams, an avenging angel who saved him from his enemies or, as now, rescued him in moments of mortal danger: "She lifted me, I could have been light as a mouse we went up, up. I could see the Square below, men running, yelling, the sheriff shooting at us, sore as hell because I was free, I was flying, I was better than any of them."[1]

This is just one of Capote's numerous accounts of Perry's rescuing bird. The parrot first appeared in Perry's dreams when he was about seven years old and was living in a Catholic orphanage. He was a persistent bed-wetter then (as he was throughout most of his life), and that was a source of considerable annoyance and inconvenience to the workers and managers of the orphanage. One of their methods for trying to bring Perry in line with the rules of the institution involved brutality.

> It was after one of these beatings, one he would never forget ("She woke me up. She had a flashlight, and she hit me with it. Hit me and hit me. And when the flashlight broke, she went on hitting me in the dark.") that the parrot appeared, arrived while he slept, a bird "taller than Jesus, yellow like a sunflower," a warrior angel who blinded the nuns with its beak, fed upon their eyes, slaughtered them as they "pleaded for mercy," then so gently lifted him, enfolded him, winged him away to paradise.[2]

Other forms of treatment for Perry's nightly incontinence in this and other orphanages and various detention facilities included beatings with a belt, submersion into ice-cold water (Perry attributes catching pneumonia to this method), and the placement of an ointment on his penis that "burned something terrible." At other times, Perry was publicly humiliated by adult-led taunting by his dormitory peers. But his bed-wetting continued. He had no one to turn to, no one to comfort him. He was alone in his suffering. Only the imaginary bird could simultaneously discharge his revenge and carry him up and away from his pain.

Before residing in orphanages, Perry had lived with his parents, who performed in the rodeo circuit under the stage name "Tex and Flo." Flo, Perry's mother, was a Cherokee Indian and a champion bronco rider. Tex, his dad, was an Irish cowboy who specialized in rope tricks. Rodeo life was difficult, despite the occasional glamour of performances. Perry was the youngest of four children who, for the most part, slept in an old truck and lived off "mush," Hershey kisses, and condensed milk. "Hawks Brand condensed milk it was called, which weakened my kidneys," Perry told Capote, "that's why I was always wetting my bed." According to Barbara, Perry's sister, mush, candy, and condensed milk were treats compared to times when the family's diet consisted of rotten bananas and stale bread. Barbara, nicknamed Bobo, believed that Perry's colic was the result of poor nutrition. She remembered times when she wept in fear of her youngest brother's death as he screamed all night.

When Perry was between four and five, injuries forced Tex and Flo to retire from the rodeo. They moved around in Nevada and then settled in Alaska for a time. Tex worked on farms, picking berries and performing any other kind of labor that was available. When conditions were suitable, he made "bootleg hooch" on the side. In the meantime, Flo became a heavy drinker. Her alcoholism got so severe that she was rarely sober, and she frequently "slept" with any man who would supply her with substances to satisfy her addiction. One time Tex caught her entertaining a group of sailors. In Perry's words,

> a fight ensued, and my father, after a violent struggle, threw the sailors out and proceeded to beat my mother. I was frightfully scared, in fact all of us children were terrified. Crying. I was scared because I thought my father was going to hurt me, also because he was beating my mother. I really didn't understand why he was beating her but I felt that she must have done something dreadfully wrong.[3]

Apparently Flo was not deterred by Tex's beatings, because Perry told Capote of a later time when he and his siblings watched a hired hand having intercourse with Flo. When Tex came home, he suspected what had happened, and a spectacular fight, the final battle, between Tex and Flo, took place. Weapons included horsewhips, scalding water, and kerosene lamps. The fight resulted in the parents' separation, and Flo took the children to San Francisco. Alcohol remained the dominant factor in Flo's life, and Perry, now completely unsupervised, was free to roam the city streets. He became a runaway, a troublemaker, a seven-year-old crook who learned the trade by hanging out with a gang of older kids. This led to a string of arrests and the beginning of his placements in orphanages and youth detention centers.

The commotion, screaming, and blood that Perry had witnessed as a child when Tex beat Flo for her extramarital sexual affairs and the whippings he was given for wetting his bed took its toll on his sexual maturation. It is clear, as well as understandable, that he associated sex with violence. Sexual pleasure resulted in life-threatening pain. He had seen it at home and had experienced it when he was beaten for his own nightly

episodes of urinating in his bed. Many have observed that there is a component of infantile sexuality involved in bed-wetting, particularly for boys,
as penal erections frequently precede the release of urine. If there was any
confusion on Perry's part regarding the source of his problem, the burning
ointment that was rubbed onto his penis in one of his institutional training
sessions marked the culprit dead center. The fearsome results of the expressing of sexual impulses put an enduring clamp on any semblance of
normal sexual development, and Perry placed vehement restrictions on
that aspect of his life. He attempted to extend his personal policy by pressing others to harness their sexual desires. Richard Hickock, his traveling
companion and partner in crime, became one of his favorite targets, and
Perry frequently argued with him about his "disgusting" relations with
women. Perry had "no respect for people who could not control themselves sexually" and was especially dismayed by Hickock's "pervert" attraction to young girls. Perry's own fantasies about enjoying female companionship were confined to envisioning himself in a place he had seen in
Japan called the Dream Pool, where women scrubbed clients from head to
toe.

The only half-serious relationship he had ever had with a woman, or
at least the only one he ever mentioned, was with Cookie, a nurse he had
met in a hospital when he was recuperating from the surgical repair of his
legs after they were fractured in a motorcycle accident. He had just been
discharged from the armed services when the accident occurred, and it
put a six-month crimp in his plans to join up with Tex in Alaska. He never
said anything about having a sexual relationship with Cookie, and, in line
with his beliefs about such matters, it is doubtful that sex was an aspect of
their companionship. But they liked each other and sometimes talked
about marriage. These conversations must have been time-fillers for Perry,
because he left Cookie when he was released from the hospital and never
contacted her again.

Perry's relationships with men were more complicated. Capote reports some evidence that Perry was sexually aroused by them on some occasions. In fact, there is some speculation that Capote and Smith did more
than just chat during Capote's extended private visits with him behind the
walls of the prison. Whether or not these recently reported hunches are
correct, Perry had more to say about sexually tinged relationships with
men than with women. He spoke of the "queens" he had met in the merchant marines and in the armed services in Korea. He believed that his refusal to "roll over" for one sergeant prevented him from moving up in
rank. This and Perry's reports of numerous encounters with other suitors
suggests at least some degree of mutual attraction.

Perry's method of guarding himself against acknowledging homosexual impulses is illustrated in the following incident. He was living in
Las Vegas in the attic of an old boarding house. A well-built railroad

worker named King lived across the hall from Perry. King never shut his door, leaving Perry with an open view of him lying naked on his bed reading comic books. Perry said that King was "O.K. Sometimes we would have beer together, and once he lent me 10 dollars. I had no cause to hurt him. But one night we were sitting in the attic, it was so hot you couldn't sleep, so I said, 'Come on, King, let's go for a drive.'"

They drove to the desert where it was cool, parked the car, and drank some beer. King got out of the car and Perry followed him. "He didn't see I'd picked up a chain. Actually, I had no real idea to do it till I did it. I hit him across the face. Broke his glasses. I kept right on. Afterward, I didn't feel a thing. I left him there, and never heard a word about it. Maybe nobody ever found him. Just buzzards."

Capote went to Las Vegas to investigate Perry's story. He was able to confirm that Perry and a black man named King had lived in the same boarding house, but there was no evidence that a murder had been committed. It was most likely a fantasy execution, one that underscored Perry's association of violence with sex.

Unfortunately for the Clutter family in Holcomb, Perry's involvement in murder was not restricted to his imagination. On the night of November, 13, 1959, he and Hickock entered through an unlocked door of the Clutter family's home, intending to rob a safe that Hickock had been told was filled with money. Hickock's informant was a fellow inmate in the prison where Dick had spent time for one of his infractions. Dick's cellmate had once worked on Clutter's Valley River Farm and drew a map of its location that also showed the whereabouts of the presumed safe, which he was confident contained at least ten thousand dollars. But Hickock failed to find the safe when he searched the walls and crannies of Herbert Clutter's home office, so he and Perry went upstairs and awoke Mr. Clutter, insisting that he direct them to the treasure. Refusing to believe his claim that there was no safe in the home and never had been, and ignoring his pleas not to harm members of his family, Perry and Dick tied up and taped the mouths of Herbert, his wife, Bonnie, and the teenagers, Kenyon and Nancy, in separate rooms to give themselves time to discover if Mr. Clutter was telling the truth.

After nearly an hour of searching the home and occasionally chatting with its terrified occupants, Perry suggested to Dick that they leave. They would be hundreds of miles from the home before anyone would discover their bound prisoners, and it would be unlikely that they would ever be caught. However, Dick's attraction to sixteen-year-old girls took precedence over that plan, and he decided that both he and Perry should "bust" Nancy. That suggestion struck a dangerous emotional chord in Perry: the idea of raping Nancy infuriated him. He blocked Dick's access to Nancy's bedroom and screamed, "You'll have to kill me first." Thereupon he escorted Dick to the basement, where Herbert Clutter was tied up, and slit the bound man's throat with a knife. It was an impulsive act that bore the fingerprints of a person who, when sexually aroused, became a wild man. Violence, specifically violence toward men, had become Perry's primary outlet for the release of sexual tension. It was the central theme in his story about King, a well-rehearsed fantasy that resulted in a live performance.

As Herbert Clutter gasped for air, Perry offered Dick the opportunity to finish him off. Dick refused, so Perry grabbed the rifle that Dick had taken from his father's home, and, point blank, blasted a hole in Mr. Clutter's head. Since no witnesses could be left behind, Perry systematically shot and killed the remaining members of the family with no feelings of remorse. He and Dick then left the home with their paltry loot—a small transistor radio from Kenyon's room, a pair of binoculars from the main floor, and a grand total of approximately forty dollars. Despite this disappointing "take," Perry was exhilarated and stayed high for many hours after the crime.

In his written confession to the killings, Perry wrote, "I didn't want to harm the man. I thought he was a very nice gentleman. Soft-spoken. I thought so right up to the moment that I cut his throat. . . . They (the Clutters) never hurt me. Like other people. Like people have all my life. Maybe it just happened that the Clutters were the ones that had to pay for it." Since Mr. Clutter was the first to "pay," let us consider the probable nature of his debt. With Freud as guide, I will pursue the idea that Perry unconsciously perceived Herbert Clutter as a stand-in for Tex.

Perry said that he had loved his father throughout his entire life. It is reported that he cried when Flo took him and her other children to San Francisco. He sometimes was heard calling out for Tex in his sleep. In fact, Tex took him away from San Francisco, and the two of them lived together in a trailer in Alaska for several years prior to Perry entering the merchant marines at age sixteen. It was an up-and-down relationship, with good times interspersed with bad. He enjoyed going hunting and trapping with his dad and learned how to cook under his supervision. He was proud of going to school and earning a third grade education. But, as we know, Tex had a temper, and Perry had to be cautious in his company. The last time Perry crossed the line with his father happened after he had been discharged from the army. He had helped Tex complete work on a hunting camp in Alaska. Few hunters came to the attractive facility, and Tex was trying to come to terms with his frustration about the expensive failure. Food was scarce, and one evening he and Perry fought over a biscuit. Tex, enraged by Perry's refusal to give him the morsel of food, pointed the barrel of his rifle at his son's head. Click. The rifle was not loaded. That gave Perry an opening to flee from the cabin, and he spent the night outside. He returned in the morning to find a suitcase that contained all of his meager possessions on the doorstep next to his guitar. That was the last time that he had any contact with his dad.

So Perry's proclaimed love for his father was undoubtedly mixed with fear, resentment, and hatred. At a very young age, he had witnessed his father beating up his mother and was horrified. Although it is unlikely that Flo was much of a mothering figure, then or ever, she was the only mother he had, and he must have feared for her life, as well as his own. He could do nothing to protect Flo, and it was easy for him to imagine Tex turning his vengeance against him or anyone else who attempted to do so. Tex was much too powerful for Perry to even consider taking on, so he repressed his anger. But, as we know, neither repressed feelings nor the objects that sparked them go away. According to Freud's model, both remain in the unconscious "as fresh as the day they were repressed," waiting for an opportunity to be released. Herbert Clutter, a father figure, and tied so tightly that he could not move, suddenly became a perfect defenseless object on which Perry could vent his bottled-up hatred. Herbert Clutter "paid for" what Tex and the adult authorities (army sergeants, police, judges, parole officers, etc.) had done to him. Perry's internal world of enemies was condensed into one object, a target who would never be able to reciprocate harm done to him.

Psychoanalytic theory assumes that when a person directs repressed feelings onto an object that merely represents the "real" one, the internal tension released is only partial. "Displacing," or taking out one's anger on a defenseless object, helps some, but not much. This premise would lead one to suspect that slaying Herbert Clutter in lieu of destroying Tex and other objects associated with his anger would act as a partial cleansing agent, but that Perry's aggressive tank would quickly fill up. However, the fact that the exhilaration that Perry felt after he murdered Mr. Clutter lingered on leads me to conclude that it was a tension-releasing, cathartic episode equivalent to the sudden eruption of a volcano whose cap could no longer contain its seething contents.

The symbolic father was now dead. The son had won the final victory. But that is just one half of the Oedipal scenario. In the ancient story, Oedipus killed a man whom he did not know was his father and became king. He then married a woman whom he did not know had given birth to him, and he lived miserably ever after. Freud brought that plot front and center as one that gives theatric expression to the "universal" dilemma experienced by sons. They want to get rid of the father so that they can gain exclusive access (for Freud, sexual access) to the mother. Where is the second part, the mother part, of the family romance script in Perry's life? It can be found, nearly line by line, in a recurrent dream that Perry described to Capote. Few of its contents need be adjusted to fit the Oedipal frame.

The dream always began in Africa, with Perry admiring a tree with diamonds growing on it. He is there to "pick myself a bushel," but "Jesus, it smells bad, that tree; it kind of makes me sick, the way it stinks." Even so, the tree is nice to look at, and Perry has to get those gems. The problem is that the tree is guarded by a snake that falls on him when he reaches up for fruit. More of the dream is reported as follows:

> This fat son of a bitch living in the branches, I know beforehand, see? And Jesus, I don't know how to fight a snake. But I figure, well, I'll take my chances. What it comes down to is I want the diamonds more than I'm afraid of the snake. So I go to pick one, I have the diamond in my hand, I'm pulling at it, when the snake lands on top of me. We wrestle around, but he's a slippery son of a bitch and I can't get a hold, he's crushing me, you can hear my legs cracking. Now comes the part it makes me sweat to even think about. See, he starts to swallow me. Feet first. Like going down into quicksand.[4]

An Oedipal classic one would think, with a few innovative twists. The tree symbolizes the mother, and Perry wants to pick her fruit. He meets two obstacles. One is the tree's awful smell that makes him sick. However, the tree is too inviting, too beautiful to look at, to make the stench insurmountable. The second obstacle is much more threatening, life-threatening in fact. A big fat snake lives in the branches and falls on Perry, cracks his legs, and begins to swallow him. Dad, the mighty father, symbolized by the snake, guards against the son's intrusion into his possession to gather its fruit and begins to consume his victim.

Support for this interpretation is not hard to come by. Perry did not have to guess what the consequences would be if he sought to gain pleasure from Flo. Tex had managed to nearly slaughter a group of sailors whom Flo had sexually entertained. Dealing with a four- or five-year-old son with romantic intentions could be done with a flip of his wrist. This and other elements of the dream fit remarkably well with the family romance script. Except for one curious component of the dream, the swallowing part. The snake in Perry's dream attempts to engulf him, to destroy him by taking him into his stomach.

There are some interesting parallels between Perry's dream and the dream that Carl Jung reported had preoccupied him throughout his life. This was the dream briefly mentioned in chapter 14, where Jung, around the age of four, descended stone-lined stairs into an underground chamber where he was startled to find a large phallic figure seated on a throne. He feared that the single-eyed creature might at any moment dismount from the throne, come in his direction, and consume him.

In Larry's imaginative story, described in the previous chapter, the hero made it all the way to womblike cavern. Neither Jung nor Perry Smith was able to complete equivalent voyages. In both instances, a large, swallowing creature stood in their way. It is reasonable to suspect that the snake that guarded the tree in Perry's dream and the man-eating fleshy tree trunk in Jung's dream symbolized the feared revenge of the father for attempting to take what he considered to be his sole possession. However, one of Freud's major insights into dreams is that symbols in them can represent more than one object. Two or more fears or wishes can be condensed into one image. Along that line, I suggest that both Jung's underground phallus and Perry's snake symbolized their fears of what would happen if they reached their final goals of returning to the safety of metaphoric wombs. They would be consumed. They would end up as clumps in the belly of a snake. Their deepest desires would be fulfilled, and they would disappear. The boundaries that comprise the self, the core self, the self that is involved in one's awareness of being a physically and emotionally alive creature, would be eliminated in the sea of the mother. As the fantasy would have it, if one were to succeed in being reabsorbed into the boundaries of the mother, one could live forever, floating in that warm and welcoming enclosure . . . and die at that same time.

Jamie Barrie's solution to this problem was to create a part bird and part human person named Peter who hovered near his mother's bedroom yearning to be let in and resisted entering the gates when they were open. Jung resolved the dilemma by inventing an eternal, never-depleted source of energy that sometimes announces its presence by way of sensations of being lifted up and looking down on the planet from on high.

What was Perry's fantasy solution? It comes at the end of his dream. Just as Perry is about to be swallowed by the snake, a parrot-faced bird swoops down and rescues him from disappearing into quicksand oblivion. She lifts him, light as a mouse, and *takes him to paradise.* In Perry's dream, paradise consists of a long table with an unimaginable amount and variety of food. Oysters, turkeys, hot dogs, enough fruit to make a million fruit cups, and, most important of all, "it's every bit free. I mean, I don't have to be afraid to touch it. I can eat as much as I want and it won't cost a cent. That shows I know where I am."

As Freud would most certainly suggest, the dream image of Perry reaching into the branches of the smelly tree to grab a handful diamonds carries with it an erotic component, particularly in view of the fact that the dreamer knows that a father serpent may at any moment slip down from the tree and punish him for his ill-begotten, erotic intentions. But I suggest that the Oedipal components of the dream were secondary to the primary wish expressed in it. It was a wish—long ago repressed but ever present beneath the surface—to return to a real or imagined time when Perry had been lifted into the arms of a nurturing mother and fed. The dream captures the bodily sensations, the physical "memories" if you will, of an infant being taken lifted from the ground to a higher place where food is abundant. No conditions, no contingencies, the food is every bit free. I am suggesting that in residence under the skin of the surly, mean-spirited man who was waiting to be hung was the wish to be a baby, to be the indisputable center of his mother's attention, to have her protect and care for him.

Perry may have had a taste of that when he was an infant, but it could not have been much of a taste. It is more likely that his oral and creature comfort cravings to be fed and held by a reliable "attachment object" were rarely fulfilled. I doubt that Flo, the bronco-riding champ whose long, flowing hair brightened Western rodeos, was ever much of a match for her child's inborn instinct to seek a need-satisfying object. Six people, two adults and four children, cramped into the back of a truck is hardly an ideal setting for the youngest child, who suffered from colic, to feel prized, to experience the kind of "intersubjective union" that Stern observes is such a vital aspect of self-development. So, I argue, what Perry wanted is something he rarely got as an infant and never received as a child of an alcoholic mother. It came about only in the form of an imaginary bird that came to him during his sleep and took him to a far better place.

I suspect that some people who have not read *In Cold Blood* or have not seen the movie based on the book have formed the mental image of Perry as tough guy. That he was, if one had seen him seated in the booth of a diner. He had a massive upper body, one that gave the impression that he could lift a truck. His enormous arms and chest were adorned with tattoos, one of which bore the name "Cookie." However, there were some jarring discrepancies that accompanied his macho physique. He had "weepy, womanly eyes" and a "whispering voice." An aura of sensitivity surrounded him much of the time, an aura that was contributed to by the prop of an ever-present harmonica, one of his prized possessions. And yet he did not convey the kind of softness that would put anyone at ease because it was often accompanied by disconcerting whining. His low-pitched whining and monotonous pleadings got on Hickock's nerves, and Dick often thought of Perry as a "wife that must be gotten rid of."

But the real shocker came about when Perry stood up. His height was that of an average twelve-year old boy. Barely five feet tall, Perry looked like a "sawed off dwarf." He was embarrassed by his size and claimed that it was the result of the damage done to his legs when they had been broken during his smash-up on his motorcycle. Perhaps so, but his height could not have been reduced by more than an inch or so.

A more likely explanation can be found in the ideas of Robert Sapolski, discussed in chapter 9, on "stress dwarfism." Under the heading "Dwarfism and the Importance of Mothers," Sapolski describes the growth-stunting effects of inadequate mothering. Sapolski observed that extreme cases of child neglect, particularly when accompanied by physical abuse, can be so stressful to the organism that the normal operation of the body's enzymes and other chemicals involved in physical maturation is so disrupted that the child ceases to grow. Sapolski, as we know, uses J. M. Barrie as an example of the condition of stress dwarfism. I agree that Barrie suffered greatly when he was no longer able to hold Margaret's attention. It was a script-determining period of Barrie's life. It became a center of gravity for themes that exercised control over his entire life. I have covered all that. But abuse? Hardly.

Perry Smith is a far more likely candidate for the diagnosis of stress dwarfism than Barrie. The violence he witnessed, his abandonment by Flo as she literally drank herself to death, the broken flashlight, the whippings, the ice-cold water and burning ointment "cures" for his nightly misdeeds— all that and more could easily account for Perry's dwarflike appearance.

During his infant and childhood years, nobody cared much for Perry, with the possible exception of his sister, Barbara. Mostly, she feared for his death. Other individuals who have been raised under equally dire circumstances somehow miraculously survive and lead reasonably healthy, normal lives as adults. Abuse and neglect are no ironclad guarantees of criminal careers. Barbara, for instance, eventually married and had children and a faithful husband. However, both of Perry's other siblings committed suicide. For his part, Perry's upper-body bravado hid his longing to be baby. His deepest wish was to be picked up and held like an infant. He wanted to be the center of somebody's loving attention. He sought a haven that no earthly source would provide him. No earthly source, that is, except himself.

In effect, Perry became his own object of glowing appreciation. He stood for hours in front of mirrors, trancelike, according to Hickock, admiring the muscles chiseled by regular weight lifting. He envisioned himself as a one-man show performing for wildly appreciative audiences on a main stage in Las Vegas. Perry O'Parsons was to have been his name, widely known as a singer and dancer who accompanied himself with a guitar and harmonica. Juxtapose that grandness against a smallish man who comforted himself by sucking his thumb, a habit from childhood that extended into his adult years. Sometimes he also cried before and during his sleep, and he nearly always wet his bed.

There are several theories about bed-wetting. *Enuresis* is its technical label. Perry attributed it to an overdose of condensed milk when he was a child. All sorts of medical explanations have been offered, and I have no doubt that, in many cases, specific physiological malfunctions can be identified as roots of the problem. But in Perry's case, a psychological explanation requires a hearing. Here is my suggestion in that regard. It takes time for babies to gain control over their bladders. Normally, around the age of three (earlier for some and later for others), diapers can be removed and the beds remain dry. Concurrent with that aspect of maturation, children who suck their thumbs gradually relinquish the habit, and nighttime crying usually subsides. Remnants of infancy are given up as most children confidently broaden the range of self-control. Perry never managed to do that.

J. M. Barrie often said that he never wanted to grow up. Perry Smith physically enacted the same sentiment. Barrie said it in words. Smith said it through his body. He cried himself to sleep as a child and continued to weep until the day he went to the gallows. He often sucked his thumb and always wet his bed. In these ways, he manifested a desire to remain a child, an infant desiring to become attached to something that would make him real. His pleas went unheard. Consciously, he was not even aware of them. But they returned at night. His repressed cravings continued to force themselves upon him, and he would cry out for help. Only a product of his imagination heard his cries. A bird, a heavenly angel, came to his rescue. She lifted him up and made him special, vastly superior to those on the ground yelling and shooting at him. Finally, she took him to his desired destination. He "knew where he was" when he saw the food and could nurse to his heart's content.

TWENTY-TWO *Tonka and His Flying Backpack*

Clive Hart[1] and Peter Haining[2] have written about the history of efforts to fly that predate the invention of the airplane. It is a richly storied topic that begins with ancient drawings of levitated objects found on the walls of caves and other items of evidence of fabled flights that appeared in legends over five thousand years ago. Pictures of drawings, statues, ceramics, and other relics indicating that flight was on the minds of their creators are gathered into plates in these volumes. Photographs of humans standing on hills or towers with various contraptions strapped to their arms and legs give a modern touch to their works. Feathers appear to have been the most commonly selected aids for aspirations to fly, but other objects have been considered as well. Among the dozens of gadgets, substances, and creatures that make their appearances in legends of flight are rowboats, pigeons (both mechanical and real), apes, gases, kites, windsocks, geese, magnets, moon springs, lice, sails, vials, and gryphons.

There was a lack of consensus throughout the ages about whether to admire, admonish, or ridicule persons who wished to fly. One of the prevailing opinions was that if God had wanted us to fly, he would have given us wings. Others believed that God's omission could be corrected by inventing artificial means for airborne transportation. The serious attention given to this idea by Leonardo da Vinci was a source of encouragement to the scientifically minded people of his day. They respected his systematic approach to the problem and celebrated the manner in which he framed the problem. He viewed birds as instruments working according to mathematical law and believed it was within the capacity of man to produce their movements. He gave much thought to the differences between the "vital" principle of the bird and the "mechanical" principle man would be required to use in emulating the flight of birds. Although Leonardo failed to achieve his dream of flying from the summit of Monto Ceceri, he produced the likeness a parachute that placed him among the true pioneers of flight.

Less mathematically inclined aviation hopefuls ventured to fly without the potential benefit of mastering mechanical principles. Some of them created theories about what would be required to fly after experiencing humiliating public failures. John Damian is perhaps the best known after-the-fact theorist. He was a vagabond Italian trickster who sought refuge in Scotland after having been expelled from Italy and France for being a schemer and land thief. Damian, proclaiming to be a physician and alchemist, had to be among the great impostors of his day. He was so beguiling at his trade that he managed to dupe none other than James IV of Scotland, whom he charmed and ingratiated himself with so thoroughly that James IV elevated Damian to the position of abbot of Tungland. The king's advisors and others objected to the honor granted this self-promoting exile. Damian must have come to believe his own grandiose lies, because he set forth to demonstrate his worthiness of rank by issuing an announcement of the day he planned to fly. Haining describes the timing of the event this way: "On the morning of 27th September, 1507, when the king was at Stirling Castle and had just dispatched an ambassador to France, Damian announced that he would put on wings and arrive in Paris before the man."[3] A crowd gathered to witness Damian's short and unspectacular flight. In fact, he did not fly at all. As recorded by Bishop John Lesley in his *Historie of Scotland* (c. 1568), Damian with "quhilkis beand fessinit apoun him, flew of the castel wall of Striveling, bot shortlie he fell to the ground and brak his thee bane." Not only did Damian "brak his thee bane," he took a nosedive into a dung heap located at the base of the Sterling Castle wall. Embarrassed but not at a loss for words, the quick-witted Damian explained to the king that his wings "were composed of various feathers; among them were the feathers of a dunghill fowl, and they, by a certain sympathy, were attracted to the dunghill on which I fell; whereas had my wings been composed of eagles alone, as I proposed, the same sympathy would have attracted my machine to the higher regions of the air."

Damian was not alone in providing material for seventeenth- and eighteenth-century novelists and satirists to write about characters whose ambitions were to fly. Francis Godwin's famous account of flight was published in 1638 under the title *Man in the Moon: or a Discourse of a Voyage Thither by Domingo Gonsales*. Godwin must have known the principles of reinforcement before they were rediscovered in twentieth century animal labs, because the hero of his story, Gonsales, taught thirty swans, or "gansas," to fly at the signal of a white cloth and transport small bundles from one hill to another. Inspired by his success, Gonsales undertook the grander task of training the gansas to carry heavier loads, loads that included him, through the air. He attempted to ease the burden by creating a system of pulleys made of cork and rope that he would use to assist in the operation. The payback for Domingo's hard work came on the occasion of his being shipwrecked and nearly drowned at sea. Suddenly his trained swans appeared in the sky above and miraculously saved their master. Unfortunately, they transported him to the moon.

The lunar theme in Godwin's novel was reworked by other authors. Elements of his story can be found in Thomas D'Urfey's comic opera *Wonders of the Sun*, Aphra Behn's farce *Emperor of the Moon*, Elkanah Settle's novel *The World of the Moon*, and Samuel Brunt's novel *A Voyage to Cacklogallinia*. Perhaps the most imaginative method for being transported to the moon appears in de Bergerac's *Historie Comique au Voyage dans la Lune*. One collects vials of dew and attaches them to one's body; the journey begins the moment the sun does its well-known feat of sucking up the dew.

The potential of explosives to send a person aloft did not escape fabulists' attention. Martagh McDermot told of placing himself and a folded pair of wings in the midst of ten wooden vessels, one inside the other, with the largest and outermost being hooped with iron. The thrust generated by seven thousand barrels of gunpowder would blast the passenger into space, where his wings would unfold and the world's first human satellite would make history.

Unaware of the flight-assisting devices that had been proposed over many centuries, Tonka started from scratch. The remainder of this chapter is about Tonka. Of course, Tonka was not the young man's real name. I dubbed him Tonka after a toy manufacturing company because it fit my image of a little boy tinkering in the basement of his home with two fans, some batteries, wire, and tape, as he attempted to create a flying backpack.

Tonka began his project when he was seven. He devoted himself to it after school and during weekends for nearly two years. A serious illness at age nine interrupted his work, and he never resumed interest in it. "As far as I know," he told me, "the junk is still in my parent's basement."

Tonka had graduated from college the year before I got to know him. He was unemployed and had lots of spare time. An advertisement that solicited undergraduates to participate in a study of lives had caught his attention. Hoping that no-cost therapy might be a result of his participation, he signed up as a volunteer.

Like Grope, described in chapter 3, Tonka had not achieved the academic success that had been expected of him. Confidence in his intellectual capacities had never been a problem. He once showed me two essays he had written in his college sophomore year marked with As. One of them contained a comment from an instructor who congratulated him on his scholarship. These two papers, however, were papers apart, in that they did not reflect his overall mediocre "gentleman's C" record. Tonka attributed his low grades to the fact that he never studied more than "two hours if I was interested. Two minutes if I wasn't." He recalled how much he had worried about his study habits throughout his four years of college. He reported that he would sit for days on end being self-critical and feeling guilty about his parents paying the college fees for a son who was doing nothing to justify the expense. "No matter how much thought-punishment I heaped on myself, nothing worked. I would just sit around, depressed and completely bored with myself. Maybe if I had been able to muster up the energy to go to a few of my classes things wouldn't have been so bad."

Tonka had been born in a suburb of Los Angeles twenty-two years prior to our discussions. He was the first of two children in his family. His mother told him that his delivery had been difficult and that he had arrived two weeks earlier than anticipated. She also informed him that he cried a lot during the first six months of his life and was breast-fed and weaned in a year. Ten months after his birth, his father completed medical school and was required to spend the next two and a half years in a branch of the armed services. Since he was stationed overseas during his tour of duty, Tonka's mother moved to a town in northern Oregon where she set up temporary residence with her father—a strict, distant, God-fearing retired minister.

Tonka was told that he had been easier to care for after his first six months of nonstop crying subsided. The fact that he didn't walk until he was twenty months old and didn't form sentences until he was over two years old were sources of concern to his family. His mother's explanation for the slow development of his language skills was that he didn't talk because he didn't have to. "She's let it be known to me more times than I can count that her services had been so good that what would have been the point of my having to talk?"

Tonka's father was discharged from military duty when Tonka was nearly four. Not quite a year after he returned, his mother gave birth to a second son. Tonka reported that he never paid much attention to the "little shit" and preoccupied himself by playing with a group of boys who made treehouses.

> I would have liked to have been the leader of the gang but I wasn't. Part of the problem was my mother and my grandfather, who by that time was living in our house, were not wholly acceptant of the other boys. They called them ruffians and warned me to keep my distance. I had the feeling that one or the other of them was on the constant lookout for where I was and what I was doing.

A solid punch in the nose delivered by one of the boys was sufficient for Tonka to heed adult advice, and he began to spend most of his time indoors.

I read a lot, watched a ton of TV, and began a building project. Did I
ever tell you about that project? I tried to build a kind of flying machine I had seen in a movie. I found a fan in a neighbor's trash and
found another one in our basement. I had a couple of batteries and I
figured that I could wire the batteries to the fans, strap them onto a
knapsack, and end up with a flying backpack. When it was completed, which of course it never was, all I would need to do would be
to press a button up she'd go! Whoosh! Looking back, I can't believe
the amount of time I devoted to the thing.

When asked if he had any idea about why he was so devoted to his
project, without hesitation he said that his efforts were based on his desire
to

get away from the hell-hole of a situation I was in at home. I used to
daydream about how much my parents, especially my mom, would
mourn my departure. There was something else too. I don't know
what it was. It is hard to describe, but I was searching for something.
It was like I was always hungry but food didn't help.

Tonka reported that he had been a bed-wetter between the ages of
seven and ten. He said that the problem was so serious that a summer
camp director sent his second-grade charge packing after only three days
of a month-long season. He also believed that his nightly routine fore-
closed any prospects of him joining the Boy Scouts.

Although I didn't like the reason for having to stay home, at least it
prevented me from suffering from home sickness. That's something I
could never figure out. Why was it that I disliked my mother so
much, but couldn't bear being away from her? Homesickness is a terrible thing. The only way I can describe it is it is a wrenching feeling,
a constant wrenching feeling of empty wants and hopelessness.

Tonka got sick when he was nine. It was a serious illness that had all
the makings of polio, but Tonka insists it was not. Whatever it was, it resulted in his being hospitalized for six weeks and missing an entire semes-
ter of school. The following excerpt from his written autobiography deals
with that period of his life.

When I was in the hospital, my mother came to see me a lot. She
brought me a lot of comics and presents. I remember crying and
being terribly frightened because there was some talk about having to
have an operation on my hip but that never happened. During most
of the time that I was home, my mother had to carry me up and
down the stairs. She carried me from room to room. She gave me
baths and even wiped my rear end. I must have liked the attention
because it took such a long time for me to be willing to walk with

crutches. After I got on crutches, they remained with me for a much longer period than was necessary.

Tonka succeeded where Jamie Barrie had failed. Jamie could never get Margaret Ogilvy to come around, to smile. Although it required a critical illness to get the job done, Tonka's mother was there when she was needed. She pampered her son and tended to all his needs. She carried her nine-year-old through the house the way one carries a baby. She showered him with gifts, and he felt prized. A baby in the body of third-grader was granted a new beginning by a frightened mother who followed what surely would have been Heinz Kohut's recommendation:[4] to mirror her son's grandiosity, made him feel special, and thereby restore his impoverished sense of self.

Although speculating about cause/effect relationships is a risky game to play, it is not unreasonable to propose that the attention Tonka's mother gave him during his illness was directly related to his scrapping his flying backpack project and terminating his bed-wetting problem. On the manifest level, Tonka believed that his flying project was driven by a desire to get out of his "hell-hole" situation at home. But where was it that he thought he might go? My now familiar answer to that question is that flying served the double purpose of escape and return. Flying away gave expression to the desire to fly back to times when "the service was good." According to Tonka's mother, the services had once been so good when Tonka was an infant and toddler that he didn't need to verbalize his desires. She had been so attuned to her son that a mere wink, nod, or whimper from him was sufficient for her to understand and obey his wishes. The cooccurrence of bedwetting with the onset of work on his flying project supports the idea that life had gotten tough for Tonka around age seven and both a symptom (bed-wetting) and a project (flying) afforded him hope for restoring more pleasurable times.

Working from transcripts of interviews with Tonka and a copy of his autobiography, I asked him to talk about what he meant by his hellish situation at home. He began by saying that he had two mothers.

> One in reality. Two in fact. By that I mean my mother could change on a dime. One minute she would be kind and pay a lot of attention to me. The next minute she would treat me like a stranger. I never knew if she might not slap me in the face like she did one time. It's not that I had nothing to do with it, I'm sure I was no angel, but if looks could kill, I would be dead hundreds of times over. It was mostly her face that worried me. The few times I was away from home, like at the summer camp I mentioned, I couldn't get past wondering what her face was doing. While other kids were swimming, playing, and joking around, I was thinking about my mother's face. Now can you beat that?

Tonka's two-mothers (is she going to love me or reject me?) quandary had formed the base of the perceptions of girls he had known as a teenager. In his autobiography he wrote that had been a frequent dater from seventh grade on. He was fond of the kissing games played at birthday parties, and he initiated a search for girls who would "pet." He lamented his lack of success by writing: "I dated a number of girls, none of whom were particularly interested in taking the lead."

He met the woman of his dreams in a library during his senior year in high school. "My thoughts are now that if I would meet someone I felt the same way I felt about Maggie, I would be tempted to get very serious about her." Tonka referred to Maggie as his "Princess" and noted how much she reminded him of Sophia Loren. She struck him as very feminine, but he couldn't decide whether she was selfish or unselfish. He described her as having been very intelligent and willing to talk about serious things. But something about her poise frightened him, and he would back away. Perhaps these thoughts helped him justify the fact that another suitor won Maggie's heart and he lost his potential "soulmate."

The two sides of Maggie were later hardened into two categories of women he dated in college. One category was reserved for women who were "poised and uncommunicative" and the other for women he perceived to be "bright, attractive, and communicative." Unfortunately, members of the first type were willing to pet, and category 2 women were uncomfortable with such activities. His dating score was this. He had been in good communication with three girls; two of them became engaged, and the other left college before graduation. Three women whom he had placed in "his poised and uncommunicative" mental slot "picked up through some subtle messages that I didn't give much of a damn and went on their merry way."

Tonka hadn't given up on the idea of marriage, but he foresaw some problems. Even if he stumbled across a potential soulmate (his word, not mine), he wouldn't be quick to act, because "*I wouldn't want to become too dependent too quickly.*"

You may have noticed that "poised" was a prominent word in Tonka's vocabulary. Here are some definitions of the word that appear in my dictionary: *ease and dignity of manner; self-assurance; composure; the condition of being calm or serene; a style of carriage or bearing of the body.* The word meant something different to Tonka, according to one of my colleagues, a member of the small team of investigators involved in studying Tonka who specialized in the administration and interpretation of the Rorschach Inkblot Test. The "test" is administered by first asking respondents to say what they see in ten inkblot cards. After that step is completed, the tester goes back over the cards and asks the respondent to show where the sighted objects are located and to elaborate on their responses if they desire to do so. In her summary report on Tonka's responses, the team member made special note of Tonka's frequent use of the word "poised," particularly in reference to various monsters he saw in the cards. For example, in one card he saw a double-headed monster. One was "poised and about to pounce on the other." He saw another monster in a different card. He couldn't decide if it was about to pounce or was just threatening, but its hands were up and it was "definitely poised, maybe ready to strike." Poised monsters were dangerous monsters for Tonka. On the other hand, *not* being poised was a good sign. For example, in one card Tonka saw two green creatures. He said that neither of them was frightening. "They look more inquisitive than frightening. Look here [he points to the card]. They aren't poised. They are not ready to attack. They aren't that kind of monster." The most benign monster observed by Tonka appeared in the final card. He called it a "crablike monster, really strange. I don't know if you can see it but that one is a symbiotic monster. She has grabbed onto the back of the other. It's on the other's back and everything will be okay. The smaller one is walking with a cane. The whole thing is harmless and fun."

The Rorschach test administrator concluded her commentary by reporting that at the end of the exercise Tonka realized that he had seen a lot of monsters. He volunteered that there are two kinds of monsters. "There are good monsters and bad monsters. The good monsters make bourbon, as much as you want. The bad monsters have their hands back and are ready to strike."

So, I'll say the obvious: two versions of one mother. One is the bourbon-producing good mother. The other is to be avoided. She's poised and ready to strike. Confronted by one (the bad one), Tonka sought permanent residence with the other, and the only way that could come about would be to return to the time before the evil monster had made her poised appearance.

I am about to violate the structural rules that govern Rorschach interpretations, but I am compelled to return to the "harmless and fun" scene Tonka's observed in card 10. There he perceived a symbiotic large crab attached to the back of a smaller one that walked with a cane. The scene can be interpreted as an ingenious condensation of memories when he had walked with crutches during the concluding days of his second round of experiences with a mother whose services had been excellent. The intimate good mother, personified as a crab, arrived on the scene to care for him, to attend to his needs. Here's the stretch. She latched herself on the smaller one's back, and everything was okay. On his back! That was where Tonka had intended to strap the contraption that was to carry him away from his "hell-hole" situation, and one may wonder if the scenario he described was his version of Perry Smith's parrot-faced, rescuing bird that transported him to heaven. "Just push the button and up she'd go! Whoosh!" The symbiotic couple, mother and son as one, inseparably flying back to the past when the service was good.

Twenty-five years after Murray published his study of Grope, he told me that hidden beneath the Icarus complex one could probably always find evidence of a mother complex. I recall posturing approval of that observation without having the slightest idea of what he meant. Perhaps you have heard a person describe another as having a "mother complex." Jung used the concept. He may have been the one who invented it. It makes its appearance in psychoanalytic literature, as well as in casual conversations, with such frequency that one may assume that it carries a shared meaning. "Oh, he has a mother complex, does he? Now I understand." The problem is that when two persons agree that such a label fits a third, they may construe its meaning quite differently and blithely carry on with the assumption that they are in full agreement. To me, it's like saying that another person "has an attitude." I know you've heard that one. It used to baffle me when students told me that someone "had an attitude." I figured that everybody has an attitude—not just one, hundreds of them. Otherwise, scores of social psychologists and public opinion polltakers who "measure" attitudes would be out of business. By now, however, my confusion about the notion of having an attitude has given way to the inadvertent tutoring of some adolescents I have come to know. I now consider myself as having been educated well enough to move into the status of at least a rank amateur in being able to spot a teenager with "an attitude." But I will remain unwilling to declare that a person has a mother complex until an agreed-on definition of the label is established.

However, there is no denying that Tonka's mother was the major figure in his life. His relationship with her was the underlying source of his division of women into good and bad objects. It influenced his ideas about the role of girls and woman during different stages of his life. During his search as a teenager for girls who would pet, he lamented the fact that he found no one who was willing to take the lead. It had a pronounced influence on his ideas about marriage. Recall his remarkable statement that he would postpone marrying a woman even if she matched the positive qualities of his former princess Maggie because he didn't want to become dependent too early in his adult life. Tonka's idea that the rite of marriage marked the beginning of a groom's dependence on his bride is so striking that it is fitting to explore how that came to be so.

When Tonka was ten months old, his father went overseas. For the following two and a half years, Tonka was raised in what amounted to a single-parent family. Tonka's account of his early years, based on his mother's report, was that her service had been excellent. But a time then arrived when the service was disrupted. To repeat an excerpt from his autobiography: "one minute she would be kind and pay a lot of attention to me. The next minute she would treat me like a stranger. I never knew if she might not slap me across the face like she did one time." I have no reason to doubt Tonka's memory of being slapped. (I was tempted to slap him a few times myself because of his habit of nonchalantly strolling in an hour or so late for his appointments.) But I would argue that the one slap she gave him served as a concrete reminder of other times when she was not happy in his company.

In direct violation of my rule against injecting information into a case study and treating that information as factual, I suspect that something like the following may have played a part in Tonka's early relationship with his mother. Mothers of sons are the early agents of society's preference for boys to be different from their mothers. Whereas daughters are encouraged to identify with their moms, boys, after a certain point of healthy nurturance has been reached, realize that they are not to be like their mothers. A mother may feel obliged to send an "enough is enough" message to a son who seeks her constant company, and the son, in his turn, may experience the shift in his mother's treatment of him as nothing less than rejection. This places mothers and sons, particularly in households where the father is absent, in a difficult situation. By her actions, Mom says, "Don't be like me, be like him." In Tonka's home, "him," was overseas and the only other "him" nearby was a distant, inaccessible grandfather. Even after Tonka's father was discharged from the navy, he was preoccupied with setting up and operating a medical practice and was rarely home.

An alternative to identifying with a male parent or parent surrogate is to interact with other boys, to become a member of a local gang of guys doing guy stuff, like erecting treehouses. But Tonka's protective mother and grandfather forbade him to play with neighborhood "ruffians," and that avenue was cut off to him.

I take Tonka's mother's concerns about his safety in the backyards of his neighborhood to be one of many examples of her being ambivalent about letting go. Probably as much as her son, she longed for the days before the bourbon's flow was interrupted by the poise she may have adopted in order to make him a man.

Whatever the early dynamics may have been between Tonka and his mother, the issue of unity versus separation was the theme that dominated his life in early adulthood. It had reached a crisis point between ages seven and nine, when he worked on his flying machine. Separation was his conscious fantasy. Reunion, however, was the unconscious goal. His year-long illness enabled him to fulfill that goal, in that it permitted his mother to unleash her devotion to him and provide him with the kind of undivided intimate attention that he had sensed had been permanently lost. No one could have designed a better therapeutic strategy. She carried her son wherever he desired to go. She bathed him and wiped his bottom, and neither of them seemed to be in any hurry for him to get back onto his feet. In the process of managing Tonka's health crisis, the mother and her son restored the intersubjective harmony of days long gone. His mother's actions and her tender devotion to him approximated the features of a working model fashioned from earlier times that had desperately sought to be restored. Tonka's damaged sense of self was partially healed, his "internal milieu" quieted down, and his sense of hopeless emptiness subsided.

After the crisis was over, Tonka no longer dwelled on what his mother's face might be doing in his absence. The energy that had been bound up by such matters was now available for him to engage in the life of a teenager that had all the signs of normalcy. But one issue remained that had the potential of undercutting his relationships with adult women. It was the issue of separation. I have emphasized the restorative influence of Tonka's reunion with his mother at age nine. By age twenty-two, the question of how to separate from her was a powerful undercurrent in his life. Tonka never addressed this issue, and it is doubtful that he was aware that it existed. But it lay at the center of the quiet storm that predisposed him to categorize women the way he did and colored his views of the consequences of marriage. The matter would not have come to my attention without the benefit of reading his TAT compositions.

To refresh your memory, the TAT consists of twenty cards containing ambiguous scenes. The task of the respondent is to create a story to go with each card. Despite never-ending disputes about the value of these stories and the dander the "test" generates among skeptics, they sometimes open direct channels to portions of the mind that otherwise are inaccessible. In chapter 22 I speculated about the "from-the-depths" nature of Larry's story about an archaeologist's discovery of a womblike cavern resting high on a mountaintop. With Tonka it is not a matter of the quality of one story. Instead it is the quantity of stories that contained repetitions of the same theme that is so striking. Eight of the twenty stories he told included a male debating whether to remain with or leave a female. Here is an example.

The formal description of card 6 says that it contains a "short elderly woman standing with her back turned to a tall young man. The latter is looking downward with a perplexed expression." That scene served as Tonka's cue for this story:

> Well, there's a relation between two people there, the mother and the son. The son looks slightly dejected where the mother might look the same way but slightly more determined. It's a situation where the son has his coat on, he's not at home so to speak and I would say that he's just said something or something's been said that causes a great deal of, of some tension. Well, I guess, for example, he says he's going to take a job and move away from the town and he's getting ready to leave. It's sort of one of those times of "Well, I'll have to be saying goodbye now." They're avoiding looking at each other and his mother does not want him to go yet all she's ever said in content is "I'd rather you stay closer [to] here."

The same theme appeared in a story about a mother poking her head into her son's bedroom to make certain he was still there. Tonka composed another story about a mother telling her son not to rush his meal with her. "Stay with me, enjoy what I have cooked for you. You know where your friends will be. You can catch up with them later." The son concurred.

An important variation of Tonka's separation theme is evident in the story he told for the eighteenth card in the TAT set. The card shows a man wearing a tie and an overcoat. The dark background makes it appear that it is nighttime. The fingers of three hands are holding on to his shoulder and arm from the back. Tonka ignored one of the hands when he composed the following story.

> Looks like a young person, maybe about thirty, very resolutely deter-mined to leave. Say he's had a quarrel with his wife *because the hands that are grasping him look mature and quite large.* He's all dressed up to go and he doesn't look particularly upset because he's so resolved to leave, perhaps to go out for the evening or to go away for a day. He's kind of surprised and nonchalant about . . . a person . . . wife grabbing him, reacting as strongly as . . . as she does . . . or has to grab him. He will, I guess, he will leave.

Tonka inferred that the grasping hands must have belonged to the man's wife because they were so mature and large. My interpretation is that Tonka perceived the hands from the perspective of a lad looking at his mother's hands. But now the little boy, wrapped in a thirty-year-old body, is resolved to leave and to get on with his life.

I bid Tonka farewell here and wish him the best on the remainder of his voyage. But before finalizing my departure, this is a convenient time to take a brief detour into folktales, because the results of an analysis per-formed on a collection of them some years ago dovetail with some of the information covered in this chapter regarding Tonka's early urge to fly. The point I want to make is that some of the things we have observed at the level of specific individuals can be detected at the broader level of cul-tural products.[5]

MATRIARCHIES AND FOLKTALE THEMES

I am unwilling to subject the reader to anything more than a general overview of how the study was conducted. It used a state-of-the-art, com-puter-driven method for analyzing the contents of written documents—a method that now would be considered terribly outdated. In the "old days," before the advent of individual computer stations, personal computers, and laptops, computer users lugged IBM cards with holes punched in them to their local mainframe computer facilities and waited in line for their turn to utilize valuable computer time. I stood in line many times during those days with several thousand cards on which the texts of 626 folktales from forty-four "primitive" cultures were recorded (i.e., "punched") on them. These stories had been compiled over many years by anthropologists, field work-ers, missionaries, and so on and were contained in Harvard's Cross Cultural Area Files, maintained by the anthropologist John Whiting. The stories had been transferred to IBM cards and loaned to me by a team of researchers who had used them in a study on the relationship between the use of alco-hol in societies and themes in their folklore.[6]

Marshall Smith, Dexter Dunphy, and I were working under the direc-tion of Philip Stone in the mid-1960s. Stone was a visionary ahead of his time who broke the tradition of using computers to analyze numbers by designing and programming a computer system for analyzing words.[7] Stone named his system the General Inquirer. Anyone who used the Gen-eral Inquirer first had to supply it with a "dictionary." This dictionary in a computer was nothing like Webster's dictionary or any of its competitors. It was much simpler, in that any General Inquirer dictionary contained a limited number of categories for defining specific words or phrases that were of interest to an investigator. For example, one of the categories in the dictionary I developed was *Ascension*. Here are some of the words that were "defined" by it: "flap," "flutter," "fly," "leap," "rise," and "go up." Each time the computer encountered one of these words in a text, the word or phrase would be tagged, or "scored," as a member of the *Ascension* category. This category was one of seventy-four contained in the dictionary I had created to cover a range of Icarian themes. Other categories were de-veloped for tracking words pertaining to fire, water, and descension. The dictionary also included categories for encoding references to emotions (e.g., sadness, fear, and anger), creatures (animals, birds, humans) and for "scoring" kinship terms, end states (e.g., success, failure, death), and a number of other concepts that I believed might be relevant to Icarian themes.

The primary purpose of the study was to group societies according to the degree to which images of fire, water, falling, and especially flying were included in their legends, and proceed to determine if the social structures of "high Icarian" societies were different from the social struc-tures of "low Icarian" societies. They were. According to an ethnographic atlas provided by George Murdock,[8] societies in which Icarian themes were abundant in their stories were matrilocal and/or matrilineal societies. That was true of fourteen out of seventeen of the societies with the highest percentages of Icarian themes in their stories. At the other end, fourteen of the seventeen societies that used the fewest percentages of words pertain-ing to flight, falling, fire, and water in their stories were coded as patrilocal and/or patrilineal in Murdock's system.

Here is what is interesting about these results. The labels *matrilineal* and *matrilocal* are applied to societies in which power is primarily under the jurisdiction of women. Family assets, places of residence, kinship relationships, and major decisions are maternally controlled in these societies, relative to societies that are indexed as *patrilineal* and *patrilocal*. Icarian themes (of which flying is a prominent component) were most prevalent in the folktales of the "matri-" societies and sparsely represented in stories sampled from societies where men are largely in control.

Cautiously interpreted, these results hint at the existence of parallel patterns of household structures that may be precursors to the insertion of Icarian themes into the lives of individuals at the "local" level, and into folklore at the cultural level. Mothers were the dominating figures in the homes of Barrie, Jung, Tonka, and, as I will show, Marc Chagall. According to Murdock's ethnographic index, women have the dominating edge over men in societies that integrate ascension themes into their legends and fables.

Before climbing aboard my argument that maternal dominance is a precursor to expressions of latent yearnings to recover sensations of interpersonal union with the mother, ardent empiricists would correctly demand more hard evidence than this study was able to offer. At best, the results obtained from the content analysis of folktales would be considered "suggestive." Nonetheless, I will relate here a further discovery I made that adds weight to the suggestive quality of the parallels I have been considering.

The final step taken in the analysis of folktales was to reduce the sample of societies from forty-four to eighteen. Nine of the eighteen were those that included the highest number of flying themes in their stories, and the other nine were societies that made the fewest references to ascension in their stories. Using a special feature of the General Inquirer, the program was instructed to identify and "retrieve" all sentences in which a word or phrase had been defined by the category *Change*. Fifty-eight sentences from "high Icarian" society stories met that retrieval specification, compared to the eighteen the computer located in stories from "low Icarian" societies. These sentences were further winnowed down to forty-one by preserving only the ones in which women were depicted as changing their form. The vast majority of these sentences (thirty-five of forty-one) were contained in the folktales of "high Icarian" societies. Here are some examples:

> I looked up and saw her change into a bear.
> Instead of divorcing her man, she pretended she was dead.
> The old woman and the girl just changed into mice.
> She suddenly became a porcupine.
> She turned into a warrior and came after me with a torch.

Tonka's mother could "change on a dime." Margaret Ogilvy changed forever when her favorite son died. "Here today and gone tomorrow" captures the traumatic manner in which Carl Jung experienced the departure of his mother. The conjoining themes of women undergoing a sudden transition—dying, in Larry's case—and of rising and levitation in folktales may be more than happenstance occurrences. Examples of what I have identified as notable features of some of the lives I have discussed have also been detected at a societal level. The empiricist side of me is relieved by the fact that some numbers can be used to support portions of my argument. The support is indirect and somewhat tangential, and no one is in a better position than I am to challenge the data (stories gathered by missionaries, field workers, and anthropologists blended into composite sets?) and the semantic assumptions that are made explicit in a computerized dictionary. But the patterns are there and demonstrate that ideas generated from in-depth case studies may not be as scientifically fruitless as critics of the approach sometimes complain.

TWENTY-THREE *A Lawn Chair*
and a Phantom Flying Saucer

Images and themes of wished-for reunions with nurturing love objects in the skies appear in poetry, music, novels, films, and other forms of art. As I will show in the next chapter, what Chagall made explicit in some of his paintings is implied in other artistic productions. For example, a metaphor for ascension contained in Federico Fellini's film $8^{1}/_{2}$ clears up some of the mystery behind the plot. The film is about a director, played by Marcello Mastroianni, who is working against a deadline and rapidly vanishing resources of impatient backers, to create a movie. The main source of tension between the director and his staff is that the director will not reveal his script. The cast has been hired, the location has been determined, but nobody has been told what the movie is to be about. From all indications, the director himself does not know. However, that does not deter him from overseeing the construction of a large scaffold for supporting a spaceship that will surely be a main feature of the production. The movie suggests that the director has in mind the prospects of entering the spaceship himself in order to escape his dilemma. In addition to the problems he has created for himself with backers and frustrated cast members anxious for starring roles, he has another one that he appears to think could be resolved by a ride into space. That problem is he cannot love. He is surrounded by women who are attracted to him—including a wife to whom he cannot be faithful—but, like J. M. Barrie, he is unable or unwilling to join with any of them in an intimate relationship. Several flashbacks in $8^{1}/_{2}$ hint that the hero is obsessed with his mother and mourns his fate of having to move into adulthood. In a leap of faith that our theory of levitation fantasies is on target, the director's half-baked plans to fly are configured and guided by unconscious images that outer space contains the solution to his longings to escape the reality of his beleaguered existence. He is trapped in the encasement of a mind and a body that cannot do what is demanded of them; the sky is waiting to enfold him in an embrace reminiscent of former times of a harmoniously partnered life.

So as not to wear readers out, I will not comment on Robert Altman's 1970s film *Brewster McCloud* (the story of an adolescent boy whose partbird maternal guardian attempts to convince him that flying is better than sex). Nor will I mention the Harry Potter books or Steven Spielberg's *E.T.*, or any of several dozen other potential reference sources. But I cannot resist quoting a passage from F. Scott Fitzgerald's novel *The Great Gatsby*:

> The quiet lights in the houses were humming out into the darkness and there was a stir and bustle among the stars. Out of the corner of his eye Gatsby saw that the blocks of the sidewalks really formed a ladder and mounted to a secret place above the trees—he could climb it, if he climbed alone, and once there he could suck the pap of life, gulp down the incomparable milk of wonder.[1]

In these two sentences, Fitzgerald makes it known that Gatsby's obsession with winning back Daisy, his former lover, was driven by a desire to restore long-lost pleasures of infancy; a fantasy that, of course, no "real" woman could fulfill.

Returning to "real life" stories, this chapter describes two men who took elaborate steps in efforts to fly. Little is known about the childhoods of either of them, and that places us in the precarious position that Freud was in when he transformed his speculations about Leonardo's early experiences into facts and proceeded to use these "facts" to support his "looking for sex" theory of flying. It is not beyond my capabilities to be seduced into a similar trap, but the total absence of early childhood information about Larry Walters and Marshall Herff Applewhite precludes any opportunity to play a connect-the-dots game. However, by now, I have a premise about flying fantasies that can be informed and elaborated on by considering the actions of Walters and Applewhite. That premise is that the ambition to rise into the air is a product of latent desires to restore ineffable body sensations that once, a long time ago, before the dawn of consciousness, had been associated with the pleasures of intersubjective union with the mother.

LARRY WALTERS

In real life, one cannot recapture a sense of intersubjective rapture by returning to a state of infancy. Even fantasies of doing so are too absurd (or threatening) to entertain. However, the concept of time travel opens some interesting possibilities. In typical time travel stories, the main character is transported, in the age and shape of his or her present body, to a different time. In a few stories, the hero's trip into the past only spans a day or so. For instance, the film *Groundhog Day* allows the character played by Bill Murray to repeat the events of the previous day over and over until he gets it right. However, most time travel stories take the main character back (or ahead) to a completely different era. Jack Finney's novel *Time and Again*[2] is about a man who was recruited for an experiment by a secret federal agency to determine if it is possible to enter the past with the concomitant prospects (and dangers) of potentially altering the future through his actions. After intensive mindset training sessions, the hero succeeds in visiting New York City as it was in the winter of 1882. He makes several trips back and forth between New York now and New York then, and at the end of the story opts for permanent residence in the earlier period. Finney uses this plot to create his vision of the physical conditions and cultural atmosphere of the city by describing the buildings, the politics, and the lifestyles of the wealthy and the desperately poor, as well as the clothes, carriages, and shops that reflected the ambience of the burgeoning community. A love story is woven into the novel, but it is secondary to Finney's exercise of depicting the local color of Manhattan in the late nineteenth century.

Finney's book inspired the script for a movie entitled *Somewhere in Time*, but the seed brought forth a quite different story. One of the major differences between the book and the film is that the film is explicitly a love story. Starring Christopher Reeve and Jane Seymour, *Somewhere in Time* takes place in the Grand Hotel in Mackinac, Michigan. Time travel episodes occur in that single location, as it appeared in 1972 and as it would have appeared sixty years earlier, in 1912.

A force draws the hero to the hotel. The film identifies that force to be an elderly woman who suddenly appears at a party celebrating the success of a college production of a play written by the hero. As she passes by Reeve, their eyes lock momentarily, and she says, "Come back to me." Her words haunt the main character for several years, to the point where he trashes his career and travels by car to the Grand Hotel, unable to understand why he is there. The hotel contains a small museum of artifacts from former periods. It includes a portrait of a gorgeous woman who performed on stage at the hotel in 1912. There is something about the portrait that Reeve clearly "recognizes," and he becomes obsessed with solving the mystery. After several days of failed attempts, Reeve manages to time travel the span of fifty years. In the hotel, now quaintly decorated, the young adult Reeve meets the young adult actress. The actress's jealous manager throws several obstacles in their way, but they overcome them and an intimate relationship gradually develops.

But all's not well in the Grand Hotel. Reeve slips back to the present, and his lover remains locked in the past. It is a tear-jerking separation.

Reeve bolts his door and stays in his room for a week. He is discovered sitting in a chair staring out a window by the hotel staff. Weak from a broken heart and starvation, Reeve is taken to a hospital, where he dies. Suddenly a vision of heaven appears above his dead body. Heaven consists of a vast, endless lake where the two lovers meet and, one is led to conclude, will coexist for all time.

Somewhere in Time is not on my list of favorite movies. But it got top billing on Larry Walters's list. He had been so deeply moved by the film that still shots from the picture covered an entire wall of his small apartment. Neither this nor any other item of information about Walters's life would be of much interest had it not been for that fact that on July 3, 1982, Walters strapped himself into a Sears, Roebuck lawn chair and, with the lifting power provided by forty-two helium-filled weather balloons, rose into the air from the small backyard of a house in San Pedro, California.

Walters's flight was not a spur-of-the-moment, impulsive, act. Nor was it a response to a bet. He had daydreamed about flying for at least ten years prior to takeoff, and his actual flight plans had been worked out in great detail. According to George Plimpton's chronicle of Walters's flight preparations, published in the *New Yorker*,[3] Walters packed the following essentials: a two-way radio; an altimeter; a compass; a flashlight; extra batteries; a medical kit; a pocket knife; eight plastic water bottles for ballast, hanging over the sides of the chair; a package of beef jerky; a road map of California; a camera; two liters of Coca-Cola; a BB gun for popping the balloons; a life jacket; and, on the insistence of his girlfriend, Carol, a parachute. Walters attached all of these items either to his person or to the chair, with one important exception. He forgot to tie down the BB gun.

Lift-off occurred with a thrust more powerful than had been anticipated. The original idea was that the contraption would gradually rise a hundred feet or so and remain there, tethered by a rope attached to a car in order to give Walters time to get his bearings. But the device rose much more rapidly than had been calculated. It went up at a rate of eight hundred feet per minute, and the tethering rope snapped within the first fifteen or twenty seconds of the flight.

Walters's plan was to cruise at an altitude of eight to nine thousand feet. Instead, the chair (which he had dubbed *Inspiration*) nearly doubled the intended altitude. When it reached fifteen thousand feet, Walters decided to pop some of the balloons. After successfully blowing holes in seven of them, he put the gun on his lap to check the altimeter. At that moment he was hit by a gust of wind, and the gun tumbled from the chair and quickly became a disappearing dark speck beneath him. The thirty-five remaining balloons lifted him to an altitude of sixteen thousand five hundred feet, where he became a flight hazard to commercial airlines. Pilots alerted air traffic controllers at surrounding airports of the dangerous situation. One controller at the Los Angeles Airport was radioed the following message: "This is T.W.A. 321, level at sixteen thousand feet. We have a man in a chair attached to balloons in our ten-o'clock position, range five miles."[4]

Just as Walters began to seriously consider using his parachute — breathing had become difficult and he was mighty cold — helium started to seep out of the balloons, and he began to lose altitude. Just as he had taken off with more force than he had anticipated, his descent was more rapid than he had expected. But his luck held out, and his fall was broken by the balloons becoming entangled in electric power lines. Fortunately, the chair missed the high-tension line and, with him still in it, it dangled about eight feet above the ground, near a swimming pool. In a day full of ironies, a pilot on his day off was lounging next to a pool and came to his rescue. Walter had flown for about an hour and a half.

The story made good copy for newspapers. It even bounced a planned headline story regarding Ronald Reagan in some papers. But news comes and goes quickly, and had George Plimpton not become interested in the story, it would have vanished altogether. Some months after Larry's adventure, Plimpton visited Larry, Larry's mother, and a few other people close to him for the purpose of gathering information suitable for an article. The interviews covered a variety of topics, including Larry's stint in the army as a cook during the Vietnam War, the development of his flight plans, the warnings and reactions of his mother and his girlfriend, and other matters suitable for arranging into a human interest story. However, shortly after the interview, Walters phoned Plimpton and asked him not to write the story. Larry feared that any piece Plimpton would publish might lessen his chances of being invited to go on a speaking tour of aviation clubs. Plimpton complied with Walters's request.

Ten years later, it was reported that Larry had died at a campsite on the side of a canyon. Plimpton, now free to tell Walters's story, returned to California and spoke with the women who had been close to him. He discovered that Walters had become pretty much a loner after his flight. He and his girlfriend had drifted apart, although they remained in touch. He had become an avid hiker and, for the most part, preferred to hike and camp out alone. Walters's mother had a few pictures of his favorite campsite, where he had shot himself in the heart. "He loved nature," his mother reported, and: "He fell in love with God." After his death, his mother found a Bible next to his bed with the following passage underlined in red: "And ye now therefore have sorrow: but I will see you again, and your heart will rejoice, and your joy no man taketh from you."

A volunteer ranger named Joyce Rios had met Larry eight years before he committed suicide, and she occasionally accompanied him on his mountain treks. Rios told Plimpton that Walters was "obsessed" with his girlfriend, Carol. He felt responsible for them drifting apart. "He felt terribly guilty about it," Joyce said. In addition to talking about Carol, Walters and Joyce also had long conversations about religion, death, and resurrection. She reported that Walters always carried a well-worn copy of Finney's *Time and Again* with him and referred to it as frequently as he referred to the Bible. "Sleep. And when you wake up everything you know of the twentieth century will be gone" was one of his favorite passages. He had marked a sentence in Joyce's personal copy of the book that read: "I now end the life that should have ended then."

In Plimpton's last conversation with Larry in 1982, he asked him what he felt after his flight was over. "Life seems a little empty, because I always had this thing to look forward to—to strive for and dream about, you know." Carol could not provide Larry with what he yearned for. Nothing in this life could fill his emptiness. In *Somewhere in Time*, an elderly woman begged Christopher Reeve to come back to her. Reeve succeeded; he found intimacy with a woman in heaven. All it cost him was his life. Larry Walters rose over sixteen thousand feet into the air in a lawn chair and returned to the ground feeling empty. The intimacy he sought was not to be found up there. Nor was it to be found on earth. He had come to believe that the gap between his timeless preconscious "then" and the "now" of objects that were unable to sate his appetite for boundless union with a maternal figure could only be filled by a time-traveling spirit that would be released upon the death of its container.

MARSHALL HERFF APPLEWHITE

In the Book of Revelation, God communicates his plan for the gruesome end of the world to his servant John. "Come up here, and I will show you things that must take place" (Rev. 4:1). Through the medium of angels, John witnesses burning mountains being thrown into the sea, whose waters are mingled with blood; the moon and stars being forever darkened; the eruption of horse-shaped locusts from a bottomless pit with teeth like lions, scorpion tails, and breastplates of iron. If that is not enough to send sinners scrambling for cover, two hundred million men riding fire-breathing horses are unleashed to wipe out unfortunate survivors. In all, not a pretty picture.

God then foretells the appearance of two witnesses to alert mankind that the end is near, that the destructive forces will soon be unleashed. "And I will give power to my two witnesses, and they will prophesy one thousand two hundred and sixty days clothed in sackcloth" (Rev. 11:3). At the end of their testimony, they will be killed by forces hostile to their message, and their dead bodies will lie in the street of a great city. After three and a half days, the breath of life from God will enter the witnesses' bodies. The two will rise from the dead, and great fear will fall upon those who murdered them. A loud voice will emanate from above, saying, "Come up here" (Rev. 11:11), at which point the two prophets will be observed ascending into heaven. In the same hour of their ascension, the destruction of the planet begins.

I recall suffering through a sermon on the topic of how the world was to end while sitting on a pew of the Presbyterian church of my childhood. The sermon wasn't so bad; no worse than the fire-and-brimstone threats that the minister of our congregation usually issued. I was accustomed to his message, but I was not accustomed to the oppressive heat and humidity that hung over the auditorium, making the exposed portions of my legs stick to the pew and perspiration from my face pour down on the jacket that was part of my required Sunday morning outfit of short pants and wool jacket. As a diversion from dwelling on my miseries and looking at my father's wristwatch every thirty seconds or so, I tried to pay attention to the minister's words. He referred to the two witnesses mentioned in Revelations as *male* prophets clothed in sackcloth sent to Earth to issue God's warnings of imminent destruction. That made sense to me.

But my pastor got it wrong, according to Marshall Herff Applewhite and Bonnie Lu Trusdale Nettles. On numerous occasions they announced that they were the incarnations of God's pair of witnesses foretold in Revelation. Not male messiahs, as my pastor had assumed and I had imagined, but a man and a woman who usually preferred to be called Bo and Peep, or Do and Ti. Less frequently they went under the names Tidily and Wink, or Winnie and Pooh. When they granted interviews, they asked to be referred to as "The Two."

If this were late March or early April in 1997, I would not have to introduce Marshall Herff Applewhite to you. His name appeared in the headlines of all national and many international newspapers during the period of several days, even weeks, after his body, and thirty-eight others, were discovered in a mansion in Rancho Santa Fe, a community located on the outskirts of San Diego, California. All of the victims had been members of the cult known as Heaven's Gate, of which Applewhite had been the guru. They were found lying on beds, fully dressed with sneakers on their feet, waiting to be rescued by a flying saucer. The spaceship was not observable by the naked eye, nor could it be seen through a telescope, because it was thought to be traveling apace with and behind the comet Hale-Bopp, whose trajectory had brought it within viewing distance of Earth. The comet was there in fact, but the saucer was there by faith, and an additional article of faith had placed Bonnie Lu Nettles (or Ti or Peep) in command of the craft. Nettles qualified as the pilot because she had died from pancreatic cancer several years earlier.

A prerequisite for being beamed up to the mother ship and a safe voyage to a higher level of existence was for all members of the household to consume lethal mixtures of vodka and phenobarbital pills and lie patiently (dead) on their beds as they waited to be taken to the next plane of existence.

The initial report of the ghastly scene discovered inside the estate on March 27 referred to the bodies of thirty-nine men. All were either bald or had extremely short hair shaved almost to the skin. Their clothing was identical—baggy black pants, long-sleeved black shirts, and new Nike sneakers. Identical packed traveling cases lay next to their bedsides. On closer examination, investigators were shocked to realize that only nineteen were men. The remaining twenty were women. And five of the males, including Applewhite, had been surgically castrated.

News agencies were abuzz with excitement. Everyone wanted to get in on the story. CNN gave on-the-spot television coverage, internet chat rooms dropped their favorite topics in favor of expressing and hearing out anonymous opinions about the unsettling event, and magazine editors assigned top reporters to cover the story. In a little over a month, the first book about the tragedy was published by Steiger and Hewes,[5] and shortly thereafter a publication written by the "Staff of the New York Post"[6] hit the bookstores. These nearly instantaneous publications were made possible by the fact that the Heaven's Gate cult had been in existence for over twenty-five years, although it had undergone several name changes. Bits and pieces of its history and items of information about its founders, including extensive interviews with The Two in the 1970s, had been retrieved from various archives and gathered together into stories. One of the most often cited resources was the group's website. They had discovered the Internet in the mid-1990s and had used their site to propagate their philosophy.

All of the accounts I have read about the life of Marshall Herff Applewhite agree on the following details. He was born in Spur, Texas, in 1932. Practically nothing is known about his childhood other than that his father was a Presbyterian minister who founded three churches during his career. Herff attended a church-affiliated college in Sherman, Texas, and studied music at the University of Colorado. While there, he landed leading roles in productions of *South Pacific* and *Oklahoma*. Encouraged by these accomplishments, he turned his eyes toward the theater capital of the world—New York City—where he hoped to establish a career as a professional singer. With the support and encouragement of his bride, Ann, the couple moved to the city, as did hundreds of other equally talented competitors hungry for employment. The best the strikingly handsome man could do was to get hired for a few commercials.

In 1952, at the age of thirty, Herff enrolled at a Presbyterian seminary in Virginia and a year later was hired as the choir director for a church in North Carolina. There the "strait-laced" couple had their first child. Eventually Ann gave birth to a second child. In 1961, Herff obtained a teaching position at the University of Alabama. As a member of the music department, he taught choral music and provided individual instruction. In May 1964, he submitted his letter of resignation. The letter was a cover for the fact that the head of his department had fired him. Herff not only left the university but left his family as well: he had become openly gay.

His transformation during his three years in Alabama had not been subtle. He flaunted his gayness. Several former male students acknowledged their sexual encounters with him. Two of them reported that he got especially charged up when he arranged to have sex with them in a room next to the bedroom where his wife was sleeping. Rumors about Herff's unethical behavior spread throughout the Tuscaloosa academic community, and nobody was pleased about his "disgraceful" behaviors. Neither was Herff, for that matter. The word "ambivalence" is too soft, too abstract, to describe his dilemma. He hated being homosexual and, at the same time, felt that he had no control over his attraction to men. One moment his mind would be flooded by self-punishing thoughts, and the next moment he would trot off to bed with a student.

By 1966, Herff had drifted back to Texas and was hired as a music teacher at the University of St. Thomas, a Catholic college in Houston. During the course of his employment there, he became affiliated with the Houston Grand Opera, where he sang over a dozen solos. But in 1970, a scandalous relationship he was having with a student resulted in his being fired from his teaching job. He covered his tracks sufficiently well to be hired as director of music at an Episcopal church in Houston. After about a year at that post, Herff admitted himself into a hospital for "emotional repair" (as he told some people) or "to correct a heart problem" (as he told his sister). Years later he revealed the truth. He entered the hospital to have his "balls chopped off." Homosexuality, all sexuality, cured.

Shortly after Herff had been neutered, perhaps during his period of recovery (although the record is not clear about that), he met a nurse named Louise (Bonnie) Lu Trusdale Nettles. Bonnie was married and had four grown children. She was four years older than Herff. She has been described as a plain-looking woman who had developed a passion for astrology and New Age religious views about reincarnation. She had been especially taken by UFO explanations of life's great mysteries.

With no second thoughts and no regrets, Bonnie left her husband and children within weeks of meeting Herff. Herff was the embodiment of the eunuch that she believed was in the cards she had been dealt, or, more accurately, had selected. His handsome appearance, wit, and talent were unanticipated bonuses.

One of the building blocks of their yin/yang compatibility was their openness in sharing feelings of alienation. These feelings were so strong in both of them that they concluded they were, in fact, aliens. They had traveled through space and time and had been planted in material containers called bodies. They called their bodies *vehicles*. Vehicles are physical objects that temporarily house souls that arrive from outer space for reasons . . . well, they didn't quite figured that one out for everyone, but they figured it out for themselves. The reason they were here was that God had sent them to fulfill His "Two Witnesses" promise in the book of Revelation.

The Two viewed fetuses, babies, children, and adults as physical containers selected and occupied by souls. Bonnie and Herff made it known that the bodies they had selected were ones that had been examined and subsequently rejected by other spirits. I must pause at that observation for a moment. Their spirits occupied vehicles or containers that other souls had rejected; this suggests that they were not particularly happy with their selections. Herff hated what his body had done when it bounced from bed to bed with male undergraduate and graduate students, and Bonnie was not pleased with her body's drab appearance. Not only had their bodies been rejected by other souls but, one suspects, various episodes of "real life" rejections on the parts of others were both defended against and explained by their mystic conclusions.

Bo and Peep concluded that the trick to life, the ticket back to a higher level of existence, was contingent on wiping out all human needs. Feelings of true awareness can only come about by way of the arduous process of becoming unattached to anything in one's surroundings. All forms of dependency must be vanquished. Sex, alcohol, drugs, and other pleasurable elixirs sponsored by Lucifer must be resisted. All attachments to other people must be severed. Love of material possessions and investments in self-defining roles serve to block entrance into the next level of existence. One must strip oneself from any connections before life eternal is granted. Pure soul is available only to those who reject or pay no attention to human emotions and avoid the distractions that constantly bombard the body and mind on the "lower level" plane of existence (Earth). The consensus of the masses regarding what is human is simply wrong.

Note that this echoes the interplay between Carl Jung's Personalities No. 1 and No. 2. He viewed his Personality No. 1 as responsible for coping with the realities of everyday life. It was the evolving result of experiential learning required to get along with other people. It was shaped and, he feared, distorted, by social, political, and religious beliefs and standards that had the potential of removing one's self from one's true Self. Jung believed that his true Self was manifested in his Personality No. 2. It was connected to something much more grand than any earthly attachments had to offer. The danger inherent in welcoming this ineffable and unknowable force was that its entrance could be so overwhelming that it could engulf the soul and sweep it away, or back, to the original sea of our existence.

Jung became one of the primary gurus for seekers of a better life. People who have garnered many of the trappings of the presumably "good" life and still feel that something is missing are ripe for his observations. His writings touch the same chord as did the preaching of Bo and Peep. The vagabond pair never had a large following, but they were able to recruit a few hundred adult followers during their fifteen-year partnership. Herff, with his penetrating blue eyes and eloquent speaking ability, spoke directly to that part of certain individuals that was screaming: "This is not it! There must be something else!" He put into words what some people felt in their hearts. They missed something that once had been and was lost. Bo and Peep managed to convince them that it could be regained. A few of them had been victims of abuse and were wandering about looking for someone to give them a sense of life's true meaning. But the majority of recruits shocked their families and communities when they abandoned them. The outwardly comfortable trappings of their lives did not grant them lives worth living. The option of returning to their real "space fetus" home offered by the dressed-alike, look-alike, middle-aged couple that called themselves The Two was irresistibly attractive to some of these people.

In the meantime, Bo and Peep practiced what they preached: no sex. They connected at a spiritual level where two souls merged into one. They nurtured each other's sense of specialness by entering into the kind of intersubjective dance written about by Daniel Stern in which neither of them existed outside their relationship. They dabbled with the notion that they had not selected their current bodies at infancy. Instead their souls had entered them when they first met. Whatever souls had been there had abandoned their vehicles, and the two messiahs prophesied in Revelation filled the vacancies. This made perfect sense to Herff. His operation had resulted in the release of his gay soul—the one that had been the source of so many of his problems. His container's new soul could make a new beginning, and Bonnie, with her mix of Christian mysticism and New Age babble, was there to help. They began and ended their project at the level of the intersubjective self. Mother and son, father and daughter, two minds operating as one. They were not part of this world and had no desire to fit in. They were part of another world, a preverbal world in which working models of intersubjective safety never failed. Heaven on earth, one might say, as they found in each other what J. M. Barrie sensed he had lost and Carl Jung believed could only be found via merger with the collective unconscious.

The Two resisted all temptations to become attached to anything except to each other; not at a physical level, of course, but at a spiritual level reminiscent of another time, an earlier time of presexual intersubjective euphoria. Their joint mission of alerting the world to God's plan for Earth's destruction became the glue that held them together and precluded any need to fashion individual identities. Their gospel directed their followers to do what they had done—to peel away their identities. The only way to return to the source of existence was to become stripped of all outside attachments and externally imposed meanings and become like innocent babes. In that way, and in that way only, could one reserve a seat on the UFO that God was sending to fulfill his levitation promise.

Herff's heaven-on-earth world was shattered when Bonnie died. He had no self-boundaries outside the partnership they had formed. The feelings of paradise on earth could only be restored by way of reuniting with the soul that had evoked those feelings . . . and she was gone. After long periods of isolating himself from his band of followers, he returned a desperate man, with a vision that the time for Earth's destruction was imminent. Salvation was on the way. Over time it became clear to Herff that salvation was to arrive in the form of a flying saucer, a spacecraft steered by none other than Ti. He envisioned his soul being transported into the "mother ship" where one plus one again totaled two, The Two. The misfits in the world below would mesh into a boundless union in the sky above and leave the fate of Lucifer's evil planet in the hands of a righteous God.

The next chapter moves this discourse from a region of pathology, deception, and despair to one of hope, optimism, and celebration; from Marshall Herff Applewhite to Marc Chagall. Many of Marc Chagall's stunning canvases blend the themes of this book into memorable images that depict realizations of the end states of ascensionistic fantasies.

TWENTY-FOUR *Marc Chagall*

In the 1960s, during the heyday of federal support for early childhood education, I worked as a member of a small team of investigators involved in studying youngsters' social development in conjunction with another team that assessed their mental skills. Of the two dozen or so children whose activities my team monitored over the course of a year, a four-and-a-half-year-old boy was among the children we drew straws for the opportunity to observe. This ruddy, articulate, and very active youngster's favorite games involved playing with airplanes. Any object could be an airplane in the hands of this boy. Grasping a block, a crayon, a toy car, or a plastic horse, he would whirl it above his head, and while making various zooming noises and copter sounds, he would leap onto chairs and tables and yell "Goodbye" to his teachers and peers. On some occasions he dropped his props and pranced from one end of the room to the other flapping his arms. Around noon, he frequently announced that he was going to fly home for lunch and then fly over to a friend's home in the afternoon and then fly back home in time for supper.

About three months into the school year, the boy introduced an ape into his imaginary landscape. He alternated between being an airplane ready for takeoff and being an ape that could hang onto the limb of an imaginary tree all day.

One morning he was observed speaking about the size and incredible strength of apes to anyone who would listen to him. Suddenly he turned to a companion and said, "You know, sometimes I feel like an ape but usually I feel like a little monkey that's scared and doesn't want to be big." This sentiment was made the same day the boy's mother had pinned a note to an extra pair of pants that said "just in case of another accident."

This charming redheaded flyboy, who viewed becoming big with some trepidation, was temporarily in the company of others whose lives I have visited. James Barrie frequently and throughout his entire lifetime declared his firm opinion about that. Not only did he object to growing up but also said he could not grow up. It was a sentiment shared by Perry Smith, who said that his life would have turned out much better had he not grown up. Tonka said, "I've been told and somehow believe that my first year was great, probably the best, and I think I hated to leave it."

Marc Chagall was more specific about his resistance to growing up when he wrote:

> As each year passed I felt myself moving towards unknown thresholds. Especially from the day when my father, wearing the talis, recited above my boyish, thirteen-year-old body, the prayer of the transfer of moral responsibility. What should I do?
>
> Remain an innocent child?
>
> Pray morning and evening and everywhere I go, whatever I put into my mouth and whatever I hear, immediately say a prayer? Or flee from the synagogue and, throwing away the books, the holy vestments, roam the streets toward the river?
>
> I was afraid of my majority, afraid of having, in my turn, all the signs of the adult male, even the beard.
>
> In those sad, solitary days, those thoughts made me weep toward nightfall, as though someone were beating me or announcing the death of my parents.[1]

Chagall's pronouncements of fear, his stated objections to advancing into adulthood, are repeated many times in his account of his childhood and adolescence.

Marc Chagall (1887–1985), one of the world's most honored artists, was born in Vitebsk, Russia. Standard biographic sketches of Chagall contain the following summary information about him. His formal studies of art began when he was twenty years old, under the direction of Leon Bakst in St. Petersburg. Three years later he moved to Paris, where he learned from the leading cubists and surrealists. He returned to Russia during World War I and remained there for eight years. During that period he was first appointed commissar of fine arts in his hometown of Vitebsk and subsequently served as the director of Russia's Free Academy of Art. By 1922, Chagall had grown weary of his style of art being frowned on by Bolshevik authorities and soon settled in France. Except when he fled its borders at the outbreak of World War II in 1941 and lived in the United States for seven years, France became his permanent home.

Today, two decades after his death, Chagall is recognized as one of the most significant painters and graphic artists of the twentieth century. His oil paintings and watercolors are among the prized possessions of museums throughout the Western world. But his art was not restricted to canvas backings; he adorned buildings with eye-catching forms. The ceiling of the Opera House in Paris, murals at the New York Metropolitan Opera, a glass window at the United Nations, and decorations at the Vatican provide more than sufficient evidence of his place in the history of modern art.

This chapter is not an attempt to "explain" Chagall's magnificent artistic achievements. The poignant quality of his works, his strong and brightly colored portrayals of the world, the simplicity of his designs, his fusion of fantasy with religious themes will not be subjected here to amateurish reductionism. I am much more inclined to appreciate Chagall's artistry than to analyze it. There is a good deal about his gifts to humankind that I hold sacred, and I am not about to minimize his accomplishments by marching to the beat of a psychoanalytic drum.

The sole focus here is to take up the question of how depictions of levitated objects initially came to be one of Chagall's trademarks. Houses, carts, people, animals, and fish don't occupy their standard places in many of his paintings. Some objects are suspended in the air or depicted as floating upside down. Some images appear to be rising and others falling. Images of fire and water, the other two elements of an Icarian theme, also make their appearances in his artwork, and both are prominent topics in his autobiography.

By this point in the book, it would seem, all that is needed is to point our radar in the direction of Chagall's mother and discover what she did to the poor fellow. Did she die when he was a youngster? Did she turn away from him at a critical time during his development? In what ways had she been inadequate, in reality or in the eyes of her son, that resulted in his craving to restore sensations that had previously accompanied feelings of unity with her? Surely Chagall's autobiography will contain information about his mother that can easily be slotted into the formula I have so diligently crafted. Freud did it for Leonardo. We can do it for Marc.

The problem is it can't be done. Believe me, I've tried, but the formula doesn't work. A critical variable is missing. It's the old-round-peg-in-a-square-hole exercise in frustration. Chagall's resistance to growing up cannot be attributed to a sense of being abandoned by his mother. Yes, he daydreamed about the pleasures of remaining completely dependent on her. And, yes, he wrote about his early struggles to get his mother to fit his picture of a totally agreeable nurturing object. I will cover that information. But it will be a prelude to a much more startling series of events that I believe fueled his ambivalence about growing up.

Chagall was forthright about having little interest in maturation when he wrote: "I often used to say that a little room with a grating in the door through which someone would pass me food would have satisfied me forever."[2] Numerous references to small enclosures, secluded nooks, and other safe places culminate in his statement that he'd "be satisfied with some sort of hole . . . I'd be happy there"—as long as he was assured there was sufficient food.

Chagall mentions food frequently in his autobiography. He speaks of it as "sort of an itch" that doesn't disappear after it is scratched. Although his family was poor (his father was a laborer in a herring warehouse), there was always a sufficient amount of food in the house for him, the eldest, and eventually his nine siblings to satisfy their hunger. His statement that "buttered bread, like an eternal symbol, was never out of my childish hands" underscores the fact that his family was never on the verge of starvation.

Eating, specifically *when* to eat, was sometimes a source of conflict between Marc and his mother. The following passage contains Chagall's account of the tug-of-war.

> As a rule, toward dinner time, I'd fall asleep, fully dressed, and Mother would come to wake her first born son.
> "I don't know what's the matter with him; the minute dinner is ready, he falls asleep. My son, come and eat!"
> "What?"
> "Some gruel."
> "Which kind?"
> "Buckwheat with milk."
> "I want to sleep."
> "Come and eat first."
> "I don't like it."
> "Come on, just try; if it chokes you, if you faint, you needn't eat anymore."
> I confess that I sometimes fainted on purpose.[3]

Chagall's battles over food are reminiscent of the mealtime squabbles that Grope engaged in with this mother, according to Murray's account of the American Icarus's early days:

> Grope's earliest memory is of dumping his supper on the floor. Seated in a high chair, he was asked by his mother if he wanted some string beans, and he, being in a bad mood, repeatedly said no, even though he usually liked string beans. She finally put the plate in front of him and it was at this point that he upset it and pushed the beans on the floor. This, he writes, "was my first feelings of grief that accompany a sort of 'martyr complex' or 'cut off your nose to spite your face complex.'"[4]

Grope's pattern of rejecting his mother's offerings extended into his grade school years. "Tempestuous quarrels" over food characterized those days. Murray believed that the struggle stemmed in part from Grope's mother's strict adherence to the then fashionable childrearing principles advocated by the behaviorist J. B. Watson. Murray writes that Grope's mother "scrupulously followed her day's dicta: (a) that children should be fed by the clock and (b) that maternal nurturance should be minimal."[5] In Murray's view, this left the infant Grope "with unsatisfied oral and affectional needs and in a state of emptiness and rage with a duration much longer than is tolerable at such a young age." He concludes that "such unrelieved intensity of need, combined with 'desertion' by the mother, is likely to result in a kind of self-protective apathy with rejection of both the giver and her gift when they ultimately arrive—too late."[6]

This is one of the few instances when Murray gives any hints about what he thinks might be precursors to fantasies of flight. His purpose in writing about Grope was to identify and define the components of the "Icarus complex," and for the most part he remained faithful to that descriptive task. In his one foray into the issues that may reside beneath the surface of the Icarus complex, he focused on Grope's "unsatisfied oral and affectional needs."

In fact, food as a symbol of being loved and accepted has arisen in several of the other cases I have considered. Take Tonka's two types of monsters, for example: one of the types, the bad, nonnurturing kind, was poised and ready to strike him at any moment. The other type, a benevolent monster, would feed him generously. Along the same line, Perry Smith's fantasy rescue by the great parrot reached its climax when he imagined himself being transported to an abundant and free supply of food in the sky. No strings attached. Just feast to your heart's content.

At this juncture a red flag goes up that cautions me not to read into the life of Marc Chagall what might have been true about the experiences of others whose lives I have written about. It would be a dreadful mistake, for example, to ignore Chagall's Hasidic cultural roots and the difficult conditions he and his family faced in Russia. From the late eighteenth century to the middle of World War I, most Russian Jews lived in and were forbidden to leave an area known as the Jewish Pale of Settlement. The Pale of Settlement comprised parts of modern Ukraine, Poland, and the Baltic States. Vitebsk was located in the northeast portion of the Pale. Jews were largely confined to living in the *shtetls*, or market districts, of the towns and had little contact with the ethnic Russian population. Jews who desired to participate in a larger secular culture of Russian life could do so only by masking or by rejecting traditional values. The prospect of rejecting traditional values was unthinkable to Chagall's parents and relatives, as the family remained steadfast in their Hasidic faith. They found spiritual satisfaction in their religion and organized their days and their identities around prayer. Their commitment to traditional Judaism and to the values that united them as a family in a community of equally devoted families

acted as a shield against the anti-Semitism and discrimination that virtually imprisoned them in the shtetl.

Chagall's early recollections of not wanting to grow up could not have
been caused by any conscious recognition of the repressive conditions imposed upon Jews by the tsarist government of Russia. His attachment to
food was not imposed on him by Russia's majority. The child yearned for
freedom, but not yet the freedom to paint the way he wished or the freedom to move about Russia whenever and wherever he wished. He desired
the freedom to control his feeding schedule, to awaken from a nap in
Mama's bed where "nothing will frighten me"[7] and be nourished from her
hand with food of his choice.

I was cautioned against emphasizing food as an idiosyncratic concern
of Chagall by a former Jewish student of mine who was raised in a small
town near Vitebsk before her family immigrated to the United States. Her
claim that food was (and still is) a prominent feature of Russian Hassidic
life was underscored when she wrote:

> From personal experience I can say that in general Jewish Russian
> people have a fixation with food. Food can solve anything. All I ever
> hear from my grandparents is, "Have you eaten?" "What did you eat
> today?" or "For Heavens' Sake. Eat something!" When I was little my
> grandmas would always hand me a piece of buttered bread before
> sending me outside to play. It may be that Chagall's obsession with
> food went further than most people's, but you must keep his culture
> in mind.

But even in the context of a culture where offerings of food function
as expressions of care, kinship connection, and love, Chagall's oral orientation to the world and its many spheres was truly exceptional. That is not
nearly as evident in his art as it is in the autobiography that he wrote as a
young man. The book is filled with references to food, eating, devouring,
teeth, and lips. He envied kerosene lamps that "drink their fill of oil." He
dreamt of food, of buns falling from his aunt's hand into his mouth. In the
world of art, he wondered if one could eat talent. When Bella, his be-
trothed, first posed in the nude for him, it was "as if a feast were spread before your eyes." Instead of going on a honeymoon, he and Bella went on a
"milkmoon." He spoke of gorging himself in museums. In Paris, Chagall's
attraction to the poet and essayist Guillaume Apollinaire made him fearful
that Apollinaire might devour him, chew him up, and "throw my bones
out the window." Thus talent, people, any kind of attractive object could
be eaten and thereby either be destroyed or made part of oneself.

We have been conditioned by psychoanalytic theory to presume that
"oral character traits" stem from unresolved early dilemmas surrounding
inconsistent mothering. "Fixation" at the oral stage of development may
manifest itself in later stages of development by way of excessive depend-

ency, extended periods of thumb-sucking, obesity, and other behaviors related to orality. It is frequently inferred that inadequate mothering lies at the heart of the problem. After one has latched onto that explanation, inadequate mothering can mean too little mothering, too much mothering, inconsistent mothering, overprotective mothering, negligent mothering . . . any kind of mothering that falls short of perfect mothering (whatever that might be).

Other than Chagall's recollection of his infantile confrontations with his mother about when and what to eat, as quoted earlier, I draw a blank when I delve into his autobiography looking for evidence that he believed that his mother somehow failed to serve his "oral and affectional needs." There are no hints of abandonment; no recollections about her being stingy with her affection or suddenly turning against him. The only demand she made of her son was that he talk with her and keep her company in the face of her husband's chronic exhaustion and urge to sleep when he arrived home from twelve- to fourteen-hour days of packing fish.

So we must look elsewhere to discover clues about why Chagall strenuously resisted developing the signs of becoming an adult. A lucky set of circumstances enabled me to convene, as it were, an ad hoc diagnostic council of persons who had written about the significance of Margaret Ogilvy's rejection of her son, Jamie Barrie; I have not found any candidates for a similar council of scholars who have independently noted the potential psychological importance of a sequence events that Chagall experienced when he was five or six years old. Chagall and I are on our own on this one.

During the preschool period of his youth, Chagall studied under the direction of a rabbi tutor whom he called "the little bed-bug." "We hadn't sent for him. He came of his own accord, the way a marriage broker comes or the old man who carries away corpses."[8] At the end of each week of studying, on Friday, the rabbi took Chagall to the baths and made him stretch out nude on a bench. "Birch-rods in hand, he examined my body closely as if I were the Bible." Chagall gives no indication that he enjoyed, objected to, or simply tolerated these inspections, and I have not been able to establish if they followed the custom of the times or were manifestations of the rabbi's weakness for young boys' bodies. In any case, a critical event occurred on a Saturday when Chagall was sent to study with the rabbi instead of being permitted to go bathing in the river. Chagall writes: "However, I knew that at that hour (immediately after lunch) the Rabbi and his wife, completely undressed, slept soundly in honor of the Sabbath. Well then, let's wait till he puts on his pants!" Hesitantly, Chagall knocked on the door and opened it, and he was immediately attacked by the rabbi's dog, "a reddish brown mongrel, old and bad tempered, with sharp teeth." The dog was infected by rabies, and it took twelve bullets to kill it. Chagall was promptly sent to Petersburg for medical attention and was given four days to live. "Charming. Everybody takes care of me. Each day brings me closer to death. I'm a hero."[9]

Miraculously, Chagall recovered and was able to return home. When he entered the house he found it full of women, grave men, and noise. Suddenly there was the piercing wail of a newborn infant. "Mama, half naked, pale, with a faint pink flush on her cheeks is in bed. My younger brother had just been born."[10]

The next scene must have solidified his association between nudity, sex, biting, blood, birth, and death. Immediately after his infant brother was born,

> An old man, murmuring the prayer, cuts with a sharp knife the little bit of skin below the newborn babe's belly. He sucks the blood with his lips and stifles the babe's cries and moans with his beard.
>
> I am sad. Silently, beside the others, I munch pastry, herring, and honey-cake.[11]

A gifted novelist would be hard pressed to invent a sequence of events more likely to result in a young boy becoming anxious about sex and pro-creation. Here is a lad who has intuited or knows by observation enough about sexual transactions to be reluctant to disturb the activities of his un-dressed teacher and his mate. He builds up his courage, knocks on the door, and is attacked by a mad dog. The boy is taken to a distant hospital and is informed that he will die. He defeats the odds, returns home, and is greeted by his mother's half-nude body and the wails and blood accom-panying the birth of a sibling, and finally witnesses an old man sucking blood from a location near the infant's belly. Little wonder that Chagall's preadolescent view of marriage contains some reservations. He writes:

> I like wedding musicians, the sounds of their polkas and waltzes.
>
> I hurry too, and I weep there with Mama. I like to weep a little when the bedchan sings and cries in his high-pitched voice: "Be-trothed, betrothed! Think what awaits you!"
>
> What awaits you?
>
> At those words my head detaches itself gently from my body and weeps somewhere near the kitchen where fish is being prepared.[12]

Chagall felt safe weeping next to Mama. Whatever awaits one who marries can wait—forever, as far as he was concerned—as he imagines his head floating in the direction of food.

The hallmark of Freud's theory regarding art is the idea that it is a product of the transformation of sexual energy into culturally creative acts. Freud would have been delighted with what Chagall said about his subli-mated alternative to masturbating. "In a classroom, I drew as S . . ., the boy next to me, indulged in his favorite pastime, thumbing under the table. What I liked best was geometry. At that I was unbeatable. Lines, angels, triangles, squares carried me far away to enchanting horizons. And during those hours of drawing, I lacked only a throne."[13]

Chagall's self-esteem needed that sort of boost, for he was not popular with his peers. He was ridiculed for being short, fearful, introspective and preferring to sit on rooftops instead of chairs. He had also begun to stammer, and that was a source of extreme embarrassment. Even though he was a dedicated student who came to school prepared with his lesson, when asked to recite, he could not. "'Come, Chagall,' says the professor, 'Are you going to recite your lessons today?' I begin: 'Ta . . . ta . . . ta.'" In these humiliating situations Chagall "felt as if a reddish dog had run up and was barking over my prostrate body. My mouth was full of dust. My teeth hardly looked white at all."

During this period, he spent an increasing amount of time alone, sometimes occupying himself by gazing in a mirror. He was curious about his appearance. His face intrigued him the most and, on occasion, he reddened his cheeks and would think about the day when he might be able to draw his portrait. He also contemplated internal images, sometimes late into the night. When he did so, Mama would call to him, saying:

> "You've burned enough oil! Go to bed. Haven't I told you to do your lessons in the daytime? You're crazy! Let me sleep!"
> "But I'm not making any noise!" I'd say.

> I think of my river, of the floating rafts, bumping about at the end of the bridge, sometimes breaking up against it.
> The planks crack, rise up in the air, but the rowers escape.[14]

In addition to thoughts about his rivers, floating objects, and things that crack and rise in the air, he thought about fires ("Oh, how I love fires!"); fires that burst up and are put out at the same time. Sometimes when he was tormented by the sight of girls, he would seek fires of longer duration by climbing onto a roof and surveying the town for signs of flames. His alternative to seeking fiery symbols of his internal sensations was to lie beneath his mother's bed. Curiously, both places, the one on high and the one beneath Mama's bed were psychologically equivalent. Both were places to hide:

> You don't know how happy I am—and I don't know why—lying under the bed or on a roof, in some sort of hiding place.
> Under the bed—dust, boots.
> I lose myself deep in thought, I fly above the world.[15]

All of the "cases" dealt with in this book found it difficult to establish mature adult relationships. They were stuck in time, struggling with ways to reunite with their mothers, to recapture earlier feelings of security and wellness associated with the weightless condition of intersubjective harmony. Tonka managed to come as close as a ten-year-old boy can come to resurrecting early conditions of being united with a mother who, in effect, mirrored his preverbal self back into existence; but he had to get sick before it happened. After a year of being the recipient of his mother's devoted caretaking, Tonka lost all interest in flying because the sensations he had sought to recover via levitation had been sated and he was ready to move on. Although intimacy remained a problem for Tonka, it was far less of a handicap than it appears to have been for Barrie and Jung. Perhaps had Barrie been able to restore the smile that he so desperately needed to fit his internal picture of a caring mother, the underpinnings of a sense of self able to engage in adult relationships might have taken root. Jung gave up on intimacy when he gave up on the idea of love and proceeded to invent, reinvent, and reify a mother substitute, an essence, that was always available to collapse his boundaries and to accept him into the collective force of nature for which time does not exist.

Unlike the others, Chagall was not developmentally crippled by his early retreat from sexuality. He blended expressions of his need to restore internal harmony into both his art and his personal relationships. His most intimate relationship was with his wife, Bella. Bella, whose maiden name was Rosenfeld, was the daughter of a wealthy Jewish jeweler from Vitebsk. The couple first met in 1909, when Bella had returned from Moscow, where she had attended a private school and had studied with Konstantin Stanislavski, the well-known theater director. Bella's parents had serious misgivings about their daughter's attraction to the son of a laborer who was eking out an existence as an artist-in-training in St. Petersburg. Nonetheless, the relationship persisted for about a year before Chagall departed for Paris, the art capital of Europe. Still poor, Chagall had found a patron, Maxim Vinaver, who, in exchange for a painting and a drawing, provided Chagall with a stipend that enabled him to spend four years in Paris. Chagall's unorthodox style caught the attention of several Parisian artists, and one of them, Guillaume Apollinaire, arranged for him to exhibit some his works in Berlin in 1914. Fearing that his four-year absence from Bella might doom their relationship, Chagall planned to visit her and the town of Vitebsk prior to returning to his studio in Paris. The "brief" visit lasted eight years. The outbreak of World War I in 1914 closed the door to Chagall's return to Paris. At the end of that bleak war, Chagall welcomed the Bolshevik seizure of power and the onset of a socialist utopia that promised full citizenship to Jews. Jewish music, literature, poetry, theatre, and other forms of art flourished during the short span of years between the Russian Revolution and the reinstitution by the Soviet Republic of the suppression of Jews.

In 1915, near the beginning of that notable era, Marc Chagall and Bella Rosenfeld were married. The marriage ended twenty-nine years later when Bella died in Paris. Chagall's written notation about her death reads: "A violent clap of thunder and a brief downpour burst at six o'clock in the evening when in September 2, 1944, Bella left this world. . . . Everything went blank before my eyes."[16] Overcome by grief, Chagall was unable to work for nearly a year.

Intimacy had not been a problem for the couple. Just the opposite—the relationship was built on intimacy. What Chagall sought and obtained from his mother, he sought and obtained from Bella. The little boy who desired to live forever in a small enclosure, who imagined his head drifting toward his mother and her kitchen when he was frightened and sad, who would wing his way back to Mama's protective body when he felt lonely, became a man who experienced himself "as one" with his wife.

This conclusion is not based solely on Chagall's mourning when Bella died and his inability to work for a lengthy period thereafter. Nor is it derived from the tender words he wrote about her in his autobiography. These facts merely support what is so evident in his visual representations of their relationship. The first example is a painting that Chagall completed in 1914, a year before their marriage. Titled *Lovers in Blue*, the painting binds the couple together by enveloping their heads in a blue haze that emanates from portions of their faces and surrounds their intimate embrace. Of the dozens of artistic renditions of his relationship with Bella, the one that most poignantly expresses their unity as a couple is titled *Lovers Over*

Marc Chagall, "Lovers Over the City," 1917. © 2003 Artists Rights Society (ARS), New York / ADAGP, Paris and Giraudon / Art Resource, NY.

the City. The painting, done sometime between 1914 and 1918, is one of Chagall's most recognizable pieces. It portrays the couple floating over the town of Vitebsk with expressions of contentment on their faces. Chagall's left arm is indistinguishable from Bella's arm. In that and other ways the figures are merged in their weightlessness. Intimacy achieved.

Chagall's near-death experience following the attack of his tutor's mad dog and his subsequent associations of nudity and sex with blood and pain led him to imagine that residence in a protective cage would be an attractive way to conduct one's life. One step removed from that would be to eat one's way through life by consuming one's surroundings. "I was born dead," writes Chagall. "I did not want to live. Imagine a white bubble that does not want to live. As if it had been stuffed with Chagall pictures. They pricked that bubble with needles, they plunged it into a pail of water. At last it emitted a feeble whimper."

When the bubble was pricked, the pictures that were stuffed into his head were released onto canvases. Many of the paintings were of Vitebsk. Although he appreciated the representational or naturalistic style of Yehuda Pen, his earliest art teacher, who recorded Hasidic life in exacting detail, Chagall painted a charmed, magical world, where characters, animals, houses, and other structures exist in unreal space, free from earthly references to time and space. He captured the spirit of the town and paid less attention to pictorial accuracy. He painted his *experiences* of his shtetl community in ways that relied less on perceptions that arrived from the outside than on ones that were internally inspired.

The pictures that were stuffed in his head during his childhood continued to spill onto his canvases many years after he left Vitebsk and many years after his shtetl had all but vanished. He relied on a fusion of imagination and memory to preserve images of his childhood. By externalizing his internal world and portraying the folk quality of his culture as preserved and rewitnessed by an adult through the eyes of a lad, he strikes a chord of recognition of things past; not only of things in his past, but things in all of our pasts; things we have forgotten; buried treasures of childhood joys brought about by family celebrations, the sense of curiosity and wonder before life became humdrum and everything became fastened to its proper place in reality. Most prominent to me and most germane to the topic of this book, many of his works evoke nonverbal and thereby only sensed memories of a lost paradise of mother/child intimacy. Perhaps the mad dog promoted Chagall's fondness for being in his mother's bed or by her side, but whatever the cause(s) may have been, a maternal figure, real in the case of Bella, imaginary at other times, presented herself as a lofty object for reunion.

Chagall's painting *The Bridge of the Seine* (1954) depicts an infant with its head turned toward the breast of a winged angel that appears to have emerged from the body of a dead woman in her coffin. It is only one variation of a theme contained in many of Chagall's works. On a few occasions, a male figure flies alone. But in the majority of cases, he is either joined by a woman in an intimate embrace or is being observed from above by protective angel. Male overseers are absent from his paintings. Even in his forays into painting religious scenes inspired by New Testament stories, God the Father is absent. The heavenly He is replaced by images of angels and goddesses, heavenly She's who watch over the town and its occupants.

In a single painting, Chagall was able to visually represent the primary observation that I have been attempting to convey here in thousands of words linearly strung out on page after page. That observation is that imaginary flight is originally inspired by and is a reflection of the desire to reunite the mother, to be graced by her protective nurturance, to become integrated as an indispensable part of her intersubjective world.

TWENTY-FIVE *A Case for Case Studies*

Courses in personality psychology are in great demand among college undergraduates. Such courses are among the first to reach capacity enrollment come registration time in many universities. Such a course is frequently staffed on an "anybody can teach that course" basis, and a distinction is made between what students want to study (lives of people) and what they should study (variables and how to measure and manipulate them). The usual compromise is to provide students with a small dose of what they want and a large dose of what is considered to be good for them.

It is difficult to sort the causes from the consequences of this situation, because both operate in tandem to create a set of circumstances whereby personality psychologists with distinct "personological" interests have become the Rodney Dangerfields of their discipline.[1] Colleagues hope these loners will soon opt for early retirement or disappear for other reasons so that vacant slots can be filled by faculty with fundable research interests.

The situation was different during the first half of the twentieth century when, according to Roy Baumeister, "it would be hard to find any other subdiscipline in the social sciences whose influence was as broad as that of personality psychology."[2] Freud's "grand theory" of personality was usually at or near the center of that influence. Concepts and principles from psychodynamic psychology flowed into literature, anthropology, sociology, and other academic disciplines where both advocates and disbelievers kept the ideas alive. Any gains in the status of psychoanalytic theory in some areas were matched by its loss of status in psychology. Psychology had struggled hard to win its independence from philosophy and align itself with science and was not about to return to a tradition of speculations.

In the right hands, psychoanalytic psychology might be of some value for work on the couch, but anecdotal support for a theory amounted to nothing in the view of a discipline that sought acceptance into the scientific community.

Psychologists were on the lookout for hypotheses and ways to test them, and few were forthcoming from psychoanalytic psychology. In the eyes of many, all it had spawned was a disgraceful thing called psychobiography, and personality psychologists scrambled to distance themselves from that source of embarrassment.

Personality psychology salvaged part of its subdisciplinary existence by developing a cadre of specialists who devoted their careers to developing scales for measuring personality variables. The majority of these variables were (and still are) traits. For a period of time it appeared that personality psychology would be able to recoup its lost status by demonstrating the usefulness of traits in accounting for behavior. But Walter Mischel[3] took the wind out of that sail when he compiled information indicating that traits were, at best, only modest predictors. He observed that *situations* are stronger than traits in accounting for behaviors. For instance, the individual traits of members of an audience at a performance are flattened by a situation that demands a degree of adherence to the sit-still-in-your-seats rule governing audience behavior. That is an exaggerated example of the more sophisticated kinds of information that Mischel extracted from research on that topic. He compiled the results of numerous investigations that damaged the trait position and opened what became known as the person/situation debate that struggled with the question of whether the person *or* the situation best explained behavior. Lines were drawn between personality psychologists (trait specialists) on one side and social psychologists (situation specialists) on the other. In the end, both sides shook hands and agreed that both an assessment of the person *and* an assessment of the situation are necessary ingredients for predicting behavior.

Personality psychology, with its new affiliation with social psychology, was back in business. An intellectual partnership between personality psychology and social psychology was formed. Social psychologists relied on the trait measurement industry to supply them with personality variables for use in their research, and to some degree that arrangement is still being played out. Baumeister points out that social psychologists have extended their range of interests into fields of cognitive psychology, developmental psychology, and, I would add, health psychology, and the discipline now occupies today's equivalent of the center of action that was vacated by personality psychology fifty or so years ago. In Baumeister's view, personality psychology is mostly off the screen as a separate discipline, largely due to its adoption of methods that typify research in social psychology.

Baumeister makes the interesting observation that there is a finite "amount of truth" to be discovered about the human psyche and hints that most of those truths may already be known. If that is the case, the remaining days of both social and personality psychology will be played out with researchers trying to find exceptions to general principles and designing research on these specialized topics so as to draw sufficient attention to maintain a dwindling number of careers.

So what's a person to do?

First of all, it is too early to drag out the coffin. Social psychology is in good shape. My office is on a floor of a psychology building that houses offices of social psychologists that are abuzz with excitement about ideas and results from their surveys and laboratory investigations. They are a happy lot. They are well versed in theory, investigate interesting topics, and are both users and inventors of a wide range of research methods. Notable for their contributions to topics of traditional concern in their field (attitudes, stereotypes, expectancy effects, and the like), they are reaching into areas that one would imagine would be the province of personality psychology (e.g., self and identity, *unconscious* foundations of biases, and other beneath-the-surface phenomena).

In the meantime, personality psychology is in danger of getting stuck with traits. Trait measurement became personality psychologists' solution to accusations of being artists in the midst of serious scientists, and I tend to share Baumeister's gloomy prognostication about the future of personality psychology if it continues down the path of business as usual. How many traits remain to be measured, and how many correlations have not already been computed?

Several decades of research on traits have resulted a working consensus that there are five basic groupings of traits that are useful for making individual and group comparisons. I mentioned these groupings or "factors" in chapter 2. These five dimensions include Neuroticism, Extraversion, Openness to Experience, Agreeableness, and Conscientiousness. J. M. Barrie's profile on these dimensions looks approximately like this: He is high on Neuroticism. (He was anxious, was often depressed, and caught nearly every cold that came his way.) He is both extraverted and introverted, placing him near the middle of that scale. (Recall that he was a crowd-pleaser who retreated to his apartment once the crowd was pleased.) I would place him on the high end of Openness to Experience, just as I would place most artists. Placement on the scale of Agreeableness is a matter of uncertainty. He was agreeable with Sylvia and disagreeable with his wife Mary, so, on balance, I give him an average score. He broke the barrier on Conscientiousness with Margaret, and as a young writer he was always on time with his Nottingham newspaper articles, but he was so careless with his money that one of his acquaintances had to step in to manage his finances. So, I place him on the high end of the middle range of Conscientiousness.

That exercise provides us with some information about Barrie that would allow his trait profile to be compared with the trait profiles of others. Some scholars are satisfied that a solid, empirical base has been established for making such comparisons, and I agree. Good science has been done in reducing a great deal of complexity into five dimensions, and like Baumeister I foresee the end of an era. We are saturated with knowledge about traits, and people are asking, "Isn't there anything more to personality than traits?"

Whether or not the trend continues, personality psychology needs to be invigorated, and invigoration will not happen if there is a broad acceptance of Baumeister's idea that most of the mysteries of the human psyche have been resolved. We have permitted our methods to dictate what mysteries come to our attention, and we have relied on our methods and measurement devices to resolve them. In the meantime, for good reasons and bad ones, personality psychologists have resisted returning to what could have been their major source of strength—"whole" person research.[4]

Among the good reasons for abandoning case studies is the rampant reductionism it bred. George Will parodied psychobiographic efforts to "explain" great deeds by great people by reducing their actions to a time of suffering at a tender age: "say, (age) seven, when his mother took away a lollipop."[5] Yes, some psychobiographies do come close to being that bad.

The tendency to "pathologize" the subject of a case study was derived from the clinical/psychiatric roots of the field. I am not a diagnostic specialist, but I would imagine that Perry Smith qualifies as a psychopath. There were also psychopathic elements in Marshall Herff Applewhite's life, but labeling these men as diseased would have shed little light on their actions. Had psychopathology been my guide, I would have emphasized the weirdness of Barrie's obsession with his mother's smile, the oddness of Jung's attribution of thoughts to rocks and stones, the neurotic quality of Tonka's motivation for working on a flying backpack, the utter strangeness of Chagall's paintings, and so on, and gone on from there in an attempt to explain their lives in terms of character defects. Psychological pigeonholing has its place, but it is not an approach that will invigorate the field of personality psychology.

While loosening the ties with the diagnostic tradition of clinical psychology and starting from scratch may represent a positive step, it leads directly to other problems. Try to understand one life, and it will confront you with many of Nature's most difficult puzzles. There will be times when the challenge will seem so overwhelming that you will want to give up. If you are an academic, the fact that the problems are hard is compounded when your colleagues look at you as though you are off your rocker. To begin at the level of a case study violates many of the rules about how science is done these days, and there will be considerable pressure to do things right—nomothetically, variable-centered right.

Words of caution may also come from kindred (case study) spirits who bristle if you stray into territory considered to be hostile (or irrelevant) to pure personology. For example, the attempt to deal with the problem of self and consciousness that resulted in my making an extended detour into current developments in brain research (part III) led to an outpouring of objections. One colleague views it as a product of my "warped" personality. He could be correct, of course—I sometimes worry about that myself—but if personology is to make any contributions to psychology it cannot remain isolated from developments in other areas of research.

Persistence in the face of one's own and others' doubts sometimes pays off. The payoff for me is a renewed interest in my discipline. Much of the credit for that goes to James Barrie, Carl Jung, and other "subjects" who have served as my mentors. They supplemented what I had already learned from Freud and a host of others by challenging various preconceptions and allowing me to consider matters that had previously been of little concern to me. Equally important, they forced me to think about old issues in new ways. For example, I have known about the phenomenon of *fixation* for a very long time. Traumas, particularly childhood traumas, can be determining factors in shaping, or *fixing*, personality. One of the primary goals of psychoanalytic treatment is to uncover repressed memories that keep such fixations in place and thereby free the person from his or her neurosis. It was abundantly clear to me that Barrie, Jung, Tonka, and some of the others studied in this book were fixated on their mothers. Their sense of having been abandoned or rejected was the source of their "problems." That would have been an easy case to make, and if I had stopped there I would have missed the genuine excitement inherent in exploring what they *did* with their problems. What they did with their problems is what we all do: they used them as sources for improvisations.

Dreams, fantasies, stories, and visions of flight were components of their improvisational work, and that, of course, is what brought them to my attention. The path I selected for understanding images of levitation led me back to their childhoods, where I noticed that most of them had suffered setbacks in their relationships with their mothers. These setbacks were more severe than having had lollipops removed from their mouths. Something good, something reassuring and comforting had either changed (e.g., Margaret's smile) or had gone away (e.g., Jung's and Larry's mothers). Donald Winnicott, a British psychoanalyst and prominent contributor to object-relations theory, uses the term *deprivation*[6] to describe the experiences of children confronted with such profound changes in their worlds. He observes that infants who have reached a "capacity to perceive that the cause of the disaster lies in an environmental failure"[7] frequently attempt to punish the environment for its misdeeds by adopting antisocial tendencies. Although they may not be able to pinpoint maternal deprivation as the root cause, they sense that something "out there" has stifled their development. Winnicott notes that this perspective on the causes of chronic misbehavior (from truancies and thefts to more serious crimes) is an extension of Bowlby's earlier report on the unstable home backgrounds of children who developed delinquent lifestyles.

An application of the linkage between deprivation and delinquency that Winnicott proposes almost certainly would benefit our understanding of Perry Smith. But feelings of deprivation also characterized Barrie, Jung, and several others whom I have studied here, and none of them attempted to punish or shape up their environments through violence. Their efforts to restore conditions of oneness with the mother by resurrecting feelings of what that was like were more innovative than smashing windows and not showing up for school. One became an author of beloved stories. Another became a theoretical innovator. One became an artist whose works are appreciated worldwide. Although others improvised less notable and sometimes tragic solutions to their dilemmas, they all, both famous and obscure, struggled with core issues of childhood that extended into their adult lives.

One result of this undertaking is that I disagree with the idea that most of the major mysteries of the human psyche have been resolved. In fact, I will go a step further than that and question the degree to which methods presently used in personality psychology enable us to even identify what the major mysteries are. In chapter 5 I quoted Henry Murray, who wrote that academic psychology "has contributed practically nothing to the knowledge of human nature. . . . It has not only failed to bring light to the hauntingly recurrent problems but it has no intention, one is shocked to realize, of attempting to investigate them."[8]

The focus on people as carriers of traits has given comparative psychology a shot in the arm. It has also led to questions regarding the origins of traits (are they inherited or learned?) and related matters like the evolution of traits (what is the survival values of traits that have been passed down from our ancestors?), but the habit of representing people as systems of traits has reached the point where inspiration is lacking. The "hauntingly recurrent problems" of human nature are not to be found by studying traits. They are more likely to be confronted by in-depth investigations using the "person" as a unit of analysis. Beneath traits are symphonies of other sorts. These symphonies are composed from a person's experiences and the subjective meanings he or she makes of these experiences. Emotions are written into the original score and give it a degree of coherence. This early coherence is subsequently modified and sometimes masked by new chords that give the music a dynamic quality that is flexibly played throughout a lifetime. These symphonies are difficult to hear, let alone decipher, from a static trait perspective. However, the themes around which they are composed are discernable if we are willing to take the time and acquire the skills to hear them.[9]

APPENDIX *Women in Flight*

Whon I decided to make fantasies of flight my point of entry into case studies, Peter Pan, Marc Chagall, and all of the others came knocking on my door. Larry Walters leapt from the pages of a story written about him by George Plimpton, and the other Larry, the long distance runner, wandered into my office looking for advice about colleges. Marshall Herff Applewhite glared at me from the front pages of newspapers, and Dumbo drifted to mind on a rainy afternoon when few rented videos presented a welcome break from a card game called war. All of these individuals and characters are men, of course, and that became a source of concern. Initially, the problem of a potential gender bias did not concern me because I believed it would only be a matter of time and patience before the gender gap would be filled. But no women (real-life[1] or fictional) "found" me, so I took steps to find them.

My intention was to locate women candidates for case studies who showed promise of matching the pattern contained in the model created from case studies of male ascensionists. When my search began in earnest, two psychoanalysts informed me that they had treated numerous female patients whose dreams and fantasies of flight contained the sorts of regressive, "searching-for-Mom" elements that I have described. Although I trusted their words, I could not simply report that information and declare the case closed. I needed a good deal more than secondhand reports about the psychodynamics of some "very disturbed" women patients to draw the parallels I had in mind.

Determined to let no stone go unturned, I conducted surveys, asked women to write about their dreams of flying (one out of three women recall such dreams), and interviewed women who agreed to speak with me about levitation fantasies as they pertain to their lives. I attended exhibitions devoted to women's art in search of paintings containing flying figures. I read about the life of Amelia Earhart and rediscovered something I already knew—pilots are not particularly noted for having the sorts of fantasies of flying that have been targeted for analysis in this book. These and other activities have not been as productive as I had thought they would be, and I am currently inclined to believe that gender *differences* may be one of the sources of my difficulty. The following "progress report" addresses this possibility.

Two thematic patterns appear to be especially common in women's fantasies of flight: the theme of *freedom* and the theme of *rescue*. Neither of these themes should be viewed as specific to women, because men generate them as well. But my informal scorekeeping gives an edge to women. The next two sections include a few (of many possible) examples of the kinds of evidence on which this claim is based.

FREEDOM

"I often see myself as a butterfly in my dreams and, more recently, in my waking fantasies," writes a thirty-two-year-old woman; in an interview with me, she said that a butterfly made its first appearance in the following dream. Making no distinction between herself and the butterfly, she told me that she was in a garden flitting from flower to flower. Suddenly some children appeared with butterfly nets and tried to capture her. She flew beyond the reach of the nets and, looking down, saw the faces of the children turn into the faces of her parents. The dream and variations of it occurred throughout her adolescence. She spoke about how strenuously she resisted the restrictions her parents placed on her activities, particularly as they contrasted with the lenient, "verging on no rules" treatment allowed her brothers. In addition, she believed that she was far more constrained than any of her peers. Her curfew was ten o'clock on her *one* weekend night, in comparison to the midnight curfews for her friends on their *three* weekend night releases.

This woman's frustration continued beyond her adolescence. As a young middle-aged adult she continued to experience constraints of a different sort, particularly in her job, and edited her butterfly dreams and waking fantasies accordingly. "I work very hard. I am good at what I do. Sometimes I get a pat on the back. But come promotion time, I become invisible. When that happens, I arm my butterflies with things that would hurt if dropped onto the heads of managers who are holding me back."

Along similar lines, another woman writes: "Flying for me is a statement of defiance. It symbolizes my desire to grow beyond the boundaries society imposes on me, or should I say, on my gender." That is close to one of the components of the plot line of Erica Jong's novel *Fear of Flying*.[2] The story's heroine, Isadora, agonizes over her career, her marriages, her liaisons, her sexuality, her body, her life, as she struggles to find her voice. Fear of flying is a metaphoric reference to the fear that accompanies the heroine's ambivalence about discovering who she "really" is and becoming that person. She variously fights against and surrenders to social forces that keep her grounded and feeling powerless.

RESCUE

Superman and other comic-book heroes are depicted as descending for the purpose of protecting the innocent and punishing the bad guys. More compassionate versions of that theme appear regularly in the private fantasies of some women. A former student of mine wrote:

> Up to the point when my parents started to scream at each other, I could count on them to look after me. But my mother was a total wreck after my parents split up and I took on the job of taking care of my little sister. I guess you could say that I became my own mother. I mothered myself and I mothered my sister. Now I mother almost everyone in my life. I almost hate to admit it but there are times when I have fantasies of flying over my town and the surrounding countryside looking for people to help.

This woman's fantasies parallel Mary Poppins's adventures as described in several books written by the Australian author Pamela Travers.[3]

As the accompanying illustration from one of the books shows, Mary Poppins descended from on high and entered the Banks family as a nanny for the four, and later, five children. She was a magical woman with several magical friends. She liked the children, sweetened their medicine when they were feeling ill, and did all she could to make up for their parents' negligence. At least that was Walt Disney's film version of one of the books. Somehow the movie left out or glossed over some of Mary Poppins's less attractive features in Travers's characterization of her. I didn't see Julie Andrews (who played Mary Poppins in the movie) "glare like a panther" at the children. Nor did I see Ms. Andrews take admiring glances at herself on nearly every reflective surface in her vicinity. She "never tells anybody anything," the children complained (in the book, that is), but never mind, they love her despite her annoying secrecy. Then, of course, when her work is done, she flies away, presumably to find other children who might benefit from a dose of her magic. Despite Mary Poppins's rough edges (again in the books), she exemplifies the theme of coming down from the skies to tend to the needs of others.

From P. L. Travers, *Mary Poppins Opens the Door* (New York: Harcourt Brace, 1943). © Harcourt Trade Publishers. Used by permission.

The theme of Mary Poppins dropping in on the Banks family can be considered a specific instance of a more general phenomenon that Robert May[4] has researched. In a study of TAT stories, May applied a scoring system for identifying two narrative patterns: ascension followed by descension, and descension followed by ascension. May refers to these patterns as "narrative cycles" and reports that the former cycle, a rise followed by a fall, is more common in men's stories than it is in women's stories. That is, male characters (constructed by males) are depicted as exaggerating their abilities or emphasizing positive emotions near the beginning of a story (scored as "enhancement" in May's system). As the story progresses, they confront obstacles they cannot overcome and begin their descent (scored as "deprivation" in May's system). By contrast, women tend to begin stories by describing central characters (heroines) who underestimate or devalue their worth (deprivation). Their victorious ascent arrives at the end of the story (enhancement). May argues that these mirror-image patterns are products of culturally conditioned gender-role differences. Briefly, here are a few details of that argument.

May's position is built on a distinction between "agency" and "communion," originally made by David Bakan.[5] Agency refers to an orientation toward separateness, independence, individuality, and personal achievement. Bakan observes that agency is the prevalent male orientation. *Communion* refers to an orientation toward developing and maintaining interpersonal relationships. It is aimed at fostering emotional closeness, intimacy, and sharing. Caring for (and taking care of) others is its hallmark, and Bakan proposes that it represents the feminine mode of existence. This distinction has gained widespread acceptance in social science literature.[6]

Taking care of others involves making self-sacrifices (May's deprivation) for the good of the family. It requires paying attention to the needs of others, and sometimes ignoring one's personal desires. Rewards for this sacrifice are feelings associated with a job well done (May's enhancement). In this context, girls and boys are given different messages. Girls are conditioned to be "like" their mothers, while boys are conditioned to be "unlike" their mothers. Nancy Chodorow[7] has written extensively about this pattern, observing that it can be the source of great consternation on the part of a male child who interprets the mother's urgings for him to be unlike her to be tantamount to rejection. Chodorow argues that this is less of a problem for girls because their relationships with their mothers are more continuous, enhancing the chances of them identifying with the mother and preparing to assume her communal orientation.

Combining May's theory with David Bakan's distinction between agency and communion and using that mixture as a base for integrating Nancy Chodorow's ideas about gender-related childrearing practices could provide a productive context for beginning a series of case studies for the purpose of working out some of the individual details of the general patterns these scholars propose.

Finally, certain that Mary Poppins is not the only figure that levitates in stories written by female authors, I compiled a list of other women based on the recommendations of others who were aware of the nature of my search. Taking advantage of Rutgers University's multiple libraries and rich collections, I borrowed several dozen books written by these authors. I read them, returned them, and ordered dozens more. The majority of these books were written for children, and to my disappointment only a few featured individuals capable of flying. Some do, however, and the majority of the main characters are *boys* or *men*. Only a handful of the books mention girls who fly. One of them, *Emma in Winter*, is written by Penelope Farmer.[8] It begins with the passage: "One night Emma dreamed she could fly again." In fact, flying dreams are almost nightly occurrences for Emma. But it quickly becomes apparent that the author is using flight as a metaphor for coping with issues of adolescent maturation. Bobby Fumpkin, the local nerd, accompanies Emma in her dreams. Remarkably, Fumpkin dreams the same dreams dreamt by Emma. Their mutual dreams appear to be shaped to reflect the status of their relationships both with each other and with their school-mates. In sum, *Emma in Winter* was a less promising lead than I originally hoped it might be.[9]

I experienced another rush a few days later when I glanced at the illustrations of a book authored by Dinah Maria Mulock Craik.[10] There she was, a girl with reddened lips, wearing a frilly dress, off on a levitated voyage (the picture reproduced here is very much like several others).

My enthusiasm plummeted when I discovered the girl was a boy, a fact I would have known if I had read the book's title (*The Little Lame Prince*) before looking at the illustrations. Even so, the central theme of the book is "on topic" here, in the sense that the adventures of the prince, Prince Dolor, elaborate on a familiar script. The prince's mother and father (the king and queen) die, and an evil uncle declares that their crippled infant son, Prince Dolor, also passed away. Prince Dolor, however, is not dead. His uncle had exiled him to the Hopeless Tower, in the middle of a desert, where, unaware of his heritage, he would have remained for the duration of this life had it not been for the magical intervention of a kindly old woman (often disguised as a bird) who, among many other things, provided him with a magic flying cloak. Upon the death of his evil

From *The Little Lame Prince and Adventures of a Brownie: Illustrated Junior Library* by Dinah Maria Mulock Craik, illustrated by Lucille Corcos, copyright 1948 by Grosset & Dunlap. Used by permission of Grosset & Dunlap, a division of Penguin Young Readers Group, a member of Penguin Group (USA) Inc., 345 Hudson Street, New York, NY 10014. All rights reserved.

uncle, Prince Dolor returned to the castle and faithfully ruled his kingdom until he retired from the throne. His favorite room in the castle was a little upper room that had been his mother's room, where she used to sit for hours watching the Beautiful Mountains. The thematic sequence of loss (abandonment), isolation, and return by flight to the mother's chambers is reminiscent of Barrie's little white bird.

This sequence is also found in some of the science fiction novels written by the award-winning author Ursula Le Guin. For example, the main character in *City of Illusions*[11] is a man named Falk whose adventures take place in a forested land that once was the landmass of the United States. The year is 4370 A.D. Falk's problem is that he has no memory. His only hope of discovering who he is and from whence he came is to travel to the city of Es Toch. Aided by a flying machine (called a "slider") and accompanied by Estrel, a woman who would eventually betray him, he makes it to the city. In the illusory city of Es Toch, Falk discovers the coordinates of his birth planet. The novel ends with Falk in a spaceship. Earth falls away as it enters into unending sunlight. Just then, the ship breaks free of time and thrusts into darkness. "Was he going home, or leaving home?" asks the author.[12]

These two books, *The Little Lame Prince* and *City of Illusions*, are among several other books written by women about boys and men who fly. Women know the script. J. K. Rowling, author of the Harry Potter[13] series, knows the script. The voyage of the hero is not a mystery to women. Likewise, women enrolled in courses in which I have assigned this book in its prepublished form understand what it is about and are enthusiastic about its contents. They tend not to fret nearly as much as men do about the absence of case studies of women. Perhaps women have grown accustomed to males writing about males and, if so, I apologize for contributing to that tradition. But I am as convinced as I can be at this point that the process of working further on the "problem" of the scarcity of female exemplars of a model created to understand male fantasies of flying will transform the "problem" into an "opportunity" that, if taken, promises to deepen our understanding of gender-based needs and orientations for satisfying them.

NOTES

CHAPTER 1

1. P. Haining, *The compleat birdman*. New York: St. Martin's Press, 1976, pp. 25–26.
2. C. Hart, *The prehistory of flight*. Berkeley: University of California Press, 1985.
3. R. P. Feynman, *"Surely you're joking, Mr. Feynman!"* New York: Norton, 1985.

CHAPTER 2

1. E. Staub, *Personality: Basic aspects and current research*. Englewood Cliffs, NJ: Prentice Hall, 1980, p. 3.
2. N. Barenbaum & D. Winter, Case studies and life histories in personality psychology: A history of ambivalence. In I. B. Weiner (Gen. Ed.) & D. K. Freedman (Vol. Ed.), *Handbook of psychology: Vol. 1. History of psychology*. New York: Wiley, 2002.
3. K. J. Gergen, Stability, change, and chance in understanding human development. In N. Datan & H. Reese (Eds.), *Life-span developmental psychology: Dialectical perspectives on experimental research*. New York: Academic Press, 1990, pp. 135–157.
4. G. W. Allport, *Personality: A psychological interpretation*. New York: Holt, 1937.
5. H. A. Murray (with staff), *Explorations in personality*. New York: Oxford University Press, 1938, pp. 142–144.
6. Barenbaum & Winter, Case studies and life histories, p. 19.

7. K. Danziger, *Constructing the subject: Historical origins of psychological research.* New York: Cambridge University Press, 1990, p. 165.

8. P. T. Costa & R. R. McCrae, Trait theories of personality. In D. F. Barone, M. Herson, & V. B. Van Hasselt (Eds.), *Advanced personality.* New York: Plenum Press, 1998, p. 114.

9. R. W. White, Exploring personality the long way: The study of lives. In A. I. Rabin, J. Aronoff, A. M. Barclay, & R. A. Zucker (Eds.), *Further explorations in personality.* New York: Wiley, 1981, pp. 3–19.

10. R. Carlson, Where is the person in personality research? *Psychological bulletin, 75,* 1971, pp. 203–219. R. Carlson, What is social about social psychology? Where is the person in personality research? *Journal of Personality and Social Psychology, 47,* 1984, pp. 1304–1309.

11. See S. S. Tomkins, *Affect, imagery, and consciousness,* Vols. 1 & 2, New York: Springer, 1962 and 1963, respectively. Another important source is S. S. Tomkins & C. E. Izard, *Affects, cognition, and personality.* New York: Springer, 1965.

12. S. S. Tomkins, Script theory. In H. E. Howe Jr. & R. A. Dienstbier (Eds.), *Nebraska symposium on motivation.* Lincoln: University of Nebraska Press, 1978, Vol. 26, pp. 201–236. This article is reprinted in a book of selected readings: Virginia Demos (Ed.), *Exploring affect.* New York: Cambridge University Press, 1995. Major sections of this book are introduced by persons who worked with Tomkins during his career. They include Brewster Smith, Virginia Demos, Irving Alexander, Paul Ekman, and Rae Carlson. The end result is a valuable overview of Tomkins's lifetime contributions to psychology.

13. See W. M. Runyan, *Life histories and psychobiography: Explorations in theory and method.* New York: Oxford University Press, 1982, and *Psychology and historical interpretation.* New York: Oxford University Press, 1988.

14. D. M. Ogilvie, The undesired self: A neglected variable in personality research. *Journal of Personality and Social Psychology, 52,* 1987, pp. 379–385.

15. D. M. Ogilvie, Life satisfaction and identity structure in late middle-aged men and women. *Psychology and Aging, 2,* 1987, pp. 217–224.

16. S. Rosenberg, Self and others: Studies in social personality and autobiography. In L. Berkowitz (Ed.), *Advances in experimental social psychology,* Vol. 21. New York: Academic Press, 1988, pp. 57–95.

17. The project, methods, and some results of my collaboration with Richard Ashmore appear in D. M. Ogilvie & R. D. Ashmore, Self-with-others as a unit of analysis in self-concept research. In R. Curtis (Ed.), *The relational self.* New York: Guilford, 1991, pp. 282–313, and in R. D. Ashmore & D. M. Ogilvie, He's a such a nice boy . . . when he is with his grandma: Gender and evaluation in self-with-other representations. In T. M. Brinthaupt & R. P. Lipka (Eds.), *The self: Definitional and methodological issues,* Albany: State University of New York Press, 1992, pp. 236–290.

18. D. M. Ogilvie, The use of graphic representations of self-dynamisms in clinical treatment. *Crisis Intervention and Time-Limited Treatment, 1,* 1994, pp. 125–140.

19. D. M. Ogilvie, Individual and cultural patterns of fantasized flight. In C. Gerbner, O. R. Holsti, K. Krippendorff, W. Paisley, & P. J. Stone, *The analysis*

of communications content: Developments of scientific theories and computer techniques. New York: Wiley, 1969, pp. 243–259.

CHAPTER 3

1. H. A. Murray, The American Icarus. In A. Burton, (Ed.), *Clinical studies of personality,* Vol. 2. New York: Harper, 1955, pp. 615–641.

2. A larger context for situating Grope's fantasies of flying and the Icarian label Murray applied to them has been provided by Karl Kilinski, an art historian at Southern Methodist University. His book *The flight of Icarus through Western art,* New York: Mellon Press, 2002, records the appearance of the myth of Icarus in art and literature over a span of twenty-five hundred years, and in theatre and opera over the past two hundred years. The durability of the theme of Icarus in various forms of art over such a long period of time suggests that Grope and several other individuals considered in this book can be thought of as personal "carriers" of an ancient theme. Each specialized in a segment of the Icarian voyage and transformed it according to the contours of their lives. In describing how and why they did so, I intend to keep in mind the possibility that they all dipped into the pool that has been the source of artistic inspirations since the advent of the original myth.

CHAPTER 4

1. D. P. McAdams, *The person: An integrated introduction to personality psychology.* New York: Harcourt, 2001.

2. B. J. Cohler, Personal narrative and the life course. In P. Baltes & O. G. Brim Jr. (Eds.), *Life span development and behavior,* Vol. 4. New York: Academic Press, 1982, pp. 205– 241.

3. H. A. Murray (with staff), *Explorations in personality.* New York: Oxford University Press, 1938.

4. H. A. Murray, In nominee Diablo. *New England Quarterly,* 23, pp. 435–452. H. Melville, *Moby Dick.* New York: Harper, 1851.

CHAPTER 5

1. H. A. Murray, Psychology and the university. *Archives of Neurology and Psychiatry,* 34, 1934, p. 806. I thank Jim Anderson for bringing this article to my attention.

CHAPTER 6

1. D. P. McAdams, *The person: An integrated introduction to personality psychology.* New York: Harcourt, 2001, p. 707.

2. E. H. Erikson, *Young man Luther: A study of psychoanalysis and history.* New York: Norton, 1958.

3. E. H. Erikson, *Gandhi's truth: On the origins of military nonviolence*. New York: Norton, 1969.

4. S. Freud, *Leonardo Da Vinci and a memory from his childhood*, J. Strachey (Ed. & Trans.). New York: Norton, 1964.

5. A. C. Elms, *Uncovering lives: The uneasy alliance of biography and psychology*. New York: Oxford University Press, 1994.

6. Freud, *Leonardo*, p. 37.

7. Elms, *Uncovering lives*, p. 42.

8. E. Jones, *The life and work of Sigmund Freud*, Vol. 3. New York: Basic Books, 1957, p. 135.

9. Elms, *Uncovering lives*, p. 37.

10. Elms, *Uncovering lives*, p. 49.

11. S. Freud, *The interpretation of dreams*. In A. A. Brill (Ed.), *The basic writings of Sigmund Freud*. New York: Modern Library, 1938, p. 522.

12. Freud, *Leonardo*, p. 75.

13. Freud, *Interpretation of dreams*, p. 390.

14. G. E. Atwood & R. D. Stolorow, *Faces in a cloud: Intersubjectivity in personality theory*. Northvale, NJ: Aronson, 1993, p. 38.

15. M. Klein, *The psychoanalysis of children*, A. Strachey (Trans.). New York: Dell, 1932/1975.

16. W. R. D. Fairbairn, *An object-relations theory of the personality*. New York: Basic Books, 1971.

17. D. W. Winnicott, *Therapeutic consultation in child psychiatry*. New York: Basic Books, 1971.

18. Freud, *Leonardo*, p. 41.

19. Freud, *Leonardo*, p. 67.

20. Freud, *Leonardo*, p. 57.

21. Freud, *Leonardo*, p. 37.

22. Freud, *Leonardo*, p. 63.

23. Freud, *Leonardo*, p. 64.

24. The following are among the numerous citations available in this regard: R. Abraham, Freud's mother conflict and the formation of the Oedipal father. *Psychoanalytic Review*, 69, 1982, pp. 442–453; Atwood & Stolorow, *Faces in a cloud*; K. R. Eissler, Creativity and adolescence: The effect of trauma in Freud's adolescence. *Psychoanalytic Study of Children*, 33, 1978, pp. 461–515; and A. C. Elms, Freud, Irma, Martha: Sex and marriage in the "Dream of Irma's injection," *Psychoanalytic Review*, 67, 1980, pp. 83–109.

25. Abraham, Freud's mother conflict, p. 442.

26. Abraham, Freud's mother conflict, p. 441.

27. Atwood & Stolorow, *Faces in a cloud*, p. 38.

28. Abraham, Freud's mother conflict, pp. 141–144.

29. S. Freud, *Civilization and its discontents*, J. Strachey (Ed. & Trans.). New York: Norton, 1930/1961.

30. S. Freud, *The future of an illusion*, J. Strachey (Ed. & Trans.). New York: Norton, 1927/1961.

31. Freud, *Leonardo*, p. 50.

32. The straw-man quality of my argument is particularly evidenced by the fact that Freud's study of Leonardo has been very nearly my sole source for extracting

his views. Alan Elms brings to my attention that Freud said other things about fly-ing fantasies in other works. For example, in *The Interpretation of Dreams*, A. A. Brill (Ed.), Freud wrote: "What is the meaning of such (flying) dreams? It is im-possible to give a general reply. As we shall hear, they mean something different in every instance; it is only the raw material of sensations in them which always de-rived from the same source" (p. 393). Freud's statement that flying dreams have different meanings is important. I may have boxed him in by attributing to him the argument that they have one meaning; to wit, a sexual meaning. But the "raw material of sensations" may not always refer to sexual sensations and, if that is what Freud implied, he and I may not be that far apart.

CHAPTER 7

1. J. M. Barrie, *Peter Pan*. New York: Puffin Classics, 1994.
2. J. M. Barrie, *The little white bird*. New York: Schribner's, 1902 (hereafter *LWB*).

CHAPTER 8

1. Freud credited Paul Federn with suggesting that an erect penis can be sym-bolically represented by the whole body in dreams. Freud elaborates on this idea in a passage in his *Introductory lectures in psycho-analysis* (London: Allen & Unwin, 1929), as follows: "The remarkable characteristic of the male organ which enables it to rise up in defiance of the laws of gravity, one of the phenomena of erection, leads to its being represented symbolically by balloons, flying machines, and most recently by Zeppelin airships. But dreams can symbolize erection in yet another, far more expressive manner. They can treat the sexual organ as the essence of the dreamer's whole person and make him fly" (p. 155).
2. J. M. Barrie, *Margaret Ogilvy by her son, J. M. Barrie*. New York: Scribner's , 1901 (hereafter *MO*).
3. A suitable translation of "windy" is "puffed up with pride," as in "I would be proud to be your mother."

CHAPTER 9

1. K. J. Gergen, Stability, change, and chance in understanding human de-velopment. In N. Datan & H. Reese (Eds.), *Life-span developmental psychology: Dialectical perspectives on experimental research*. New York: Academic Press, 1990, p. 142.
2. D. M. Ogilvie, The problem of opinions without evidence in psychobio-graphic research. *Clio's Psyche*, 8, 2001, pp. 132–134.
3. T. Schultz, The Prototypic Scene: A Method for Generating Psychobio-graphical Hypotheses. In D. McAdams, R. Josselson, & A. Liblich (Eds.), *Up close and personal: Teaching and learning narrative methods*. Washington, DC: APA Press, 2003, pp. 151–175.

4. I. Alexander, Personality, psychological assessment, and psychobiography. *Journal of Personality*, 66, 1988, pp. 265–294.

5. A. C. Elms, *Uncovering lives: The uneasy alliance of biography and psychology.* New York: Oxford University Press, 1994.

6. J. Singer & P. Salvoy, *The remembered self: Emotions and memory in personality.* New York: Free Press, 1993.

7. See D. P. McAdams, *The person: An integrated introduction to personality psychology.* New York: Harcourt, 2001, p. 691.

8. H. A. Murray (with staff), *Explorations in personality.* New York: Oxford University Press, 1938, pp. 604–605.

9. D. G. Mackail, *The story of JMB.* New York: Scribner's, 1941 (hereafter *JMB*).

10. *JMB*, p. 51.

11. *JMB*, p. 23.

12. R. Sapolski, *Why zebras don't get ulcers: An updated guide to stress, stress-related diseases, and coping.* New York: Freeman, 1998.

13. Sapolski, *Zebras*, p. 91.

14. Sapolski, *Zebras*, p. 92.

15. J. Wullschlager, *Inventing Wonderland: The lives of Lewis Carroll, Edward Lear, J. M. Barrie, Kenneth Graham, and A. A. Milne.* New York: Free Press, 1995.

16. Wullschlager, *Inventing Wonderland*, p. 131.

17. Wullschlager, *Inventing Wonderland*, p. 118.

18. Wullschlager, *Inventing Wonderland*, p. 119.

CHAPTER 10

1. *JMB*, p. 26.

2. *MO*, p. 25.

3. *MO*, p. 207.

4. *MO*, p. 51.

5. J. Wullschlager, *Inventing Wonderland: The lives of Lewis Carroll, Edward Lear, J. M. Barrie, Kenneth Graham, and A. A. Milne.* New York: Free Press, 1995, p. 118.

6. *MO*, p. 32.

7. *MO*, p. 115.

8. *JMB*, p. 5.

9. *MO*, pp. 165–166.

CHAPTER 11

1. Yogi Berra was a major league (Yankee) baseball player and coach who is beloved for his clever sayings.

2. J. Bowlby, *Maternal care and mental health.* Geneva: World Health Organization, 1951.

3. S. S. Tomkins, *Affect, imagery, and consciousness*, Vols. 1 & 2. New York: Springer, 1962 and 1963, respectively. Another important source is S. S. Tomkins & C. E. Izard, *Affects, cognition, and personality.* New York: Springer, 1965.

4. E. Goffman, *The presentation of self in everyday life*. Woodstock, NY: Overlook Press, 1959/1973.

5. S. S. Tomkins, Script theory. In H. E. Howe Jr. & R. A. Dienstbier (Eds.), *Nebraska symposium on motivation* (Vol. 26 pp. 201–236). Lincoln: University of Nebraska, 1978.

CHAPTER 12

1. *JMB*, p. 77.

2. *JMB*, p. 218.

3. J. Wullschlager, *Inventing Wonderland: The lives of Lewis Carroll, Edward Lear, J. M. Barrie, Kenneth Graham, and A. A. Milne*. New York: Free Press, 1995, p. 120.

4. J. M. Barrie, *Tommy and Grizel*. New York: Press Readers Club, 1943.

5. A. Birkin, *J. M. Barrie and the lost boys: The love story that gave birth to Peter Pan*. New York: Potter, 1979, p. 40.

6. Birkin, *J. M. Barrie and the lost boys*, p. 1.

CHAPTER 13

1. C. G. Jung, *Memories, dreams, reflections*. New York: Vintage Books, 1965, p. 42 (hereafter *MDR*).

2. C. G. Jung, *Flying Saucers*, R. F. C. Hull (Ed. & Trans.). London: Routledge and Kegan Paul, 1959, p. 67.

3. C. G. Jung, *The undiscovered self*, R. F. C. Hull (Ed. & Trans). Boston: Little, Brown, 1957, p. 85.

4. Jung, *Flying Saucers*, p. 101.

CHAPTER 14

1. G. E. Atwood & R. D. Stolorow, *Faces in a cloud: Intersubjectivity in personality theory*. Northvale, NJ: Aronson, 1993. The quotation from Murray appears in the book's foreword.

2. C. G. Jung, *Collected works of Carl Jung*, W. McGuire (Exec. Ed.). Princeton, NJ: Princeton University Press, 2000.

3. *MDR*, p. 293.

4. P. Homans, *Jung in context: Modernity and the making of a psychology*. Chicago: University of Chicago Press, 1979.

5. Homans, *Jung in context*, p. 99.

6. B. J. Cohler, Personal narrative and the life course. In P. Baltes & O. G. Brim Jr. (Eds.), *Life span development and behavior* (Vol. 4, pp. 205–241). New York: Academic Press, 1982.

7. *MDR*, p. 8.

8. *MDR*, p. 44.

9. *MDR*, p. 18.

10. W. McGuire, *The Freud/Jung letters: The correspondence between Sigmund Freud and C. G. Jung*. Cambridge, MA: Harvard University Press,1988.

11. Homans, *Jung in context*, p. 52.

12. Homans, *Jung in context*, p. 65.

13. Homans, *Jung in context*, p. 77.

14. It is noteworthy that the voice was usually heard from above. In Jung's earliest dream of descending into an underground chamber that contained a phallic figure seated on a throne, he heard "from outside and above" his mother's voice warning him that the figure was a man-eater. Jung also referred to feminine voices and images on several occasions in a series of seminars given in 1925. (These lectures are in William McGuire (Ed.), *Analytical psychology*, Princeton University Press, 1991. For example, Jung spoke of a dream wherein a white bird descended and was transformed into a girl who tenderly placed her arm around his neck (p. 40). The frequency with which women's voices interrupted his work by speaking words of comfort and advice led Jung to consider the prospect of God being female, as he "thought for a time that perhaps the anima figure was a deity" (p. 46).

15. C. G. Jung, *Two essays on analytical psychology*. New York: Meridian, 1965, p. 71.

16. Jung, *Two essays*, p. 187.

17. Jung, *Two essays*, p. 202.

18. MDR, p. 295.

19. MDR, p. 297

20. J. Campbell, *The hero with a thousand faces*. Princeton, NJ: Princeton University Press 1949.

CHAPTER 15

1. I. P. Pavlov, *Lectures on conditioned reflexes: The higher nervous activities of animals*, H. Gannet (Trans.). London: Lawrence and Wishart, 1928.

2. H. F. Harlow, The nature of love. American Psychologist, 13, 1958, pp. 673–683.

3. J. Bowlby, Forty-four thieves: Their characters and home life. International Journal of Psychoanalysis, 13, 1944, pp. 107–127.

4. J. Bowlby, *Maternal care and mental health*. Geneva: World Health Organization, 1951.

5. J. Bowlby, *Attachment and loss. Vol. 1: Attachment*. New York: Basic Books, 1969.

6. M. D. S. Ainsworth, Patterns of attachment behavior shown by the infant in interaction with his mother. Merrill-Palmer Quarterly, 10, 1964, pp. 51–58.

7. D. M. Ogilvie & R. D. Ashmore, Self-with-others as a unit of analysis in self-concept research. In R. Curtis (Ed.), The relational self (pp. 282–3130. New York: Guilford, 1991, and in R. D. Ashmore & D. M. Ogilvie, He's a such a nice boy . . . when he is with his grandma: Gender and evaluation in self-with-other representations. In T. M. Brinthaupt & R. P. Lipka (Eds.), The self: Definitional and methodological issues (pp. 236–290). Albany: State University of New York Press, 1992.

CHAPTER 16

1. D. N. Stern, *The interpersonal world of the infant: A view from psychoanalysis and developmental psychology*. New York: Basic Books, 1985, p. 12.

2. Stern, *Interpersonal world*, p. 110.

3. Here and elsewhere, there is a great deal of overlap between Stern's ideas about RIGs and Silvan Tomkins's concepts of scenes and scripts described in chapter 11. In effect, a RIG can be viewed as a magnified scene in Tomkins's terms and a script serves as the individual's guide to action in the context of a familiar scene. A detailed and thoughtful comparison of these two theoretical frameworks would probably result in striking similarities.

4. Stern, *Interpersonal world*, p. 126.

5. Stern, *Interpersonal world*, p. 163.

6. Stern, *Interpersonal world*, p. 10.

7. H. S. Sullivan, *The interpersonal theory of psychiatry*. New York: Norton, 1953.

8. A. H. Maslow, *Toward a psychology of being* (2nd ed.). New York: D. Von Nostrand, 1968.

9. Freud objected to the idea of oceanic feelings and distanced himself from anything that came close to resembling it. In this note I shall consider why he did so, because it may help to understand why the path to understanding imaginary flight that I am exploring here was one that he seemed to come close to entertaining but dismissed on his way to developing his sexual sublimation theory of levitation fantasies.

In the concluding portion of chapter 6, I proposed that Freud read his own unconscious and unresolved "issues" into the paltry amount of information available about Leonardo's early life and proceeded to treat his "projections" as indisputable "facts" of the case. For example, Freud's interpretation of Leonardo's "vulture fantasy" was that it echoed his "suckling days." Suckling days remain "indelibly printed on us" as original sources of all pleasure. Elsewhere, I have noted Freud's observation that the infant's ties to its mother are "altogether the most perfect, the most free from ambivalence of all human relations." But seventeen years after what Freud saw so clearly as a strong unconscious force in Leonardo's life (and in most lives, according to his general statement), Freud could not locate any hints of suckling day sensations in himself. As a consequence, he concluded that oceanic feelings refer to something made up, to sensations that don't and never did exist.

Freud's opportunity to present his case came when he received a letter from an acquaintance named Romain Roland. Roland's letter contained comments about Freud's book *The Future of an Illusion*, which was about the irrational foundations on which all religions are based. Roland wrote that he agreed with Freud's judgments about religions but, according to Freud, "was sorry that I had not properly appreciated the true source of religious sentiments." According to Roland, the true source was a peculiar feeling, a sense of eternity, an unbounded, unlimited sensation—"as it were, 'oceanic.'"

Freud wrote that he would continue to respect his friend but in this instance felt that he was mistaken. "Oceanic feelings" might be acceptable words to use in religious parlance, but scientifically they refer to nothing that has the slightest bearing on the reality of human experience. He wrote that his friend's views "caused me no small difficulty." The source of his difficulty was that "I cannot discover this 'oceanic' feeling in myself" and, as a consequence, "cannot convince myself of the primary nature of such a feeling."

Freud published these comments near the beginning of *Civilization and Its Discontent*, his treatise on the necessity of mankind suppressing and diverting instincts in order to conform to the demands of society. True to form, the essay is primarily about sons' relationships with their fathers, the need to renounce sexual rivalry, and the costs (loss of freedom) and benefits (a "civilized" existence) of curbing the instincts of sex and aggression. Men against men and the cultural consequences of squelching Oedipal hostilities had become Freud's special theme. Whatever it was that had been "indelibly printed" in the minds of infants during their suckling days was a thing of the past. He had changed his mind because he could neither locate nor recall such feelings in himself.

My point is this: over time, Freud's blind spot in regard to his ambivalent relationship with his mother continued to harden up. As I mentioned in chapter 6, he entertained the theory that Leonardo missed his mother but backed off from elaborating upon it because it hit too close to home. In order to preserve a purified, "all good" image of his mother, his intensive, ongoing self-analysis skirted any memories of maternal disappointments. Instead, he focused on boys' relationships with their fathers. It was an important topic, and what Freud wrote about it remains tremendously influential. It also got him off the hook. It explains why he veered in the direction of interpreting images of flying to be sublimated expressions of sexual energy and gave no further consideration to the wish to recover feelings associated with sensations of oneness with the mother.

10. M. Lewis & J. Brooks-Gunn, *Social cognition and the acquisition of self*. New York: Plenum Press, 1979.

11. W. James, *Psychology*. Greenwich, CT: Fawcett, 1892/1963, p. 166.

CHAPTER 17

1. A. Damasio, *Descartes' error: Emotion, reason, and the human brain*. New York: Avon Books, 1994.

2. A. Damasio, *The feeling of what happens: Body and emotion in the making of consciousness*. New York: Harcourt Brace, 1999, p. 287.

3. The manner in which Jaak Panksepps conceptualizes his and others' research is particularly notable in this regard. Panksepp's theory of subjective self-development has a good deal in common with Damasio's theory, but there are a few areas of disagreement with regard to how (and where) the brain monitors the body's emotional states. Panksepp's theory of self is presented in chapter 16 of his book *Affective neuroscience: The foundation of human and animal emotions*. New York: Oxford University Press, 1998.

4. See, for example, J. Fodor, *The mind does not work that way: The scope and limits of computational psychology*. Cambridge, MA: MIT Press, 2000.

5. O. Sacks, *The man who mistook his wife for a hat and other clinical tales*. New York: Harper, 1970.

6. Damasio, *The feeling of what happens*, p. 154.

7. Joseph LeDoux (*The emotional brain: The mysterious underpinnings of emotional life*; New York: Simon and Schuster, 1996) writes about the brain stem's exquisite structure as revealed in research from his and other animal labs. In careful and readable detail, LeDoux, a neuroscientist, describes the no-choice, reflex responses that occur when an organism (in this case, a rodent) senses a match between an external condition that it is genetically programmed to avoid. For instance, the appearance of a cat alters the internal state of a rodent. Rodents are prewired to freeze at the sight of cats. In terms of natural selection, this makes sense because a moving object is easier for a predator to see than one that is motionless. In addition to freezing, rodents' hearts beat faster, their blood pressure rises, and other physiological changes occur that prepare them for action, either fight or flight. They also emit a high-pitched screech, outside the hearing range of a predator, that functions as an alert to other rodents that trouble is brewing. These actions occur immediately, within milliseconds, before the rodent is even aware that danger lurks. In the event that its defensive freezing fails to conceal it from the predator, the animal is physiologically prepared to act decisively.

One of the components of the rodent's brain is the amygdala, a critical portion of the midbrain that is centrally involved in the emotion of fear. When the amygdala is activated by neurotransmitters that descend into it from one or more sensory systems, it, in turn, delivers split-second information to other portions of the body that alters its condition and places it in a state of alert. The animal makes no decisions. None of this is intentional. In rough-and-ready language, this is how that happens. First, the rodent senses the presence of the cat. This visual information is transmitted by way of the optic nerve to the visual cortex for processing. Along the way, it passes through the thalamus and activates neurons with axons that descend into the amygdala. When external stimuli match a preprogrammed (that is, inherited) configuration of a life-or-death situation, the animal becomes braced for action. The amazing thing is the animal's organism is already on alert before the visual processing has been completed; that is, before it "sees" the cat.

One other important thing takes place. Another part of the rodent's brain called the hippocampus records information about its spatial location: for example, a trash can over there, a particular scent in the air, a drainpipe a few feet away. This snapshot of the context of the-cat-almost-ate-me situation forms neural circuits with other parts of the brain linked with the amygdala in a way that enhances the likelihood of the animal experiencing fear reactions whenever there is a match between what is recorded in the snapshot and the objects in its present environment. In that way the animal learns (or in more technically precise language, is conditioned) to avoid the location where there is a combination of a drainpipe, a trashcan, and a particular aroma. The animal will also avoid or at least be cautious in other settings that provide similar "cues." The presence of even one of the cues in a different setting, for example, the detection of the aroma in the alley where the confrontation first took place, may prevent the creature from entering the fear-provoking setting.

In other words, rodents are prepared to adjust their behaviors according to their feelings. Like other mammals, they possess emotional systems that operate in subcortical or "deep" regions of their brains. Largely because of the work of LeDoux, the fear system has been mapped out in great detail. It makes sense that the parameters of the fear system, now that they have been discovered, are so well delineated, because the emotion of fear is so critical to survival. Other negative or unpleasant emotional systems that sponsor feelings of distress, anger, disgust, and sadness are at the early stages of being worked out. Explorations of primary emotions involved with pleasurable feelings like enjoyment, excitement, surprise, and (I would add) relief are lagging behind.

8. W. James, *Psychology*. Greenwich, CT: Fawcett, 1892/1963.

9. A fascinating account of the brain's archaeological record is contained in Paul MacLean, *The triune brain: Role in paleocerebral functions*. New York: Plenum Press, 1990. MacLean refers to the brain stem as the reptilian brain. It monitors and automatically adjusts the internal condition of the body, controls territorial and mating behaviors, and functions in other primitive ways to maximize the organism's chances of participating in the survival of its species. Over millions of years of evolution, the paleomammalian brain was formed; it consists of the brain stem plus layers of cells (billions of them) that form a ring around the more ancient reptilian brain. MacLean calls this "new" section of the brain the limbic system. Viewed as the "seat of emotions," the limbic system gives mammals an edge on survival by virtue of its ability to integrate feelings with what happens in the environment and to store information about what feelings were previously evoked in a particular environment setting.

The final stage of development that led to the emergence of the *neomammalian brain* involved the addition of billions more cells that make up the cerebral cortex. The cerebral cortex is most fully developed in human beings and can loosely be referred to as the "seat of thinking." MacLean's triune theory is considered to be out of fashion by many neuroscientists, some of whom, for example, have serious reservations about the so-called limbic system. Despite these reservations, MacLean was the first brain scientist to take a "big picture" approach to the evolution of the brain. Although recently developed information challenges parts of his theory, I believe that his most important observations regarding the history of the brain's development will withstand the test of time.

10. Damasio, *The feeling of what happens*, p. 130.

11. D. N. Stern, *The interpersonal world of the infant: A view from psychoanalysis and developmental psychology*. New York: Basic Books, 1985, p. 126.

12. Stern, *Interpersonal world*, p. 132.

13. Stern, *Interpersonal world*, p. 127

14. I have borrowed this term from Panksepp, *Affective neuroscience*, p. 313.

CHAPTER 18

1. The vast amount of literature on the topic of attachment seems to assume that children grow out of the stage of parental attachment to parents and into a stage of attachment to peers. Even adult relationships are studied from an attachment framework. I think that is a mistake. Attachment theory has taken on some of the qualities of an industry that has overgeneralized Bowlby's ideas regarding attachment systems and has extended them to the breaking point of their usefulness. Bowlby said that attachment systems are normally quiescent. They become active only under conditions that are experienced as threats to the young organism's sur-

vival. The specificity of Bowlby's concept of attachment systems is lost when *all* major and even minor relationships throughout the life span are viewed as manifestations of attachment behaviors. The perspective that seems to be carrying today's extensive literature on the topic implicitly assumes that attachment systems are constantly in the "on" position and this engine determines how we relate to most people in our lives. This strikes me to be a distortion of Bowlby's contributions, and I would like to see a reduction in the use of the phrase "attachment styles" in referring to various patterns of relating to others. Call them "relationship styles," not "attachment styles," because most interpersonal relationships have no bearing on Bowlby's original formulation of infant attachment. In summary, it appears to me that many attachment researchers and theorists have become overly attached to the concept of attachment.

2. *JMB*, p. 51.
3. *JMB*, p. 24.
4. Damasio, *The feeling of what happens*, p. 130.
5. *MO*, p. 32.

CHAPTER 19

1. Grimm's Brothers, *The complete Grimm's fairytales*. New York: Random House, 1972, pp. 23–29.
2. J. Campbell, *The hero with a thousand faces*. Princeton, NJ: Princeton University Press, 1949.
3. H. A. Murray, American Icarus. In A. Burton, (Ed.), *Clinical studies of personality* (Vol. 2, p. 632). New York: Harper, 1955.

CHAPTER 21

1. T. Capote, *In cold blood*. New York: Signet, 1965, p. 299 (hereafter *ICB*).
2. *ICB*, p. 110.
3. *ICB*, p. 308.
4. *ICB*, p. 110.

CHAPTER 22

1. C. Hart, *The prehistory of flight*. Berkeley: University of California Press, 1985.
2. P. Haining, *The compleat birdman*. New York: St. Martin's Press, 1976.
3. Haining, *The compleat birdman*, p. 63.
4. H. Kohut, *The restoration of self*. New York: International Universities Press, 1977.
5. D. M. Ogilvie, Individual and cultural patterns of fantasized flight. In G. Gerbner (Ed.), *The analysis of communication content: Developments in scientific theories and computer techniques*. New York: Wiley, 1969, pp. 243–259.
6. R. Kalin, W. N. Davis, & D. C McClelland, The relationship between use

of alcohol and thematic content in folktales. In P. J. Stone, D. C. Dunphy, M. S. Smith, & D. M. Ogilvie (Eds.), *The general inquirer: A computer approach to content analysis.* Cambridge, MA: MIT Press, 1967, pp. 569–588.

7. Stone et al., *The general inquirer,* 1967.

8. G. Murdock, Ethnographic atlas, *Ethology, 14,* 1962–65.

CHAPTER 23

1. F. S. Fitzgerald, *The great Gatsby.* New York: Scribner's, 1995, p. 117.

2. J. Finney, *Time and again.* New York: Simon and Schuster, 1970.

3. G. Plimpton, The man in a flying lawn chair. *New Yorker, 74*(14), 1998, pp. 62–67.

4. G. Plimpton, The man in a flying lawn chair, p. 62.

5. B. Steiger & H. Hewes, *Inside Heaven's Gate.* New York: Signet Books, 1997.

6. Staff of the *New York Post, Heaven's Gate: Cult suicide in San Diego.* New York: Harper, 1997.

CHAPTER 24

1. M. Chagall, *My life.* New York: Orion Press, 1960, p. 46 (hereafter ML).

2. *ML,* p. 95.

3. *ML,* p 25.

4. H. A. Murray, American Icarus. In A. Burton, (Ed.), *Clinical studies of personality* (Vol. 2, p. 618). New York: Harper, 1955.

5. Murray, American Icarus, p. 639.

6. Murray, American Icarus, p. 640.

7. *ML,* p. 27.

8. *ML,* p. 43.

9. *ML,* p. 44.

10. *ML,* pp. 45–46.

11. *ML,* p. 46.

12. *ML,* p. 29.

13. *ML,* p. 51.

14. *ML,* p. 51.

15. *ML,* p. 68.

16. M. Chagall, *Chagall by Chagall.* New York: Abrams, 1979, p. 244.

CHAPTER 25

1. Rodney Dangerfield is a popular standup comedian in the United States whose trademark comment is "I don't get no respect."

2. R. F. Baumeister, On the interface between personality and social psychology. In L. A. Pervin & O. P. John (Eds.), *Handbook of personality: Theory and Research.* New York: Guilford Press, 1999, p. 371.

3. W. Mischel, *Personality and assessment.* New York: Wiley, 1968.

4. New interest in person-centered research is evidenced by recent publica-

tions of books that advance methods of narrative analyses. An example of this trend is D. McAdams, R. E. Josselson, & A. Liblich (Eds.), *Up close and personal: Teaching and learning narrative methods*, Washington, DC: American Psychological Association, 2003.

5. G. Will, The "Truman Paradigm." *Newsweek*, September 7, 1992. This reference is cited by A. C. Elms in *Uncovering lives: The uneasy alliance of biography and psychology*. New York: Oxford University Press, 1994, p. 4. The full quotation is as follows: "In 'psychobiography' the large deeds of great individuals are "explained with reference to some hitherto unsuspected sexual inclination or incapacity, which in turn is "explained" by some slight the individual suffered at a tender age—say, 7, when his mother took away a lollipop."

6. Winnicott has written about maternal deprivation on several occasions. See, for example, D. W. Winnicott, *The maturational processes and the facilitating Environment*. New York: International Universities Press, 1965, p. 226.

7. D. W. Winnicott, *Through paediatrics to psychoanalysis*. New York: Basic Books, 1975, p. 313.

8. H. A. Murray, Psychology and the university. *Archives of Neurology and Psychiatry*, 34, 1934, p. 806.

9. Excellent examples of the value of the sorts of things that can be learned by way of intensive studies of individuals are in C. Magai & J. Haviland-Jones, *The hidden genius of emotion: Lifespan transformations of personality*. London: Cambridge University Press, 2002. The authors of this thoughtful book have devoted most of their careers to the topic of emotions. They are among the few who comprehend the intricacies of Silvan Tomkins's work and, from that vantage point, perceive its relevance to modern-day "dynamic systems" theory. Until this publication, neither author was noted for her contributions to personology. But their psychobiographies of Carl Rogers, Albert Ellis, and Fritz Perls change all that, and their inspiring work has strong potential for providing new ideas and new methods to a discipline in need of both. They have set an agenda for research that endorses the role of affect as the central organizing force of personality, and personologists would do well to follow their lead.

APPENDIX

1. One missed opportunity continues to haunt me. A woman, probably in her mid- to late twenties, worked out daily in the weight room of a gymnasium I frequented before I got lazy. This woman's body featured shoulders that were objects of envy even among the male "regulars," whose primary mission in life was to chisel eye-popping physiques. The most notable piece of this woman's workout schedule was to grasp a chin-up bar with her hands and hang motionless for twenty minutes. Rumor had it that she had mentioned to the weight room supervisor that she was building up her shoulder strength in the hopes of being able to fly. Rumor also had it that she was not receptive to attempts to converse with her. I let the matter rest until an occasion to speak with her arose when I was entering the facility and she was leaving. An elderly man who regularly drove her back and forth from the gym accompanied her. I had been told that he was her father. I smiled and introduced myself to them. The hand I offered to be shaken was ignored, and they

walked out the door. I followed them into the parking lot and attempted to speak with them about my admiration of the remarkable feats of strength I had observed on the part of the daughter. Undaunted by their reluctance to respond and pretending not to be rattled by the awkwardness of the situation, I persisted by asking if it might not be possible for us to set up a time to talk about various ways to exercise. The father stopped and sternly took me aside. He told me his daughter "had problems" and, in no uncertain terms, informed me that I was to leave her alone. So much for that. Science is one thing. Stalking is quite another.

2. E. Jong, *Fear of flying: A novel*. New York: Holt, Rinehart, and Winston, 1973.

3. The following books are included in the Mary Poppins series by P. L. Travers: *Mary Poppins opens the door*. New York: Reynal and Hitchcock, 1943; *Mary Poppins in the park*. New York: Harcourt, Brace, and World, 1952; and *Mary Poppins*. New York: Harcourt, Brace, and World, 1962.

4. R. May, *Sex and fantasy: Patterns of male and female development*. New York: Norton, 1980.

5. D. Bakan, *The duality of human existence*. Chicago: Rand McNally, 1966.

6. For instance, the psychologist Carol Gilligan has written extensively about gender differences in regard to the distinction between agency and communion. She argues that, in general, women are more oriented toward relationships (i.e., communion) than are men. See, for example, C. A. Gilligan, *In a different voice: Psychological theory and women's development*. Cambridge, MA: Harvard University Press, 1982.

7. N. Chodorow, *The reproduction of mothering: Psychoanalysis and the sociology of gender*. Berkeley: University of California Press, 1978.

8. P. Farmer, *Emma in winter*. New York: Harcourt, Brace, and World, 1966.

9. Mary Louisa Molesworth (better known as simply Mrs. Molesworth) was born in 1839 and died in 1921. She wrote over one hundred books for children. In one of these books, *The cuckoo clock* (1877; reprint, New York: MacMillan, 1893) Griselda, the heroine, develops a relationship with an imaginary friend, a cuckoo that lives in a clock. He visits her, mostly at night when she is asleep, and on various occasions carries her on his back as they travel to fantasy locations the cuckoo wants Griselda to visit. Griselda's mother had died and she had been sent to live with two aunts. They were kind to her and also quite demanding. (They were also upper-class snobs, but that unquestioned virtue pervades many of Mrs. Molesworth's books.) Some maternal qualities are attributed to the cuckoo, as he makes sure that Griselda's head is comfortably positioned when they fly and he wraps one of his wings around her to keep her warm. But unlike Peter Pan, who did not want to grow up, Griselda looks forward to maturation, and the cuckoo provides assistance in that regard. In fact, he arranges for Griselda to meet a boy named Phil. The friendship between Griselda and Phil terminates the cuckoo's visits, and he resumes permanent residence in the clock.

10. D. M. M. Craik, *The little lame prince*. New York: Grosset and Dunlap, 1948.

11. U. K. Le Guin, *City of illusions*. New York: Ace Books, 1967.

12. Le Guin, *City of illusions*, p. 160.

13. J. K. Rowling, *Harry Potter and the sorcerer's stone*. New York: Scholastic, 1997.

SELECT BIBLIOGRAPHY

Abraham, R. (1982). Freud's mother conflict and the formulation of the Oedipal father. *Psychoanalytic Review, 69*, pp. 442–453.

Ainsworth, M. D. S. (1964). Patterns of attachment behavior shown by the infant in interaction with his mother. *Merrill-Palmer Quarterly, 10*, pp. 51–58.

Alexander, I. (1988). Personality, psychological assessment, and psychobiography. *Journal of Personality, 66*(1), pp. 265–294.

Allport, G. W. (1937). *Personality: A psychological interpretation*. New York: Holt.

Ashmore, R. D., & Ogilvie, D. M. (1992). He's such a nice boy . . . when he is with his grandma: Gender and evaluation in self-with-other representations. In T. M. Brinthaupt & R. P. Lipka (Eds.), *The self: Definitional and methodological issues* (pp. 236–290). Albany: State University of New York Press.

Atwood, G. E., & Stolorow, R. D. (1993). *Faces in a cloud: Intersubjectivity in personality theory*. Northvale, NJ: Aronson.

Bakan, D. (1966). *The duality of human existence*. Chicago: Rand McNally.

Barenbaum, N. B., & Winter, D. G. (2002). Case studies and life histories in personality psychology: A history of ambivalence. In I. B. Weiner (Gen. Ed.) & D. K. Freedheim (Vol. Ed.), *Handbook of psychology. Vol. 1: History of psychology*. New York: Wiley.

Barrie, J. M. (1888). *Auld licht idyls*. New York: International Book.

Barrie, J. M. (1896). *A window in Thrums*. New York: Dodd and Mead.

Barrie, J. M. (1901). *Margaret Ogilvy by her son J. M. Barrie*. New York: Scribner's.

Barrie, J. M. (1902). *The little white bird*. New York: Scribner's.

Barrie, J. M. (1994). *Peter Pan*. New York: PuffinClassics.

Barrie, J. M. (1919). *Sentimental Tommy*. New York: Scribner's.

Barrie, J. M. (1928). *The plays of J. M. Barrie*. New York: Scribner's.

Barrie, J. M. (1932). *Farewell, Miss Julie Logan*. New York: Scribner's.

Barrie, J. M. (1943). *Tommy and Grizel*. New York: Press Readers Club.

Baumeister, R. (1999). On the interface between personality and social psychology. In L. A. Pervin & O. P. John (Eds.), *Handbook of personality: Theory and Research*. New York: Guilford Press.

Birkin, A. (1979). *J. M. Barrie and the lost boys: The love story that gave birth to Peter Pan*. New York: Potter.

Bowlby, J. (1944). Forty-four thieves: Their characters and home life. *International Journal of Psychoanalysis, 13*, pp. 107–127.

Bowlby, J. (1951). *Maternal care and mental health*. Geneva: World Health Organization.

Bowlby, J. (1969). *Attachment and loss. Vol. 1: Attachment*. New York: Basic Books.

Campbell, J. (1949). *The hero with a thousand faces*. Princeton, NJ: Princeton University Press.

Capote, T. (1965). *In cold blood*. New York: Random House.

Carlson, R. (1971). Where is the person in personality research? *Psychological Bulletin, 75*, pp. 203–219.

Carlson, R. (1984). What is social about social psychology? Where is the person in personality research? *Journal of Personality and Social Psychology, 47*, pp. 1304–1309.

Carroll, L. (1992). *Alice in Wonderland*. New York: Norton. (First published in 1864).

Chagall, M. (1960). *My life*. New York: Orion Press.

Chagall, M. (1979). *Chagall by Chagall*. New York: Abrams.

Chodorow, N. (1978). *The reproduction of mothering: Psychoanalysis and the sociology of gender*. Berkeley: University of California Press.

Cohler, B. J. (1982). Personal narrative and the life course. In P. Baltes & O. G. Brim Jr. (Eds.), *Life span development and behavior* (Vol. 4, pp. 205–241). New York: Academic Press.

Costa, P. T., & McCrae, R. R. (1998). Trait theories of personality. In D. F. Barone, M. Herson, & V. B. Van Hasselt (Eds.), *Advanced personality*. New York: Plenum Press, pp. 104–121.

Damasio, A. (1994). *Descartes' error: Emotion, reason, and the human brain*. New York: Avon Books.

Damasio, A. (1999). *The feeling of what happens: Body and emotion in the making of consciousness*. New York: Harcourt Brace.

Danziger, K. (1990). *Constructing the subject: Historical origins of psychological research*. New York: Cambridge University Press.

Demos, V. (1995). *Exploring affect*. New York: Cambridge University Press.

Dinnerstein, D. (1976). *The mermaid and the minotaur*. New York: Harper and Row.

Eissler, K. R. (1978) Creativity and adolescence: The effect of trauma in Freud's adolescence. *Psychoanalytic Study of Children, 33*, pp. 461–515.

Elms, A. C. (1980). Freud, Irma, Martha: Sex and marriage in the "Dream of Irma's injection." *Psychoanalytic Review, 67*, pp. 88–109.

Elms, A. C. (1994). *Uncovering lives: The uneasy alliance of biography and psychology*. New York: Oxford University Press.

Erikson, E. H. (1958). *Young man Luther: A study of psychoanalysis and history*. New York: Norton.

Erikson, E. H. (1969). *Gandhi's truth: On the origins of military nonviolence*. New York: Norton.

Fairbairn, W. R. D. (1952). *An object-relations theory of the personality*. New York: Basic Books.

Feynman, R. P. (1985). *"Surely you're joking, Mr. Feynman!"* New York: Norton.

Feynman, R. P. (1989). *What do you care what other people think?* New York: Bantam.

Finney, J. (1970). *Time and again*. New York: Simon and Schuster.

Fitzgerald, F. S. (1995). *The great Gatsby*. New York: Scribner's.

Fodor, J. (2000). *The mind does not work that way: The scope and limits of computational psychology*. Cambridge, MA: MIT Press.

Freud, S. (1938). The interpretation of dreams. In A. A. Brill (Ed.), *The basic writings of Sigmund Freud*. New York: Modern Library, pp. 183–541.

Freud, S. (1964). *Leonardo da Vinci and a memory from his childhood*. J. Strachey (Ed.). New York: Norton.

Freud, S. (1961). *The future of an illusion*, J. Strachey (Ed. & Trans.). New York: Norton.

Freud, S. (1929). *Introductory lectures in psycho-analysis*. London: Allen and Unwin.

Freud, S. (1961). *Civilization and its discontents*. J. Strachey (Ed. & Trans.). New York: Norton.

Gergen, K. J. (1977). Stability, change, and chance in understanding human development. In N. Datan & H. Reese (Eds.), *Life-span developmental psychology: Dialectical perspectives on experimental research* (pp. 135–157). New York: Academic Press.

Gilligan, C. A. (1987). *In a different voice: Psychological theory and women's development*. Cambridge, MA: Harvard University Press.

Goffman, E. (1959/1973). *The presentation of self in everyday life*. Woodstock, NY: Overbook Press.

Graham, K. (1965) *The wind in the willows*. New York: Scribner's. (First published in 1924).

Grimm's Brothers. (1972). *The complete Grimm's fairytales*. New York: Random House.

Haining, P. (1976). *The compleat birdman*. New York: St. Martin's Press.

Harlow, H. F. (1953). Mice, men, and motives. *Psychological Review, 60*, pp. 23–35.

Harlow, H. F. (1958). The nature of love. *American Psychologist, 13*, pp. 673–683.

Hart, C. (1985). *The prehistory of flight*. Berkeley: University of California Press.

Homans, P. (1979). *Jung in context: Modernity and the making of a psychology*. Chicago: Chicago University Press.

James, W. (1892/1963). *Psychology*. Greenwich, CT: Fawcett.

Jones, E. (1957). *The life and work of Sigmund Freud*. Vol. 3. New York: Basic Books.

Jong, E. (1973). *Fear of flying: A novel*. New York: Holt, Rinehart, and Winston.

Jung, C. G. (1965). *Two essays in analytical psychology*. New York: Meridian Press.

Jung, C. G. (1957). *The undiscovered self*. R. F. C. Hull (Ed. & Trans.). Boston: Little, Brown.

Jung, C. G. (1959). *Flying saucers*. R. F. C. Hull (Ed. & Trans.). London: Routledge and Kegan Paul.

Jung, C. G. (1965). *Memories, dreams, reflections*. New York: Vintage Books.

Kalin, R., Davis, W. N., & McClelland, D. C. (1967). The relationship between use of alcohol and thematic content in folktales. In P. J. Stone, D. C. Dunphy, M. S. Smith, & D. M. Ogilvie (Eds.), *The general inquirer: A computer approach to content analysis* (pp. 569–588). Cambridge, MA: MIT Press.

Kilinski, K. (2002). *The flight of Icarus through Western art*. New York: Mellon Press.

Klein, M. (1932/1975). *The psychoanalysis of children*. A. Strachey (Trans.). New York: Dell.

Kohut, H. (1977). *The restoration of self*. New York: International Universities Press.

Le Doux, J. (1996). *The emotional brain: The mysterious underpinnings of emotional life*. New York: Simon and Schuster.

Lear, E. (1987). *The owl and the pussy-cat*. New York: Clarion Books. (First published in 1871).

Lewis, M., & Brookes-Gunn, J. (1979). *Social cognition and the acquisition of self*. New York: Plenum Press.

Mackail, D. G. (1941). *Barrie, the story of JMB*. New York: Scribner's.

MacLean, P. (1995). *The triune brain: Role in paleocerebral functions*. New York: Plenum Press.

Magai, C., & Haviland-Jones, J. (2002). *The hidden genius of emotion: Lifespan transformations of personality*. London: Cambridge University Press.

Maslow, A. H. (1968). *Toward a psychology of being*. (2nd ed.). New York: Von Nostrand.

May, R. (1980). *Sex and fantasy: Patterns of male and female development*. New York: Norton.

McAdams, D. P. (2001). *The person: An integrated introduction to personality psychology*. New York: Harcourt College.

McAdams, D. P., Josselson, R. E., & Liblich, A. (2003). *Up close and personal: Teaching and learning narrative methods*. Washington, D.C.: American Psychological Association.

McGuire, W. (1988). *The Freud/Jung letters: The correspondence between Sigmund Freud and C. G. Jung*. Cambridge, MA: Harvard University Press.

McGuire, W. (2000). *The collected works of C. G. Jung*. Princeton, NJ: Princeton University Press.

Melville, H. (1851). *Moby Dick*. New York: Harper.

Milne, A. A. (1954). *Winnie-the-Pooh*. New York: Dutton. (First published in 1924).

Mischele, W. (1968). *Personality assessment*. New York: Wiley.

Murdock, G. (1962–65). Ethnographic atlas. *Ethnology*, 1–4.

Murray, H. A. (1934). Psychology and the university. *Archives of Neurology and Psychiatry, 34*, pp. 803–817.

Murray, H. A. (with staff) (1938). *Explorations in personality*. New York: Oxford University Press.

Murray, H. A. (1951). In nomine Diablo. *New England Quarterly, 23*, pp. 435–452.

Murray, H. A. (1955). American Icarus. In A. Burton (Ed.), *Clinical studies of personality* (Vol. 2, pp. 615–641). New York: Harper.

Ogilvie, D. M. (1969). Individual and cultural patterns of fantasized flight. In G. Gerbner (Ed.), *The analysis of communication content: Developments in scientific theories and computer techniques*. New York: Wiley.

Ogilvie, D. M. (1987). The undesired self: A neglected variable in personality research. *Journal of Personality and Social Psychology, 52*, pp. 379–385.

Ogilvie, D. M. (1987). Life satisfaction and identity structure in late middle-aged men and women. *Psychology and Aging, 2*, pp. 217–224.

Ogilvie, D. M. (1994). The use of graphic representations of self-dynamisms in clinical treatment. *Crisis Intervention and Time-Limited Treatment, 1*, pp. 125–140.

Ogilvie, D. M. (2001). The problem of opinions without evidence in psychobiographic Research. *Clio's Psyche, 8*, pp. 132–134.

Ogilvie, D. M., & Ashmore, R. D. (1991). Self-with-other representations as a unit of analysis in self-concept research. In R. Curtis (Ed.), *The relational self*. New York: Guilford Press, pp. 282–314.

Panksepp, J. (1998). *Affective neuroscience: The foundation of human and animal emotions*. New York: Oxford University Press.

Pavlov, I. P. (1928). *Lectures on conditioned reflexes*: Vol. 1. *The higher nervous activities of animals*. (H. Gantt, Trans.). London: Lawrence and Wishart.

Plimpton, G. (1998). The man in the flying lawn chair. *New Yorker, 74*(14), pp. 62–67.

Rosenberg, S. (1988) Self and others: Studies in social personality and autobiography. In L. Berowitz (Ed.), *Advances in experimental social psychology* (Vol. 21, pp. 57–95). New York: Academic Press.

Runyan, W. M. (1982). *Life histories and psychobiography: Explorations in theory and method*. New York: Oxford University Press.

Runyan, W. M. (1988). *Psychology and historical interpretation*. New York: Oxford University Press.

Sacks, O. (1970). *The man who mistook his wife for a hat and other clinical tales*. New York: HarperPerennial.

Sapolski, R. (1998). *Why zebras don't get ulcers: An updated guide to stress, stress-related diseases, and coping*. New York: Freeman.

Schultz, T, (2003). The prototypical scene: A method for generating psychobiographical hypotheses. In D. McAdams, R. Josselson, & A. Liblich (Eds.), *Up close and personal: Teaching and learning narrative methods* (pp. 151–175). Washington, DC: APA Press.

Singer, J, & Salovey, P. (1993). *The remembered self: Emotion and memory in personality*. New York: Free Press.

Staff of the New York Post. (1997). *Heaven's gate: Cult suicide in San Diego*. New York: Harper.

Staub, E. (1980). *Personality: Basic aspects and current research*. Englewood Cliffs, NJ: Prentice-Hall.

Steiger, B., & Hewes, H. (1997). *Inside Heaven's Gate*. New York: Signet Books.

Stern, D. N. (1985). *The interpersonal world of the infant: A view from psychoanalysis and developmental psychology*. New York: Basic Books.

Stone, P. J., Dunphy, D. C., Smith, M. S., & Ogilvie, D. M. (1967). *The general inquirer: A computer approach to content analysis*. Cambridge, MA: MIT Press.

Sullivan, H. S. (1953). *The interpersonal theory of psychiatry.* New York: Norton.

Tomkins, S. S. (1962). Affect, imagery, and consciousness. (Vol. 1). New York: Springer.

Tomkins, S. S. (1963). Affect, imagery, and consciousness (Vol. 2). New York: Springer.

Tomkins, S. S. (1987). Script theory. In H. E. Howe Jr. & R. A. Dienstbier (Eds.), Nebraska symposium on motivation (Vol. 26, pp. 201–236). Lincoln: University of Nebraska Press.

Tomkins, S. S., & Izard, C. E. (1965). Affects, cognition, and personality. New York: Springer.

White, R. W. (1981). Exploring personality the long way: The study of lives. In A. I. Rabin, J. Aronoff, A. M. Barclay, & R. A. Zucker (Eds.), Further explorations in personality (pp. 3–19). New York: Wiley.

Winnicott, D. W. (1965). The maturational process and the facilitating environment. New York: International Universities Press.

Winnicott, D. W. (1971). Therapeutic consultation in child psychiatry. New York: Basic Books.

Winnicott, D. W. (1975). Through paediatrics to psychoanalysis. New York: Basic Books.

Wullschlager, J. (1995). Inventing Wonderland: The lives of Carol Lewis, Edward Lear, J. M. Barrie, Kenneth Graham, and A. A. Milne. New York: Free Press.

INDEX

References in *italics* refer to illustrations.